UNHOLY TRINITY

SUNY series in Latin American Cinema

Ignacio M. Sánchez Prado and Leslie L. Marsh, editors

UNHOLY TRINITY

State, Church, and Film in Mexico

REBECCA JANZEN

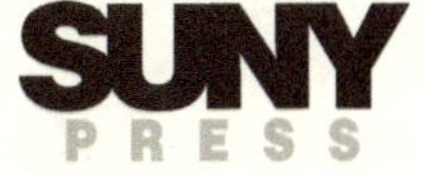

Cover image: Filming St. Joseph's Catholic Church. © Rebecca Janzen.

Published by State University of New York Press, Albany

Printed in the United States of America

For information, contact State University of New York Press, Albany, NY
www.sunypress.edu

Library of Congress Cataloging-in-Publication Data

Name: Janzen, Rebecca, 1985– author.
Title: Unholy trinity : state, church, and film in Mexico / Rebecca Janzen.
Description: Albany : State University of New York Press, 2021. | Series: SUNY series in Latin American cinema | Includes bibliographical references and index.
Identifiers: LCCN 2020053464 | ISBN 9781438485317 (hardcover : alk. paper) | ISBN 9781438485300 (pbk. : alk. paper) | ISBN 9781438485324 (ebook)
Subjects: LCSH: Motion pictures—Mexico—History—20th century. | Motion pictures—Mexico—History—21st century | Religion in motion pictures. | Motion pictures—Political aspects—Mexico.
Classification: LCC PN1993.5.M4 J | DDC 791.43/0972—dc23
LC record available at https://lccn.loc.gov/2020053464

10 9 8 7 6 5 4 3 2 1

To Sara, Ilana, Rebecca, Cheyla, and Amanda for their support

CONTENTS

ILLUSTRATIONS

ACKNOWLEDGMENTS

I would like to thank my family, friends, and colleagues for helping make this book possible. My parents, Marlene Toews Janzen and Bill Janzen, and my brother and sister-in-law, Phil Janzen and Rachel Powers. I would also like to thank extended family and friends including Ghenette Houston and Brian Ladd, Steve and Gloria Houston, Jane Willms, Ben Willms, Paul Siebert and Moira Toomey, Dave Siebert, Ally Siebert, and relatives who have taken a special interest in this project, Clara Toews, Ed and Bev Toews, and Sol Janzen. Many thanks to my coven, Becky, Christy, Emily, Erin, Lindsay, Jenny, Carly, Laura, Liz, Mary, Allie, Rachel, Kristin, and Lauren. Thankful to friends for support in the final months of this project, which coincided with the pandemic—Janet Teuber, Nathan Rouse, Kieley Sutton, Erin Carlson, Alanna Breen, TJ Kimel, and Casey Carroll. And for the friends who took up hiking with me during this time: Grace Yan, Nick Watanable, Sarah and Jon Carroll, Eve Ross, and Jie Guo.

I am thankful for support from my writing group, Emily Hind, John Waldron, Sophie Esch, Carmen Serrano, and Carolyn Fornoff, and lady locusts, Amanda Petersen, Cheyla Samuelson, Ilana Dann Luna, Sara Potter, and Rebecca Ingram, to whom I have dedicated this book. Special thanks to Ilana for advice when starting the project.

Colleagues in Mexican studies, whether part of the UC-Mexicanistas or the more informal MexicanEast series of conferences, have provided invaluable feedback and opportunities for exchange about these ideas. In fact, due to the pandemic, the only forum where I shared these ideas was at the MexicanEast conference in Chapel Hill in fall 2019 organized by Oswaldo Estrada. Brian L. Price, Pedro Ángel Palou, Shelley Garrigan, and Anna Nogar offered important feedback at that conference. Thanks also to Brian Gollnick, David S. Dalton, Roberto Cruz Arzabal, Marisol García Walls, Fran Dennstedt, Julia Brown, Ariel Wind, Ivan Aguirre Darancou, and, as always, conversations with my thesis advisor Susan Antebi for assistance with this project. Thanks also to Olivia Cosentino for incredible insights on film that she shared as a guest speaker at the University of South Carolina campus in early 2020.

I have presented about portions of this work in classes to graduate and undergraduate students at the University of South Carolina. I'm thankful for continued good experiences with colleagues in my department, particularly in the Spanish program (Andrew C. Rajca, Mercedes López Rodríguez, Nina Moreno, Eric Holt, Paul Malovrh, Jorge Camacho, and Francisco Sánchez), as well as research support from librarians in that workplace. Thanks to the Walker Institute for providing support to conduct research in Mexico and the College of Arts and Sciences for support to finish the book. This allowed excellent freelance editor Sean Grattan to finalize the manuscript.

Final thanks to series editors Ignacio M. Sánchez Prado, a mentor since I was a PhD student, and Leslie Marsh, as well my fantastic editor at SUNY, Rebecca Colesworthy.

INTRODUCTION

I will never forget how, on my first visit to Mexico City, I saw an altar to the Virgin of Guadalupe attached to an electricity pole on the side of the road.[1] The altar consisted of a small statue of the Virgin, adorned with flowers, inside of a small metal cage. Though simple, it was obvious that someone took care of it. A few weeks later, I went to the Basilica dedicated to the Virgin of Guadalupe, at the site of her apparition to an ordinary man, Juan Diego, in December 1531. There I could stand on a moving sidewalk, along with hundreds of her devout followers, and see images of her initial apparition. These ways of expressing devotion to the Virgin were different from the practices of the Catholic people in the neighborhood where I grew up in Ottawa, Canada.

Though Catholicism is present in nearly every country in the world, in each country it has a character of its own. In Mexico, it includes both popular dimensions, in the sense that it is practiced by many people, and orthodox dimensions, in the sense that it is approved by the church hierarchy.[2] Both dimensions were very evident at the Basilica of Our Lady of Guadalupe: the orthodox in the official narrative of the Virgin's apparition, and in the many statues, decorations, and architecture of the Basilica and the buildings that surround it; and the popular in the thousands of people who come, not only as visitors but as pilgrims, kneeling in prayer at various places, and in the many objects containing images of the Virgin that they could purchase. The popular dimension is evident throughout the country, from the altars to the Virgin on many city streets and in people's homes to the crosses that stand prominently on hilltops and mountain ranges. Indeed, the largest Christ statue in North America is at the top of the Cerro de las Noas, in Torreón, in the state of Coahuila.[3]

Though the Catholic Church in Mexico has far more adherents than any other religion, it is not the only one. According to the 2010 census, approximately 82 percent of the people claimed to be Catholic, but this was significantly less than the almost 97 percent who identified that way in 1940 (Instituto Nacional de Estadística y Geografía [México]; Instituto Nacional de Estadística, Geografía e Informática 3). Other interpretations of Christianity, such as the Mennonite tradition, which I have written about elsewhere, arrived in Mexico with immigration early in the twentieth century. Baptist and other Protestant and Evangelical forms of Christianity also have a substantial history there; in 2010 they represented around 10 percent of the population (Instituto Nacional de Estadística y Geografía [México]). Mormon missionary work has gained over a million Hispanic followers. Jewish people represent less than 1 percent of the population but their faith has been in Mexico since the colonial period when crypto-Jews, that is, Jewish people who practiced their religion in secret to avoid persecution, arrived in Mexico (Luna 120; Instituto Nacional de Estadística y Geografía [México]). In addition, Indigenous people practice religious traditions that predate colonization.

These and other religious traditions all have a place in Mexican culture, but in this monograph, I focus primarily on Catholicism. As already noted, it has a large role in popular culture. Its long history, dating back to the Spanish conquest, is evident in the many remarkable colonial-era images of the Virgin, now exhibited in the Museo Nacional de Arte (National Art Museum). It continues to be evident in Mexican popular music, which has countless references to Catholic ideas and religious figures, for example in "Camino de Guanajuato" ("Road to Guanajuato") by well-known singer José Alfredo Jiménez, and in the recent "Nana Guadalupe" ("Mother Guadalupe") sung by Natalia Lafourcade, Lila Downs and Lupe Esparza as part of the documentary film *Hecho en México* (*Made in Mexico*) (Duncan Bridgeman, 2012).

In film, religion is represented in various ways, "run[ning] the gamut from devotional praise to a wholesale critique of religion, particularly Roman Catholicism" (Plate 98). Some films, such as the *La virgen de Guadalupe* (*The Virgin of Guadalupe*) (Alfredo Salazar, 1976), which is analyzed by Antonio D. Sison in "Postcolonial Religious Syncretism: Focus on the Philippines, Peru, and Mexico," encourage religious devotion, in this case to the Virgin of Guadalupe (188–92). The trio of films by Miguel Zacarías, *Jesús el niño Dios* (*Jesus the Christ Child*) (1969),

Jesús, María y José (*Jesus, Mary and Joseph*) (1969) and *Jesús nuestro Señor* (*Jesus our Lord*) (1970), also encourage devotion, in this case to the particular Biblical figures on which they focus (García Riera, *Breve historia* 270). Also illustrative of this devotional orientation is a book by Luis García Orso, a Jesuit priest at the ITESO, a Jesuit University in Guadalajara, entitled *Imágenes del espíritu en el cine* (*Images of the Spirit in Film*). He holds that films can be used for spiritual improvement, that is, so that people can better follow the Catholic faith (71–73). A fellow Jesuit at the same institution, Raúl H. Mora Lomelí, makes a similar argument, noting that God can be found in a variety of films, even ones that do not have an explicitly religious plot or character (7–12).[4]

My purpose in this monograph, *Unholy Trinity*, is different. It is not to promote religious devotion; rather, it is to examine films that represent some aspect of religion, and how films critically engage with their context through the representation of religious imagery and symbols.[5] This analysis will add to the understanding of the role of religion in Mexico, the conditions for film production, and the involvement of the state in its extensive support for film production. In pursuing these goals, this monograph builds on the work of other scholars. Craig Detweiler, for example, connects the representation of religion in films to the way these films engage with their context of production. Specifically, Detweiler discusses the 2002 film by Carlos Carrera, *El crimen del padre Amaro* (*The Crime of Father Amaro*), which portrays corrupt priests and devout people in a small Mexican town; he then argues that this film alludes to the corruption among Catholic leaders in Mexico (116). I also dialogue with the work of critics of Spanish film like Elizabeth Scarlett and Jorge Pérez who connect religion in film to changes in Spanish history. Scarlett, for example, argues that modernization measures in Spain could not obliterate religion (20). Pérez, for his part, observes that by focusing on religion as seen in film we can gain a more complete understanding of modernization as an incomplete process (14).

I will examine nine films made at various times from the 1930s to the present. The first ones are from 1933 to 1964, sometimes known as the Golden Age of Mexican film. Others are from the 1960s and 1970s, when the state became remarkably active in creating new institutions to train filmmakers and in funding the work of filmmaking. Still other films are from the more "neoliberal" economic conditions of the 1990s and 2000s. The representations of religion that I examine vary considerably: one involves a sex worker worshipping at an altar in her room in a brothel in Luis Alcoriza's *El oficio más antiguo del mundo* (*The Oldest Profession*) (1970); another involves the title character in Emilio Fernández's 1944 film, *María Candelaria*, who takes an image of the Virgin of Guadalupe from her home altar to a public shrine. Others include fictionalizations of priests in their historical context, as in the case of a Fr. Méndez who rescues sex workers in the1970 film by José María Fernández Unsáin's *Las chicas malas del padre Méndez* (*Father Méndez's Bad Girls*), and Carlos Carrera's 2002 film *El crimen del padre Amaro*, about Fr. Benito, who colludes with a local drug cartel. In the case of Felipe Cazals's 1976 *Canoa: Memoria de un hecho vergonzoso* (*Canoa: A Shameful Memory*), I suggest that the film criticizes a priest and, by extension, various other leaders in the film's context. I follow critic Ilana Luna who posits that this film draws "a direct parallel between government repression of student movements and pernicious religious discourse" (22). Two other films that I discuss represent explicitly religious spaces, or spaces that become religious when certain rituals take place there. These are Guita Schyfter's 1994 film *Novia que te vea* (*Like a Bride*), about the Hashomer Hatzair, a socialist Zionist youth group for university-age students, and Dana Rotberg's 1992 *Ángel de fuego* (*Angel of Fire*) about a travelling puppet show.

A number of scholars have referred to the presence of religion in Mexican films, but to date there is little by way of a focused analysis. Emilio García Riera commented on religious representations in both his 1969 multi-volume survey of Mexican film, *Historia documental del cine mexicano* (*Mexican Film History in Documents*) (see, for example, vol. 1, 22), and in his shorter *Breve historia del cine mexicano: Primer siglo 1897–1997* (*Brief History of Mexican Film: First Century, 1897–1997*), published in 1998.[6] García Riera (*Breve historia* 89) also noted that religion was present in Golden Age classics like Juan Bustillo Oro's 1935 *Monja, casada, virgen y mártir* (*Nun, Wife, Virgin, and Martyr*), which portrays the Spanish Inquisition.[7] He also mentions B-movies of the 1970s like *El oficio más antiguo del mundo*, where sex workers rescue a priest (García Riera *Breve historia* 270).

Also significant is the 1978 thesis of María Luisa López-Vallejo y García, "La religión en el cine mexicano (ensayo)" ("Religion in Mexican Film [An Essay]"), in which she catalogues the presence of religion in Mexican film from 1930 to 1960. She notes three kinds of films that commonly represent religion which, in her case, is synonymous with Catholicism: films that glorify the Catholic Church; films that deal with priests; and films that are historical-religious melodramas (309–10). López-Vallejo y García concludes that perhaps a quarter of the films produced each year have some religious component (309–10), and adds that as the number of Mexican films produced each year increased, so too did the number of films that dealt with Catholicism in some way.

Some film directors have garnered close analysis on their representation of religion. Alicia Adriana Morán, in her 2007 thesis "La crítica de un irreverente: el catolicismo en diez obra mexicanas de Luis Buñuel (1950–2006)" ("Criticism of an Irreverent: Catholicism in Ten of Luis Buñuel's Mexican Works [1950–2006]"), examines Catholicism in the multiple films of the famous Mexican-Spanish film director Luis Buñuel (1900–1983). Morán shows how Buñuel's films presented good and evil in ways that conform somewhat to Catholic doctrine, where good characters go to heaven (47, 132). Bad characters, rather than going to purgatory or hell, are punished on earth (184). Scarlett, whose approach to religion in Spanish film I mentioned earlier, also analyzes the religious and spiritual elements in Buñuel's oeuvre. She suggests that they criticize the Catholic Church and seek to rescue the mystery inherent in Catholic beliefs (21). The exhibit "Buñuel en México" ("Buñuel in Mexico") displayed at the Cineteca Nacional in Mexico City in the fall of 2019 confirmed these observations, as it dedicated significant space to the prevalence of religious themes in this director's work. The work of these scholars confirms that religion has been present in Mexican film, in various ways, for many decades, in the work of multiple film directors.

A simple explanation for film directors refering to religion in their films is that often it is helpful for communicating with their intended audiences. John Lyden has stated: "Films may present religious ideas explicitly or implicitly, and in this way express a religious perspective associated with a historic religion" (4). Lyden goes on to say that filmmakers "draw from the religious traditions of their countries even when they have a more secularized perspective themselves" (4). Director Guillermo del Toro has described the influence of religion on his secular perspective, saying that his life is somewhat of a reverse catechism, that he grew up with belief and then left it behind. In a 2010 interview, he said that he has gone backwards and is now agnostic (Ashbrook). Nevertheless, his oeuvre includes various references to religion. For instance, his 2013 film *Pacific Rim* includes a character called Stacker Pentecost, a name that commemorates the important Christian holy day of Pentecost. Del Toro, like most Mexican filmmakers, refers primarily to the Catholic Church when he represents religion.

Filmmaking, it has been said, is a technology for making meaning and providing structure and form for daily life. Sergio de la Mora has noted that it gives rise to forms of identification, in his case, as they pertain to masculinity (*Cinemachismo* 6). Lyden makes a similar observation about religion, stating that its presence in film can reinforce a specific understanding of gender roles or, he adds, a particular set of prejudices (4–6). I extend these claims and propose that Mexican films, when they make religious references—be it with characters like priests or nuns who have a religious vocation, religious figures like the Virgin of Guadalupe, or religious spaces like churches—can help to either uphold or critique social norms, and likewise to support or critique the government, its leaders, or the Church. The use of such religious references will help the films to communicate, whether subtly or explicitly, with their audiences. This makes it important to understand the relationship of the Mexican state with its filmmaking industry, and the relationship of the state with the Catholic Church, noting the interests at play as both of those relationships changed over the course of the last century.

The relations between the Mexican state and the Catholic Church has been uneven and often tense. Early in the twentieth century there were instances of open conflict. The revolution that led to the 1917 Constitution emphasized secularism and represented a significant repudiation of the Church. Among other things, the Constitution called for secular public education, which led to open conflict between forces that supported the government and those who supported the Church in the 1926–1929 Guerra Cristera (Cristero War). Tensions over public education continued in the 1930s and, at times, broke out in more violence (Kloppe-Santamaría 507–10).

Late in the 1930s, however, a certain mutual accommodation between church and state emerged. Perhaps the government recognized that many of the people remained quite religious. The Church was then allowed to reopen its schools, but the government would have a substantial role in them. The Church would no longer be the exclusive and primary provider of education in the country; also, the state would look after various social concerns (Blancarte, *Historia* 24). Then, in 1940, prior to taking office, president-elect Manuel Ávila Camacho declared himself a *creyente* (believer) in an interview with the journalist José C. Valadés (Monsiváis, *El Estado* 130). He gave the presidential seal of approval to the thawing relationship between the Church and the state. Although Mexico remained an officially secular country, that is, one without a state religion, after this declaration, cooperation replaced conflict to a significant extent.

In the middle of the twentieth century, the Church gained acceptance as a moral voice in society. There was unrest as people in many places advocated for change both in society and in the Church. In the Church, things changed significantly after the Second Vatican Council convened in Rome in the mid-1960s. This led to a greater role for laypeople and enlarged the concern beyond religious devotion in the Church to justice in wider society. Priests and nuns would no longer be required to wear their traditional garb; they could now dress more like regular people in society. And priests, when presiding at the Eucharist, would no longer have to use Latin; they would now use the language of their society. Further, at mass, priests would now face the people, not away from them, and the people would take both the bread and the wine and were no longer required to kneel at the altar rail (Hughes 148–49). Understandably, some in the Church criticized these and other reforms, but others—those more aligned with the protest movements—suggested that they did not go far enough. In the ensuing decades, the Church made various pronouncements that appealed to a broad spectrum of the people; among other things, it rightly criticized the government's failure to implement policies that would better the lives of Mexican people (Blancarte *Historia* 22). In all likelihood, this general orientation helped the Catholic Church to remain an important presence in Mexican life.

If the relationship of the Mexican state with the Catholic Church changed over time, so too did the state's relationship with the arts, including filmmaking. Funding for filmmaking became significant in the 1930s and 1940s, under the presidencies of Lázaro Cárdenas (1934–1940) and Manuel Ávila Camacho (1940–1946), in what became known as the Golden Age of Mexican film. Funding continued under many of the subsequent administrations, always with the aim of creating and promoting a coherent vision of what it meant to be Mexican (Fox 143). Cárdenas and Ávila Camacho also drew on other funding sources, such as the Rockefeller Foundation (King 47), resulting in public-private arrangements that helped private companies to produce a large number of films. Most were for popular audiences and portrayed stock characters like *charros* (rural cowboys or cattle rancher figures) and long-suffering mothers; others took the form of variety shows (King 47).

In order to support film, various administrations created new institutions. In 1942, the Ávila Camacho administration of created the Banco Nacional Cinematográfico (National Film Reserve) (BNC). The administration then invested heavily in the Banco and, as a result, more Mexican films were produced (King 53, 130; Amador and Ayala Blanco 373–78).[8] In addition, the government passed laws to ensure that Mexican people would watch Mexican films as opposed to foreign films. Its first film law, passed in 1949 and revised in 1952, ensured that at least half of what was shown on screen in Mexican cinemas was Mexican (Tuñón *Mujeres* 51). Another step in fostering film development was the creation, in 1957, of the Comisión Nacional de Cinematografía (National Film Commission) (Tuñón *Mujeres* 51).

In the 1960s and 1970s, the government moved further; it encouraged educational institutions to train filmmakers. Universities could now expand their programs so as to include filmmaking techniques and the place of Mexican culture in film. In 1963, the Universidad Nacional Autónoma de México (Mexican National Autonomous University) (UNAM) established a film school, the Centro Universitario de Estudios Cinematográficos (University Center for Film Studies) (CUEC). Now students, instead of apprenticing in film unions, could train at these educational institutions. This was significant. Many of these institutions taught not only on technical skills but provided a broader intellectual and theoretical knowledge. They encouraged students to consider filmmaking beyond the scope of the nation and gave them an awareness of international trends as well as opportunities to forge relationships with their peers (Thornton 72).

In 1970, when Luis Echeverría became president, he increased support for filmmaking even more. In his case there were particular reasons: he wanted to draw attention away from Mexico's growing social problems, as well as from his own role in orchestrating the 1968 Tlatelolco massacre when he was minister of the interior.[9] He then strategically appointed his brother, Rodolfo Echeverría, as head of the Mexican Film Bank, which was the main funding arm for film in Mexico. Rodolfo had been a union leader prior to taking this position and so many filmmakers were receptive to his involvement in the industry (Pérez Turrent, "Crises and Renovations" 100–3). His brother's appointment and the general increase in funding provided by President Echeverría showed that culture and the arts, especially the film industry, were "pivotal to his populist project" (Noble 19).

In 1975 the Echeverría government set up the Centro de Capacitación Cinematográfica (Center for Film Training) (CCC) under the Instituto Nacional de Bellas Artes (National Institute of Fine Arts) (INBA) (Luna 25). This led to the creation, that same year, of two film production companies, the Corporación Nacional Cinematográfica (National Film Corporation) (CONACINE), and Corporación Nacional Cinematográfica de Trabajadores y Estado (National Film Corporation of Workers and State) (CONACITE) I and II (Lay Arellano 59). These measures helped President Echeverría to tie his presidency to the 1917 Revolution and to the 1930s presidency of Lázaro Cárdenas, who was widely seen as carrying the mantle of the Revolution. Echeverría did this even as own administration eroded many revolutionary projects.[10] These various increases in support in the decades of the 1960s and 1970s meant that many low-budget spectacles flooded the Mexican film market.

The trend, however, was not sustainable. This expanding state support for filmmaking could not continue indefinitely. The problems came to a head with the 1982 oil crisis and the 1985 earthquake (Lay Arellano 62–63), but they had been noted earlier. In a 1976 report, at the beginning of the presidency of José López Portillo, the Mexican Film Bank had stated: "Al iniciarse la presente administración, la crisis de la industria cinematográfica mexicana en lo económico era evidente" (When the current administration began, the economic aspect of the Mexican film crisis was evident) (Banco Nacional 27).[11] In response to the issue, the government undertook a gradual but extensive restructuring, reflecting both a consolidation and a diversification.

In 1983, as part of this restructuring, the government established the Instituto Mexicano de Cinematografía (Mexican Film Institute) (IMCINE), to encourage film directors and producers to seek funding not only from state sources but also from private companies (Mora 191). Then, in 1988, the new government of President Carlos Salinas de Gortari (1988–1994) established the Consejo Nacional para la Cultura y las Artes (National Council of Arts and Culture) (CONACULTA). CONACULTA would include IMCINE, the film institute, and would be placed inside the Secretaría de Educación Pública (Ministry of Education) (SEP), moving it out of the jurisdiction of the Secretaría de Gobernación (Secretary of State) (SEGOB). The CCC gained an additional sub-entity, the Centro de Producción de Cortometraje (Short Film Production Center) (MacLaird 27). Both CONACINE and CONACITE were dissolved (MacLaird 27).

These structural changes were to encourage entrepreneurship in film. This was said to be more feasible, given that by now government and academic programs had trained many filmmakers in a variety of genres. It would also enable more filmmakers to avoid unionized environments and thus enjoy more freedom. Now, grants from CONACULTA required filmmakers to seek a mixture of funding sources (MacLaird 22–23). In spite of these changes, or because of them, many films from this time presented a relatively optimistic view of Mexican culture (MacLaird 47).

In 1994, when NAFTA was passed, there were significant cuts in state support. Mexican films would no longer enjoy subsidized ticket prices or be guaranteed distribution of their films in Mexican movie theaters (Sánchez Prado, *Screening* 79). Quotas for the number of Mexican films that had to be shown in Mexican theaters were eliminated. The law from 1952 to 1992 had stated that 30 percent of films shown in a given theater had to be Mexican. This was lowered by 5 percent per year from 1993 to 1997 and remained at 10 percent thereafter (MacLaird 27–28). The government then sold its chain of movie theaters, COSTA, its television station, Imevisión, as well as its film studio and production company, Estudios América (MacLaird 27). Filmmakers could still get some support from the government, but they now also had to find private investors.

These changes had implications. Producers would now make films that appealed more to audiences that had money to pay the unsubsidized ticket prices. And since the government no longer had its own theaters, people had to go to multiplexes, usually located in wealthier neighborhoods. Because of their locations and the higher prices, theaters were now accessible only to about half the population (MacLaird 34). The primary audiences of films now were the middle and upper classes, but interestingly, one of their preferred genres was the romantic comedy (MacLaird 46; Sánchez Prado, *Screening* 83). Then, in 1996, IMCINE began the Fondo de Producción Cinematográfica de Calidad (Fund for Quality Film Production) (Foprocine). This led to more films being produced in Mexico by the end of the 1990s than at the beginning of the decade (Sánchez Prado, *Screening* 92). Mexican directors like Guillermo del Toro, Alejandro González Iñárritu, and Alfonso Cuarón became famous on the world stage, and the three directors won a total of five Academy Awards for best director from 2013 to 2019 (de León).

I have referred to the state's twofold relationship with the Church and the film industry, but the relationship between the Church and the film industry must also be noted. Pérez says that "until the epoch of the Vatican II Council, more than 130 papal documents discussing the role of film in society had been disseminated" (6). Catholic leaders and faithful Catholics in Mexico would have followed these developments closely. This "embrace" of film as a valid means of education and formation, may, at times, have meant that the Church could use its influence to ensure that it was portrayed in positive ways (Peredo Castro 75). It also allowed people to criticize the Church's past, particularly its ties to the conquest and the colonial era, while still remaining faithful Catholics (Ramírez Berg 27).

In the middle years of the twentieth century, the relationship between church and state changed significantly. This is when the Catholic Church reclaimed a role as Mexico's moral authority, and it was helped in this by the administration of Adolfo Ruiz Cortines (1952–1958). As Claire F. Fox explains, in 1953, his government implemented Plan Garduño in order to decrease the influence of US movies in Mexico and to promote a strict moral code (143). Now the Church supported films like Mauricio de la Serna's 1959 anti-abortion film, *El derecho a la vida,* and Julián Soler's 1959 anti-divorce film, *Mis padres se divorcian* (García Riera, *Breve historia* 214). In a sense, these were responses to the 1936 criticism of Pope Pius XI of the film industry's damage to morality and religion (7) and the 1955 exhortation of Pope Pius XII that filmmakers portray the good and beautiful aspects of reality (35).[12]

CHAPTER 1: NEGOTIATING A PLACE FOR RELIGION IN A DEVELOPING ECONOMY: CATHOLICISM IN THE GOLDEN AGE

The first chapter of this monograph examines film from the Golden Age of Mexican film (1933–1964). It argues that films align with the state's goals for the country as they receive state funding and thus Golden Age films were largely produced by state-supported film companies. They also often supported the state's vision for creating a new and better Mexico by presenting characters who embodied their vision. Catholic religious beliefs had already influenced these ideals. I analyze three films, Emilio Fernández's *María Candelaria* (1944) and *Río Escondido* (1948) and Roberto Rodríguez's *El seminarista* (1949). In this analysis I suggest that the explicit use of Catholic religious spaces, characters, and rituals in films from this period allows them to communicate more effectively, and that part of what they communicate is the state's understanding of the post-revolutionary nation.

The primary way I think that the films use Catholic symbols and images to further state goals is through the way they present the revolutionary family. Catholic beliefs underpin this schema in the historical context and on screen, and Catholic religious rituals legitimize it. These "representations of family units mirrored the paternalistic structure of the government" (Luna 16). Men would imitate the president, heading up families of new Mexicans, and women would serve their husbands, raising their children for the betterment of the nation (Hershfield 29). Catholicism is a "silent presence" in many films from this period (Ramírez Berg 26). Ana M. López adds that the Mexican nation was defined by Catholicism, particularly because the Virgin of Guadalupe was its patron saint (150). The Virgin of Guadalupe is the Virgin Mary's most important miraculous appearance in Mexico. People pray to the Virgin mother to intercede on their behalf before God. Catholicism's "values and precepts—sacrifice, self-abnegation, and passive acceptance of 'God's will'—are underlying assumptions of Mexican life" (Ramírez Berg 26).

Catholic religious rituals performed by priests, such as marriage, were the way a legitimate family began (even though Catholic religious rituals did not have any legal weight), and other rituals, like initiating children into the community through baptism, cemented it. On screen, a *charro* becomes a legitimate head of the family through marriage, as in *El seminarista.* Female characters, for their part, uphold the Catholic Church's vision for women as devoted wives and mothers (Franco xiii; Tuñón, *Mujeres* 185). Films portray female characters in positive ways when they behave like the Virgin. Rosaura in *Río Escondido*, for example, is lauded for her self-sacrifice (Hershfield 49). Similarly, the protagonist of *María Candelaria* is portrayed in a positive light because she is devoted to the Virgin and because she eschews the attentions of men who are not her intended.

CHAPTER 2: CATHOLICISM AT ITS WIT'S END: PRIESTS, MADAMS, AND SEX WORKERS

In the 1960s, there was an influx of popular films in Mexico that continued in the 1970s. In the 70s, thanks to increasing training programs and presidential interest in cinema, the number of art house films also increases. This chapter examines two films aimed at popular audiences, *El oficio más antiguo del mundo* and *Las chicas malas del padre Méndez*, and a third, *Canoa*, which yielded significant critical acclaim. These films present a critical view of Mexican society. As critic Charles Ramírez Berg observes, Catholicism was one aspect of "the general failure of the system to address real Mexican problems" (35). It follows that imagery associated with Catholic traditions and institutions was part of these films' social critique.[13] Films crit icized priests more openly and gender norms for men and women on screen were slightly less restrictive. On screen, male characters' machismo was less powerful and female characters broke away from restrictive roles for women (Ramírez Berg 34–35).

Films align with these changing views, and this chapter focuses on the ways that these three films do this through their representations of Catholic clergy. When they represent priests, explicitly religious characters, they show that some have been able to change with the times, like the priest in *Las chicas malas* who rescues sex workers without condemning them. In other cases, films overtly criticize the Church through their representation of the clergy, as with the false priest character in *El oficio*. They also subtly criticize the state through its representations of the clergy, as in *Canoa*.

CHAPTER 3: COMPLEX RELIGIOUS EXPRESSION WITHOUT REDEMPTION: CATHOLICISM, SYNCRETISM, AND JUDAISM

This chapter looks at films that emerge from a context that emphasizes public-private partnerships. Mexicans sought out romantic comedies at home and certain directors became renowned abroad. While fewer Mexicans identified as Catholic in the 1990s, its imagery continues to be used in Mexican films. Filmmakers also represent other interpretations of Christianity and other religions in films that are widely viewed. This chapter looks at three films, *Ángel de fuego*, *Novia que te vea*, and *El crimen del padre Amaro*. Like the films MacLaird discusses from the 1990s like *Amores perros* (Alejandro González Iñárritu, 2000), they are also edgier, with more violence and more sex (101). The films I look at employ religious imagery and present traditional Catholic and Jewish rituals and spaces, as well as unique syncretic religious practices. I propose that they do so in order to critically engage with their context of production, one of uneven economic development, a widening wealth gap, and massive numbers of murdered, disappeared, or missing women in border cities like Ciudad Juárez (Luna 223).

CHAPTER ONE

NEGOTIATING A PLACE FOR RELIGION IN A DEVELOPING ECONOMY

Catholicism in the Golden Age

Films from the Golden Age of Mexican Cinema (1933–1964) engage with their economic and political context. Part of this engagement is through representations of religion, which is one of the ways that these films criticize the Mexican government. As these films represent religious figures, scenes, and spaces, they also allude to and upend traditional understandings of gender roles for women and men. Many scenes also employ religious imagery to refer to the government's relationship with the Catholic Church. Paradoxically, even as the films criticize the government, its close relationship with the Catholic Church, and the gender roles favored by both church and state, they were funded, at least in part, by the Mexican government's cultural programs.

Three films from this period, *María Candelaria* (1944), *Río Escondido* (1948), and *El seminarista* (1949), present particularly compelling examples of religious imagery as they engage with the contexts in which they were produced. This use of religious imagery means that the films would have been legible for their initial audiences. This includes the films' critical representation of Mexico's economic growth, the role of Catholic Church, and the country's many social and political changes, including changing gender roles and an evolving understanding of the role of rural Mexico.

The first film discussed in this chapter is *María Candelaria*. It portrays a young woman called María Candelaria (Dolores del Río) who lives in Xochimilco, to the south of Mexico City, in the early twentieth century. She is the daughter of a sex worker and is somewhat of an outcast in her community as a result. The film's plot centers around María Candelaria's desire to marry a young man called Lorenzo Rafael (Pedro Armendáriz), and their need to save money for their wedding. This situation is complicated by the fact that María Candelaria is forbidden from entering community spaces, such as the local Catholic Church and the market, because of her mother's reputation as a sex worker. In spite of these challenges, she earns money for her wedding in many ways. One of these is by posing for a painting. Yet, after the painter tells María Candelaria that he wants her to pose nude, she refuses to do so. So, he finds a replacement to model an equivalent body. The painter then exhibits the nude painting in Xochimilco, which still has María Candelaria's face. The people there are so enraged they form a mob and kill her.

The second film I discuss in this chapter, *Río Escondido*, also focuses on the life of a female character. This woman, Rosaura (María Félix), is a teacher with a heart problem. She is sent by then-President Miguel Alemán (1946–1952) to a small town called Río Escondido to teach in its public school.[1] Upon her arrival, she realizes that many people in the town live in substandard conditions that cause illness. Rosaura convinces local leaders to conduct an immunization campaign. The film concludes as she succumbs to a heart condition that even a young medical intern (Fernando Fernández) cannot cure.

The third film that I examine in this chapter, *El seminarista*, stars a young male seminarian called Miguel (Pedro Infante). At the beginning of the film, he has to leave seminary because he has contracted typhoid. He returns to the family ranch where his uncle resides in order to recover. As Miguel recovers, he teaches music in the local convent school. In addition to teaching a group of adoring young women, he falls in love with one of them, Mercedes (Silvia Derbez). As the film's posters from the time period advertised, "Se le cruzó en el camino el diablillo del amor" (Cupid's arrow crossed his path [to priesthood]) (*El seminarista* poster). After some complications, the film ends with the marriage of Miguel and Mercedes.

GOLDEN AGE CONTEXT

All three films were released during the Golden Age of Mexican film, which, as I described in the introduction, was a period of significant increase in film production, as well as changes in the country's political milieu. In the 1930s and 1940s, the Mexican government attempted to consolidate power through a single political party. This began with President Lázaro Cárdenas (1934–1940) and the Partido Revolucionario Mexicano (Mexican Revolutionary Party). When Manuel Ávila Camacho came to power in 1940 under the Partido Revolucionario Institucional (Institutional Revolutionary Party) (PRI), he began a single-party dictatorship that would last the remainder of the twentieth century.[2] His presidential administration coincided with the beginning of a period of economic prosperity that is often called the Mexican Miracle of economic development (1940–1968). It was also marked by the fact that Mexico joined the Second World War as an allied force. This led to the US investing in Mexican production of wartime propaganda, and so the Mexican film industry was able to advance in a technological sense (Tierney, *Emilio* 24–25). The film production that had begun under Cárdenas's administration increased significantly under the presidency of Ávila Camacho and throughout the 1940s and 1950s.

This chapter explores the ways that religious imagery in these films coincided with and implicitly supported state goals. One of these goals was the state's vision of the family, which involved specific gender roles for men and women. The desirable role for men was as a benevolent patriarch. He would be modeled after the president, who was the pre-eminent patriarch at the helm of the revolutionary family and the father of the Mexican nation (Pilcher 161–163).[3] This role coincided with what Robert McKee Irwin calls a strong social need to regulate heterosexuality through marriage and through certain acceptable forms of male homosocial bonding (5, 8). Vinodh Venkatesh echoes these remarks as he confirms that this iconic male role was crucial to Mexico's nation-building and modernization projects (5). In this iconic role, men would imitate the president, acting as *hombres honrados* (honorable men) who would head their families and act as good fathers, husbands, and providers (Luna Elizarrarás 20). Films portray characters who embody this role in positive ways.

Films also represent the macho *charro* (rural cowboy) figure. These male characters were the "quintessential virile image of the post-revolutionary Mexican nation, an image widely circulated through film, popular music (*rancheras, mariachi*), performance, sports (rodeo, equestrian), the graphic arts (Jesús de la Helguera's famously illustrated calendars, for example), and literature" (de la Mora, *Cinemachismo* 2). The leader of these groups of *charros* often overlaps with a *cacique* (rural strongman), the formal or informal leader of most small towns. According to Carlos Monsiváis, these *charros* were forged in the cantina, the church, and the bedroom; they went to brothels, where their purportedly noble souls were sullied ("Sociedad" 118). Characters like don Damián in *María Candelaria* embody this figure by controlling what happens to the town of Xochimilco, and subordinate characters, like the town's priest, embody characteristics associated with the role of the benevolent patriarch.

At the same time, some films portray characters who embody the *charro* role who change. This aligns with Sergio de la Mora's understanding that *charros* could change; he examines films from the 1930s onward and shows that "the *charro*, strongly associated with the pre-revolutionary landowning elite, is paradoxically celebrated, elevated onto a pedestal, and transformed into the quintessential embodiment of the post-revolutionary nation" (*Cinemachismo* 83). Religious imagery that accompanies these changes helps us understand that they were thought to be positive. For example, in *Río Escondido*, the *charro* don Regino undergoes a conversion and lets the saintly protagonist Rosaura do her job, even promoting an immunization campaign that she has started.[4] Religious ideas of conversion and a protagonist who embodied acceptable womanhood suggest that *charros* could also be ideal fathers and husbands.

Religious imagery also accompanies positive portrayals of women on screen. These portrayals are of characters who remain virgins until marriage, and, after marriage, become self-sacrificing mothers. Octavio Paz's landmark 1950 essay "The Labyrinth of Solitude" describes this vision of femininity as it existed in his context of production, meaning that his comments are relevant for analyzing Golden Age films. The acceptable role for women was that of a universal mother: "la intermediaria, la mensajera entre el hombre desheredado y el poder desconocido, sin rostro" (The intermediary, the messenger between disinherited men and the unknown, inscrutable power) (Paz, *El laberinto* 93–94; *Labyrinth* 85).[5] This echoes President Alemán's understanding of women's role in helping men raise the revolutionary family. In 1946, for example, he stated that he would extend the right to vote to women because it would not change their role as loyal sisters, self-sacrificial wives, or incomparable mothers (Alemán 51). This acceptable role for women depended entirely on how she would assist the revolutionary husband and father. In film, as in other parts of Mexican culture, positive portrayals of female characters included a likeness to the Virgin Mary, especially to the Virgin of Guadalupe. Their behavior aligns with this woman, who, in the Biblical text, passively accepted God's will. These characters might also represent the Catholic teaching that was prevalent in Mexico at that time. According to this teaching, women were to obey their husbands and were to use their moral capacity to influence the men around them to restore Christian order in Mexico (Boylan 201–3). Indeed, many female characters in Mexican film embody this role. According to critic Adriana Pacheco, multiple films from the 1940s and 1950s portray female characters as "una especie de martirio que se ajusta perfectamente con el melodrama que el catolicismo mismo implica en la abnegación, el pecado y la purificación" (a type of martyr that is perfectly adaptable to the Catholic melodrama of self-denial, sin, and purification) (Adriana Pacheco 44). One of the ways that *María Candelaria* positively portrays its protagonist is through her devotion to the Virgin Mary and the way that her actions imitate the Virgin's selflessness.

Films represent female characters in negative ways when they do not meet this ideal. In the Mexican representational and symbolic scheme, the opposing end of the virgin-whore is often modeled after Malintzin or Malinche, a woman who was the Spanish conqueror Hernán Cortés's translator, guide, or rape victim.[6] In the popular imagination, propagated by the work of Octavio Paz, she is called *la chingada* and understood as the woman who sold out Mexico.[7] Women like María Candelaria's mother are devalued because of their likeness to Malinche.

MARÍA CANDELARIA

María Candelaria was directed by the famous director Emilio Fernández and starred Dolores del Río and Pedro Armendáriz, three important figures in the Golden Age of Mexican film.[8] The immensely popular director reportedly created *María Candelaria* to apologize to Dolores del Río for the way he had treated her while making a previous film (Vallejo 2). This film, like other examples of Fernández's oeuvre, was both artistic and had mass appeal (Tierney, *Emilio* 72). Many of these films included references to religion in some way, and *María Candelaria* is no exception (Hershfield 70–71). Early on, it portrays the protagonist traveling to a shrine dedicated to the Virgin of Guadalupe, while holding an image of the Virgin. María Candelaria also interacts with the local priest on multiple occasions. This is in keeping with the observations of critic Elena Feder that the Virgin of Guadalupe is an important element in many of Fernández's films (249). This imagery and these interactions are part of popular expressions of religion, which Fernández's films usually represent in a more favorable way than the Catholic Church's hierarchy. These examples of popular religiosity were likely normal for their initial audience, as at that time the overwhelming majority of Mexico was Catholic.

My analysis of this film hones in on representations of religion because, as I explain, careful attention to these scenes will offer insight into changes in the Mexican political and social context. I propose that it furthered the state's goals of a specific understanding of the ideal Mexican family, and the way it planned to consolidate power over rural Mexico, through scenes in which characters satisfy what were then prevailing understandings of gender roles and of rural Mexico. Although the director received significant funding from Mexican state cultural programs throughout his career, *María Candelaria*, as well as his other films, did not exclusively uphold the state's ideals (Tierney, *Emilio* 2–3).[9] The film presents close relationships between the Catholic priest and the local *cacique*, and these relationships evoke patterns from the colonial period, pointing to the ways that Catholic power evolved in the film's context to be concerned primarily with spiritual matters and understandings of gender roles that would be acceptable for the Church and the state.

The film centers on the life of María Candelaria, whose mother's profession marginalizes her in the town of Xochimilco. She would like to marry a young man called Lorenzo Rafael, but they are unable to do so because they owe money to the local *cacique*, don Damián. To make enough money to pay off their debt, which will allow them to get married in the local Catholic Church, María Candelaria and Lorenzo Rafael raise a pig. Unfortunately, before they can sell the pig, María gets sick. To help her, Lorenzo goes to the local store and steals both the medicine needed to cure her and the wedding dress she has ordered but not yet paid for. Lorenzo is caught and sent to the local jail. María needs money more than ever. To earn enough to get Lorenzo released, María poses as a model for a famous artist, modeled after Diego Rivera and his studio in San Ángel, in the south of Mexico City (Tuñón, "Femininity" 91). After she refuses to model nude, he combines the completed painting of her head with a different woman's body and exhibits the final work in Xochimilco.[10] A mob of townspeople respond and, before Lorenzo can break out of prison to stop them, they kill her.

Water imagery welcomes the audience to the film, creating an experience outside of ordinary time or experience. This is significant when we consider the importance of water in the Catholic religious context: water is part of baptism, the rite of initiation into the Christian community, and holy water is usually found in a font or basin just inside the front door of a Catholic Church. In Mexico, people usually dip a finger into the holy water on their way in or out of a church. Following theological reasoning, this action reminds people of their baptism, or, following popular reasoning, it wards off evil.

The film is set in 1909, when the primary means of transportation in Xochimilco was canoes in local canals. The film's representation of these canals during the opening credits initiates the viewer into a different time. As critic Julia Tuñón has observed, this "lends an ethereal, timeless and lyrical tone to the narrative, presenting it as a mythical tale" ("María" 45). Eventually, a screen full of text summarizes the film's plot and establishes that it represents a tragedy that has taken place several decades earlier. Brass music plays as the text flashes on screen, and its sounds add to the impression of viscosity. The sequence is also highly repetitive. The combination of water, sounds, and credits creates the impression of rolling along a canal and moving backwards to a different time.

These canals are also central to popular religious expression in the film, that is, to the way that María Candelaria expresses her devotion to the Virgin. Having established that María Candelaria and Lorenzo Rafael have financial issues, the film presents María Candelaria taking her troubles to the Virgin Mary. In a traveling shot, the film shows María Candelaria as she walks along canal banks, carrying a small photograph-sized image of the Virgin with her. This type of prayer card venerating a religious figure like the Virgin Mary is common in Mexico. It offers the devout person a greater connection with the figure venerated on the card, so this figure will then intercede more powerfully on the person's behalf before God. A person may seek to improve this intercession by having a priest bless the prayer card, or may take it to a special worship place. María Candelaria, like someone in both the mid-twentieth century context of production and the early twentieth century context of the film, would pray at the shrine with this image and return home with the understanding that the figure on her card would intercede more strongly on her behalf. Her desperation for outside intervention and relief found in prayer is relevant to the arc of the story as well as the film's audience in the 1940s.

The protagonist's watery journey to pray at this shrine leads to one of the film's central conflicts, between María Candelaria, an Indigenous character played by a white actor, and an Indigenous woman. María Candelaria reaches the shrine and the anonymous woman yells at her, insulting her in what we are meant to understand is an Indigenous language. This affront is likely based on the fact that she believes that María Candelaria is not worthy of praying to the Virgin, because the Virgin will only respond to the petitions of the innocent faithful. In the same scene, the camera shifts from María Candelaria's face to rest on the face of the Indigenous woman, who tells her, "Que coraje traes" (You have guts), as if she is unable to believe how bold María Candelaria is by coming to the shrine. The scene continues as this woman states, "Yo no tengo la culpa de que seas lo que eres" (It is not my fault that you are what you are). The Indigenous woman implies that María Candelaria is doing something bad by going to the shrine, whereas she, the speaker, is blameless. María Candelaria is so beyond help that she will remain a bad woman regardless of her actions.

This religious conflict affords greater insight into the ways that the film upholds an existing racial hierarchy and challenges a prevailing understanding of sexual purity. In scenes shot from above, the film makes it clear that the banks of the canals used for transportation on foot are precariously close to the water. And so, it is easy for María Candelaria to push the other woman into the canal. María Candelaria, "la buena salvaje" (the good savage), stands above the Indigenous woman (Palou 34). This scene places a potentially impure character over the pious Indigenous woman, which mirrors and reverses the relationship between the Virgin of Guadalupe and Malinche. In this cinematic reinterpretation, Maria Candelaria is likened to the Virgin and, as the other woman falls into the canal, she becomes like Malinche, whose actions were thought to cause the downfall of her people. The film places its protagonist in a positive light as it restores a pigmentocratic hierarchy based on whiteness. This follows what Tierney has already observed in terms of the positioning of some Indigenous people as good, and some as bad, in ways that align with increased light on certain actors, as well as the actors' proximity to whiteness (*Emilio* 90–91). The fact that the white-passing, supposedly Indigenous woman (and daughter of a sex worker) pushes the Indigenous-appearing, supposedly pure character into the water reminds us that these archetypal roles are unstable. In addition to the way this scene plays with the gender roles for women, we can also consider that María Candelaria and the Indigenous woman appear in a way that is similar to the original apparition of the Virgin of Guadalupe to Juan Diego when he was in an area full of flowers. On screen, the Indigenous woman is close to the flowers she and María Candelaria sell, physically below the virginal María. This interpretation cements María Candelaria as a virginal character, in a scene that has already muddied the division between the gender roles available for women.

The film presents an opportunity for us to further explore the cinematic allusions to these roles in the two characters' second conflict. Water plays a different but no less important role here. María Candelaria eventually garners sufficient courage to attend church with her little pig, likely attending church for the feast of St. Francis of Assisi on October 4, when animals are often recognized by the Catholic Church. Yet pigs, which have historically been considered unclean animals, are not usually permitted in this type of ceremony. That the priest character had encouraged María Candelaria to bring her animal to this event was a gesture of goodwill. Some observers criticize this scene as unrealistic. In 2011, Delia Selene de Dios Vallejo claimed that the priest in the film was "extravagante, ridículo, fuera de cualquier realidad pueblerina. Curas como ése no hay en México" (extravagant, ridiculous, and beyond any conceivable reality in a small town. Priests in Mexico are not like him) (10). That being said, the priest in the film, no matter how far removed from a realistic portrayal of a priest, is the social authority in the town (López-Vallejo García 23). When María Candelaria shows up outside the church with her pig, it causes a scene. The same Indigenous woman who had yelled at her at the shrine yells at her in the entrance to the church. She claims that if María Candelaria and her pig are allowed inside, everyone else's animals will die without receiving the priest's blessing. The priest then hears the commotion and asks the Indigenous woman what she is doing. The anonymous woman responds by reminding the priest of María Candelaria's mother. The priest responds by saying that the church is the "casa de Dios y él que en ella ofenda a un hermano es como si escupiera el agua bendita . . ." (House of God and he who offends a brother within the church is like someone who spits in the [basin of] holy water). The reference to *agua bendita* adds a religious dimension to the women's conflict. The priest's disapproval of the woman's remarks, moreover, places him, and the official Catholic Church, in a positive light. It also confirms that María Candelaria is behaving in line with her inherent purity and goodness and that she should not be judged because of her mother's profession.

In spite of the priest's ability to resolve María Candelaria's problem here, he cannot solve all of her problems. In a scene following the one in front of the church, she becomes ill. She falls over almost as if out of nowhere. As we examine the role of water in this scene and those that follow, we see the ways that popular religious practice works with traditional medicine rather than with the Catholic priest. After she falls down, Lorenzo Rafael carries María Candelaria inside the house and sets her on a pallet. She is thus situated for healing and Lorenzo Rafael, as benevolent patriarch, employs a number of methods to heal her. First, he finds the local *huesera* (bone-setter) and brings her to their home. When she arrives, she pours liquids into a pot on an open fire. Now that this type of healing has begun, Lorenzo Rafael moves on to other methods. The camera moves outside their humble abode and shows a heavy rain. Lorenzo, wearing a raincoat that evokes pre-conquest and pre-Gore-Tex technologies, gets in his canoe and goes to the local store. Once near the store, the camera jumps between his body and the storefront. After he enters the building, it shows the word "QUININA" (QUININE) in large capital letters. He returns home, having stolen the medicine and María Candelaria's wedding dress. Then, he prays to the Virgin for María Candelaria to get better. The film has shown portions of this shrine to the Virgin on earlier occasions, but this is the first time that it focuses on a character praying in front of it. The camera shows Lorenzo Rafael in an angled profile that displays his back and arms rather than a profile shown strictly from the side. After he picks up a candle from a small shelf, lights it, and places it in front of a framed picture of the Virgin, the film shows his atypical stature of devotion (see figure 1.1). His neck and back do not change position because Lorenzo Rafael does not bow before her, nor does he kiss the image. The film shows that he simply speaks from his heart, crying as he tells the Virgin "haz de mi lo que tú quieras" (do with me what you wish). Lorenzo Rafael is willing to do almost anything to help his betrothed. The imagery of water from the storm, the *huesera*'s liquids, María Candelaria's sweat, and the canal

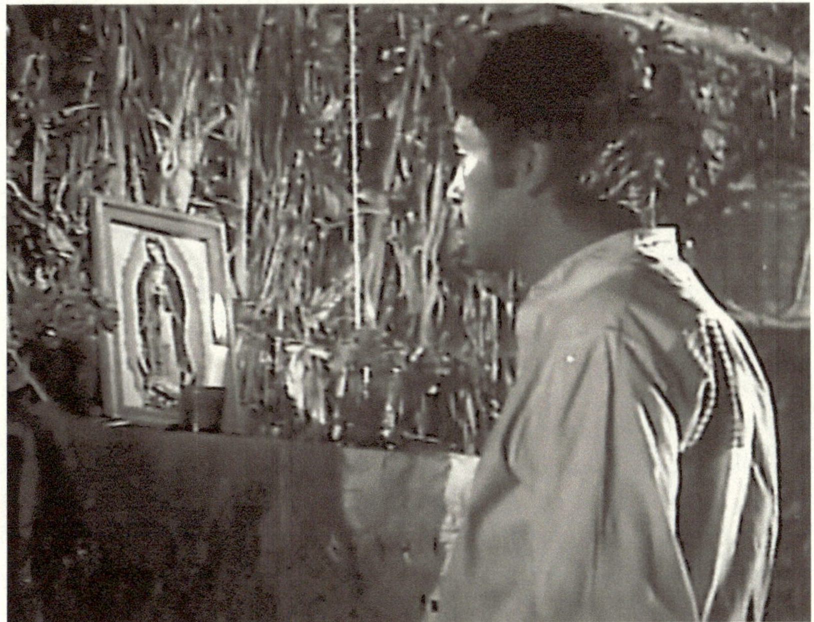

Figure 1.1. Lorenzo Rafael prays while María Candelaria is sick in *María Candelaria*. *Source*: *María Candelaria*, fair use.

make his performance of the role of a benevolent patriarch who will do anything to assist his partner more believable.

The scenes that follow illustrate the Catholic Church's relationship with other powerful entities, through the priest's relationship with the local *cacique* and commercial power. Once María Candelaria has recovered, she and Lorenzo Rafael try to get married in a ceremony that takes place just outside of the church's doors. They almost succeed. At the last minute, don Damián, the local *cacique* and store owner, interrupts the ceremony. He and a group of men take Lorenzo away because he had stolen quinine and María Candelaria's dress. Even though the priest is above don Damián in the community's spiritual hierarchy, he cannot stop this the arrest (Cañada Martínez 86). The priest's actions, however, align with the secular power structure that is more important in Mexico than the spiritual hierarchy by the 1940s, when the film was produced.

The priest does maintain a monopoly over spiritual and emotional matters, and the religious environment of the church sanctuary comforts a sobbing María in a way that keeps her in a position for women approved by both state and Church. After Lorenzo is arrested, María Candelaria runs to the priest and cries. They walk towards the church and are featured in profile as if they were on equal footing. As is common in Mexican Catholic churches, this building has pews, or benches, and at the front of the church there is a pulpit for the priest to use when speaking. There is also a table where he will perform the Eucharist, which is the ritual of consecrating the bread and wine so that, in the Catholic understanding, they become the body and blood of Jesus Christ. María Candelaria walks through the church building and tentatively approaches the steps that lead up to the Eucharist table, filmed as if from the aisle on the other side of the pews. She is surrounded by statues that remind the faithful of the most important Catholic figures, such as Jesus, the Virgin and El Niñopa (Divine Child Jesus), and the saint after whom the church is named. Images of the Divine Child are prominently featured in the sanctuary.[11] The camera shows María Candelaria in the middle of the foreground as she rests her knees on the steps that lead to the altar. She bends down so that her forehead touches the ground, and she cries. The *rebozo* (large shawl) that covers her head in the church, as well as her upper body, lie in the left-hand side of the foreground. The prominently displayed fabric makes María seem more similar to the rest of the church as it evokes the other textiles in the frame, such as a cloth banner hanging from a wall that honors the Divine Child on the left-hand side of the background, and the part of the priest's elegant robes that are visible on the right-hand side in the foreground (see figure 1.2).

The priest tells María Candelaria, "Llora hijita, desahógate" (Cry, my little daughter, vent). María Candelaria replies that she cannot bear her cross anymore and that she wants to yell until her throat is dry. María's behavior displays the character's remarkable comfort inside the church building, where, according to the film's plotline, she was had not been allowed to enter prior to this scene. Then, all of the sudden, María stops crying. The camera shifts from her and the priest to display a statue of the Virgin, which fills the entire left half of the screen. The camera then goes back to display María Candelaria, shifting between the two as María Candelaria accuses the Virgin of not listening to her prayers. This contrasts sharply with Lorenzo Rafael's statement that the Virgin could do with him what she wished. In the church. the priest warns María Candelaria not to talk to the Virgin in that way, shaming María Candelaria for doing something that would upset the Virgin.

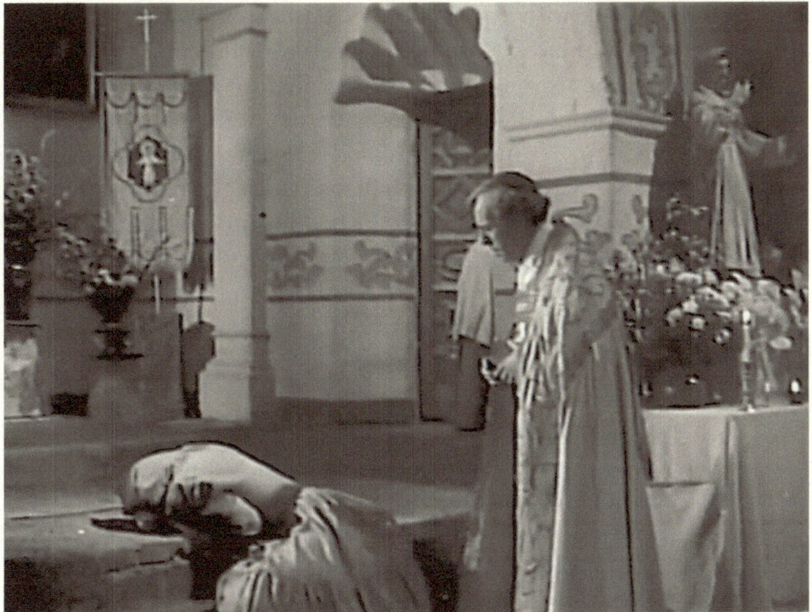

Figure 1.2. María Candelaria cries in the church in *María Candelaria. Source*: *María Candelaria*, fair use.

He points out, "Mira como lloran sus ojos [de la Virgen]" (Look at how her [the Virgin's] eyes are crying). It is obviously impossible for a statue to cry; it is not, however, impossible for the faithful to assign human attributes to inanimate objects. In so doing, the priest highlights a similarity between this venerated figure and María Candelaria. The scene ends with a shot from above, and the statue of the Virgin diminishes in size to occupy a third rather than half of the screen. This scene illustrates the priest's compassion towards María Candelaria, the comforting presence of the interior of the church, and the way that the priest uses María's tears to keep her submissive to the Catholic Church. This behavior relates to its context. It confirms that the priest, and the Catholic Church, play continue to occupy an important spiritual and emotional role for people, and that they promote behavior for women that is in line with the state's views on appropriate gender roles.

The scenes that follow further emphasize the close relationship between the Church and the state. In addition to promoting gender roles acceptable to both in the film's context of production, the priest's actions on screen show he is complicit with characters that represent state power, namely, with don Damián. Don Damián is the virile rural strongman in this film who also holds some governmental responsibilities. The way he holds power, and the fact that the film is set in 1909, means that his actions allude to ways *caciques* held power before the Mexican Revolution. Yet his role remains relevant and understandable for the film's initial viewers in the 1940s, as critics like de la Mora have observed, because the rural strongman is both pre-revolutionary and an integral part of the post-revolutionary project of building a new and better Mexico (*Cinemachismo* 83). Indeed, don Damián is part of every significant event in the film. As critic Adriana Cañada Martínez astutely states:

> Es posible darse cuenta de la complicidad que mantenían la Iglesia y el Estado, para mantener el sometimiento de la población, pues si el sacerdote sabía que don Damián era una persona prepotente y arbitraria, éste nunca intenta hacer conciencia en Lorenzo Rafael para que exija sus derechos sino, por el contrario, por medio de la religión lo manipula y se convierte en un ser pasivo, quien deja en manos de Dios la solución de sus problemas.
>
> (We realize that the Church and the state were complicit with one another. This [relationship] kept the population in a submissive position. The priest knew that don Damián was an overbearing and arbitrary person; yet, he [the priest] never encourages him [Lorenzo Rafael] to exercise his rights. Rather, the priest manipulates him [Lorenzo Rafael] through religion and so [Lorenzo] leaves his problems in God's hands.) (83)

That is, the priest knowingly allows don Damián to treat Lorenzo Rafael badly. Following Cañada Martínez's observations, when he reminds Lorenzo Rafael of God's providence, he is in fact keeping him in a subservient position. The priest does not intervene at Lorenzo Rafael's sentencing either. In a courtroom scene, don Damián stands next to the judge and, once Lorenzo is sentenced, don Damián reaches for something in his pocket. This allusion to paying off the judge implies that he has co-opted the legal system. This calls to mind corruption and complicity in the context the film represents, and the ways that this behavior remained unchanged some three decades later, when the film was produced.

The subsequent scenes further demonstrate the negative influence of this confluence of religious and secular power. When María visits Lorenzo in his jail cell, the film provides an overhead shot of his cellblock under the *palacio municipal* (municipal building). This is an administrative building across the *zócalo* (public square) from the church. Its large hallway and rooms to each side look like the sanctuary of a Catholic Church and the small shrines to various other saints that are set off in small alcoves in most Mexican Catholic churches. This is no accident. Both the church and municipal building were constructed in the colonial period, where the Catholic Church was an integral part of the Spanish imperialist project. In this way, the film shows how the Church and the state were complicit with one another (Cañada Martínez 83). The scenes in the cellblock confirm this complicity. The sound of water dripping from the ceiling, for instance, echoes María Candelaria's tears in the church. Moreover, once she arrives at Lorenzo Rafael's cell, she looks at him in the same way that she had looked at the statue of the Virgin in the church building. This imagery confirms the devastatingly close relationship between secular and religious power in the film, and the Church's subordination to the state in the film's context.

Men from entities not directly tied to either Church or state then collude with one another to keep María Candelaria in a subservient position, which both powerful entities would approve. Lorenzo Rafael had not managed to cure María with the stolen quinine, his desperate prayers, or by calling the *huesera*. She was restored to health after a man interested in painting María Candelaria had paid for a doctor. In the patriarchal scheme, it follows that he would ask Lorenzo Rafael, her intended husband, to access her body and her time. After Lorenzo Rafael gives the artist permission to paint María Candelaria, she travels with the artist to Mexico City. As discussed in the film summary, she refuses to be painted nude. Then, when the artist exhibits the painting in Xochimilco, he does not tell anyone that he created his painting using two models: María Candelaria for the face and head and another woman for the body. In a scene of heightened emotions, María Candelaria walks along the marshy edges of a canal and falls in. She pulls herself out of the water with great difficulty and makes her way to the jail to find Lorenzo Rafael. As she walks, a mob led by the anonymous Indigenous woman, with whom María has had several conflicts, throws things at her. Ultimately, the people of Xochimilco interpret María Candelaria's supposed actions as the epitome of *malinchismo* (Feder 251). In one sense, she is like Malinche, because a man forces her to appear as if she has betrayed her people. At the same time, she can also be interpreted as similar to the Virgin she venerates, because she has refused to pose nude. Her behavior in these scenes suggests that even when a female character attempts to live within the boundaries prescribed by the patriarchy, she will inevitably fail.

The scenes surrounding María Candelaria's death confirm the confluence of religious and secular power. The camera focuses on María Candelaria as she stands in the *zócalo* at the edge of the municipal building where Lorenzo Rafael is being held. A cross, likely a shadow from the church, appears above her head. As if blessed by the Catholic faith—or foreshadowing a death like that of its crucified savior—Lorenzo Rafael breaks out of the jail. He holds María Candelaria as the mob looks on and she dies in his arms. The priest rings the church bell and Lorenzo Rafael places her body in a canoe and paddles away. The film's final scenes shift between his face and María Candelaria's body in the canoe, her head surrounded by flowers. The priest does not stop the people, and he only offers limited comfort to the broken-hearted Lorenzo. He willingly abdicates moral responsibility to stop the mob. This would have maintained a good relationship with its likely leaders, and their alliances with don Damián and his secular and commercial power in the film. By paying attention to scenes involving religious figures, spaces, and symbols in this film we see that religion largely upholds secular power.

The film lulls the viewer into a sense that its events take place in an alternative timeline, with watery religious imagery flooding its opening scenes. Throughout the film, we see a contrast between characters deriving meaning from popular religious rituals and those that take place within the church's walls. The rituals that take place outside of the church, such as Lorenzo praying to an image of the Virgin when María Candelaria is sick, or María Candelaria walking to a shrine, upend certain established hierarchies. Lorenzo's prayers do keep him within the boundaries of acceptable masculinity, even though they give him more emotion that we might have expected. María Candelaria's prayers, and her conflict with the Indigenous woman outside of the shrine and the church, for their part upend some parts of the dichotomy between an idealized virginal character and a condemnable whore. The priest, who represents the official Catholic Church, condemns the anonymous Indigenous woman for her prejudices against María Candelaria. Beyond that one instance, however, the priest largely acts in line with what we would expect from historians' understanding of the role of the Catholic Church in Mexico in the 1940s, where the Church's authority was confined to spiritual and emotional matters. He is subordinate to other powerful character, the *cacique* don Damián, who paid off the judge, and the painter who paid for María Candelaria's doctor. The priest provides solace for María Candelaria but he does so in ways that ensure that she continues to occupy a role for women deemed acceptable by the Church and by the state. He does not challenge the mob's opinion of her either, and only rings the bell in the church when María Candelaria dies. This ultimate failure gestures towards the limits of religious power in the film's context.

RÍO ESCONDIDO

Río Escondido was also directed by Emilio Fernández and is in many ways similar to *María Candelaria*. It won a number of awards, including nine Arieles in 1949 (Tierney, *Emilio* 25).[12] The film stars the famous María Félix in the role of a young teacher called Rosaura. The president sends her to teach in a small town called Río Escondido in rural Mexico in spite of persistent heart trouble. The movie was filmed in Tultepec, in Mexico State, and in the Estudios Azteca film studios, and the title may refer to a river by the same name in the state of Coahuila (García Riera, *Historia* vol. 4 144). There, she revitalizes the local school and with the "help of a student doctor, Felipe (Fernando Fernández) . . . successfully rids the town of smallpox, and rehabilitates the drunken local priest (Domingo Soler)" (Tierney 144). She ultimately succumbs to her chronic heart problems.

The film is full of religious imagery, and focusing on it points to the ways that secular and religious power work together in the film's context. The film begins as an almost-divine-sounding narrator places the film's events in the arc of Mexican history, as then-President Alemán commissions Rosaura to teach in Río Escondido. Once she arrives in town, Rosaura embodies the acceptable female behavior of teaching and healing. The film portrays Rosaura's struggle to educate and vaccinate rural Mexican people in ways that liken her behavior to the religious figure of the Virgin Mary and to religious leaders like priests. This would have communicated central plot points in a straightforward way to the film's initial audience.

The film begins with imagery that gives the revolutionary goals of education colonial and Catholic overtones. After the opening credits, the film presents a still image of a woodcut print, or lithograph, which calls to mind illustrations in colonial manuscripts of chronicles of conquest or priests' recordings of Indigenous beliefs. In addition to evoking the conquest, these lithographs remind us of the Taller de Gráfica Popular (Revolutionary Visual Arts Workshop) which presented revolutionary ideas to the public.[13] For this reason, I propose that the film creates a subtle parallel between the colonial and revolutionary projects.

It follows that the film does not have an exact historical equivalent, but rather, as critic Anne Doremus asserts, takes place in a time when Mexico was in the process of becoming modern (157). The words that appear on the screen after the opening lithographs confirm this:

> Esta Historia no se refiere precisamente al México de hoy, ni ha sido nuestra intención situarla dentro de él. Aspira a simbolizar el drama de un pueblo que, como todos los grandes pueblos del mundo, ha surgido de un destino de sangre y está en marcha hacia superiores y gloriosas realizaciones.
>
> (This Story is not precisely about Mexico today, nor is it our intention to situate this [Story] within it. It aspires to symbolize the drama of a people who, like all the great peoples of the world, has arisen through blood and is marching towards its great achievements and glorious destiny.)[14]

This modernization has some religious overtones, as blood enabled the transformation to a new understanding of Mexico.

The film then narrates the first scenes in a way that likens the protagonist to people who were important to Mexico's history and who had a close relationship to the Catholic Church. This places Rosaura and her work to modernize Mexico in a religious light. A narrator with a deep and commanding voice describes Mexican history in the opening scenes and sounds like some kind of divine being. This use of the human voice was part of Fernández's style as an "oratorical image-maker" (Dever 25). After displaying several lithographs, the film jumps to the *zócalo* in downtown Mexico City, and shows images of the Mexican flag and the Metropolitan Cathedral. It then displays a woman rushing along the left-hand side of the screen, next to the Palacio de Gobierno (National Palace), which is located in the *zócalo*. The camera moves between her face and a bell and the deep-voiced omniscient narrator explains, "Soy la campana de la libertad, soy la campana de Dolores" (I am the bell of liberty, I am the bell of Dolores). In this way, the film creates a similarity between the protagonist's face and Mexico's independence movement. The bell of Dolores refers to the bell that Fr. Miguel Hidalgo rang at a decisive point in the nineteenth-century struggle, and the bells that now ring each year on the night of September 15 to commemorate this action. This narrator's easy slip from the government building to bells reminds us of the role that the Catholic Church played in the struggle for independence. The voice continues, "En mi voz late la eternidad de México" (Mexico's eternity beats in my voice). This explicitly connects the legacy of independence with the narrator's present, and the hope that its context, the post-revolutionary period, will be eternal. The film continues to show Rosaura walking along, and she eventually enters the National Palace. There, this divine narrator further ties this character to important figures from the colonial period and the nineteenth century. The voice tells us that Rosaura is entering the "plaza de Cortés and Juárez . . . es el corazón de la patria" (Cortés and Juárez's plaza . . . [which] is the heart the nation). By mentioning Hernán Cortés (1485–1547), who is recognized for conquering what is now Mexico between 1519 and 1521, the film places Rosaura as an heir of the conquest. He also relates her to Benito Juaréz (1806–1872), who was Mexico's first president of Indigenous descent (1858–1872), and who was largely credited for the 1857 reforms that officially made Mexico a secular country. In spite of being known for his commitment to liberal ideals, the narrator describes this figure as an example of faith and patriotism. The divine voice's interpretation of Mexican history concludes by stating that Rosaura is at the vanguard of Mexico's future. He claims that as a teacher, she will sow seeds that will germinate as "almas limpias que han de forjar el future glorioso de la patria" (clean souls that will forge the nation's glorious future). The omniscient narrator's voice carries strong religious implications. This, coupled with the fact that the opening scenes the film employ imagery from the colonial period and the nineteenth century, suggest that the film's protagonist will fulfill the dreams of all prior periods of

Mexican history through the revolutionary project of education. The narrator's voice and the way that he highlights religious roles, as well as his omniscience, lends credibility to the ways that the film promotes revolutionary ideals.

The divine voice explicitly commissions Rosaura to teach in a series of scenes that follow.[15] There, too, religious imagery gives the educational mission divine overtones. The narrator, speaking directly to Rosaura, and then the president who commissions her, implies that she will be a missionary on behalf of the Revolution. The film shows Rosaura as she runs down the hallways of the National Palace, and the narrator tells her to be fearless. In spite of this omniscient encouragement, she is late. When she finally arrives in the president's office, the other teachers have already left. A guard eventually lets her in to the president's office. Rosaura steps into a new room. She is roughly in the center of the screen, surrounded by impressive furniture and decorations. A man, whose face we do not see, appears on the right-hand side of the screen. This figure, played by President Alemán himself, alludes to his modernization project (Tierney, *Emilio* 145). His divine voice and not-quite-human appearance suggest that his office is somewhat like a church. Critic David S. Dalton adds that even though "we never see his 'holy' face . . . he presides over the nation's 'benevolent' projects of indigenous incorporation" (108). As he speaks, his voice is one of a "Dios invisible o casi (o sea, el presidente) [que] encomienda a su hijo (María Félix, ángel de belleza y bondad) que lleve su palabra a los mortales, o sea el pueblo mexicano" (an invisible or almost invisible God (that is, the president) [who] orders his son (María Felix, angel of beauty and goodness) to bring his word to the morals, that is, the Mexican people) (García Riera, *Historia* vol. 4 146). I suggest that critic García Riera employs biblical language as he describes the president's behavior in this scene because the symbolism is so palpable. The president invites Rosaura to sit down. He tells her that rural areas are not productive because they live in the "tinieblas de analfabetismo" (darkness of illiteracy). So, to fix these problems, he is calling on public school teachers to bring health, water, highways, literacy, and official morality to rural Mexico. Rosaura tearfully agrees to comply with the president's almost impossible charge. Critic García Riera again employs religious language as he describes this scene. In his view, "la maestra rural, tan arrogante y bella (es María Félix) como humildemente pura (usa rebozo) hará triunfar a la Instrucción sobre los Males de la Patria (el caciquismo, la arbitrariedad, el fanatismo, la insalubridad, la ignorancia)" (the beautiful and arrogant rural teacher (it is María Felix) is also humbly pure (she uses a shawl) and will make Education triumph over the Evils of the Nation (*caciquismo*, arbitrariness, fanaticism, lack of health [and hygiene], ignorance) (*Historia* vol. 4 146). The scene, as well as these remarks, give the sense that Rosaura is to be a secular evangelist for revolutionary modernization. The allusions to Catholicism throughout these opening scenes likely inspire sympathy in the revolutionary project the film portrays.

Rosaura bravely brings about modernization at great cost to herself, a type of behavior that likens her to the ideal woman in secular and religious contexts. President Alemán's speeches lauded self-denying women and the Catholic Church praised women who acted like the Virgin Mary and bravely accepted God's will. Throughout the film, Rosaura places the goal of modern Mexico above her own needs. For instance, as soon as she leaves the president's office, a doctor tells her that she cannot go to rural Mexico because her heart condition means that she is not well. Rosaura responds that she has to go because it is her mission. Then, while she is traveling by train to the town of Río Escondido, her illness becomes a problem. Rosaura gets off the train in a beautiful scene that portrays her tiny figure in the wide-open expanse of sky and desert. As she walks across the empty plain, she falls down and a character called Felipe, who we later learn is a veterinary student doing social service, rescues her. He repeats what the doctor in Mexico City had said: that she is too delicate to go to Río Escondido. Rosaura repeats that she has to go where the president has sent her. She is so committed to eradicating the sickness the president had called the darkness of illiteracy that she ignores her own needs. She is a self-sacrificing woman, much like the Church and the state's understanding of an ideal woman who would remain a virgin until marriage and, after that, a selfless mother helping her husband.

The scenes that surround Rosaura's arrival in Río Escondido characterize this character in religious ways. Indeed, she is portrayed in ways that evoke women's role in the colonial project as nuns who were teachers or nurses and who, like Rosaura, cover the heads. This sympathy and likeness are an important part of the way the film portrays this rural area. "Los Males de la Patria" (The Evils of Nationhood), religion and rural tradition, control the town, and mean that it contrasts sharply with the opening scenes in the National Palace.[16] As critic Ernesto Román states, "No hay nada más ilustrativo sobre el 'México profundo' que contrastar estas primeras imágenes del filme que recorren la construcción del Palacio Nacional y los murales de Diego Rivera, con ese mundo rural que desconoce por completo que ya existe" (There is nothing that illustrates 'deep Mexico' more than the contrast between these first images on film that cover the construction of the National Palace and Diego Rivera's murals, with this rural world that is completely unaware that they exist) (58). The first part of Río Escondido that the film shows is its church, and, in this way, implies that the Catholic Church is the most important entity there. It then shows a *charreada* (cattle show) in the town square. Rosaura enters the fray and tries to prevent the local *cacique* don Regino from killing a horse, which ties rural tradition to violence. In this opening scene, the cross looms large over the town square, implying that the Church and rural tradition are the primary powers in the town. The fact that the film presents these Catholic symbols alongside a violent *charreada* would have made audiences sympathize with her mission to change it through the modernizing forces of education.

Subsequent scenes, where Rosaura tries to establish the local school, confirm that the rural tradition of *caciquismo* is the most powerful force in the town. After unsuccessfully challenging the *charreada*, Rosaura falls on the ground with tears in her eyes. When she gets up, she finds a man leading a caravan of horses and donkeys out of the town, and he warns her that she will never be able to change it. The film fades from this discouraging remark to another location, which the film soon discloses as the local school. It displays Rosaura's back as she faces a broken-down building. It occupies the majority of the frame and, even though one of the doors is blocked with lumber, it is an imposing structure. The music and her posture in her simple dress and black *rebozo* emphasize her determination (see figure 1.3). The camera shifts to her face, which presents a perplexed look. It moves to show the word "ESCUELA" (SCHOOL) and then pans out to show that the pile of rocks and gravel is a rudimentary ramp that leads to its door. Undaunted, she knocks. A man opens it and tells her that this is the stable used by don Regino, the local *cacique* and *presidente municipal*, who was also the man with whom Rosaura had tried to interfere in the *charreada*. The *cacique* has managed to gain a position within the post-revolutionary structure of government. Another man adds that "don Regino no es un cristiano . . . es peor que los animales" (don Regino is not a Christian . . . he is worse than the animals). He spends a lot of time in the local bar with his men and, even though he occupies a position in the municipal government, he rails against

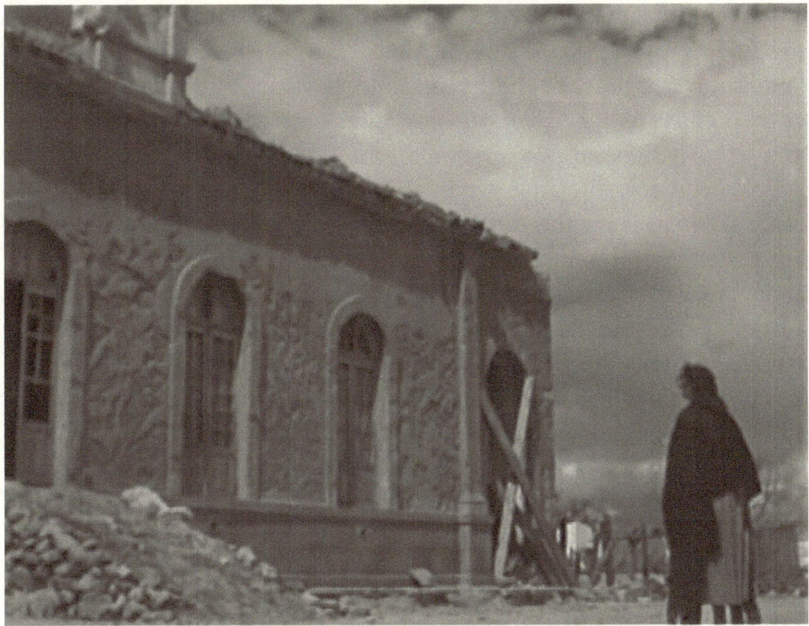

Figure 1.3. Rosaura looks at the school building in *Río Escondido*. *Source*: *Río Escondido*, fair use.

the new government's programs. Like other *charros* that critic de la Mora analyzes in *Cinemachismo*, don Regino has adapted to the new political processes. He has developed a relationship with these newer political powers and maintains control in the town of Río Escondido.

Then, Rosaura attempts to courageously transform the small town. In these scenes, the film reinforces the idea that Rosaura is like the Virgin of Guadalupe, which makes her more palatable to other characters in the film and to the audience. This interpretation of Rosaura as the Virgin follows Dalton's observation that the film equates Rosaura with the divine, because, in his view, the film imbues Rosaura with a secular moral authority (119). It also builds on García Riera's acknowledgement of her impenetrability, which he states was a requirement for nuns and for the Virgin of Guadalupe (*Historia* vol. 4 147). One way the film likens Rosaura to the Virgin is that early in her time in Río Escondido Rosaura miraculously facilitates the healing of another character. This is similar to the way someone praying to the Virgin could understand that she would intervene on the petitioner's behalf before God and facilitate their healing. Rosaura walks along the streets of Río Escondido carrying a satchel and tubes that could hold posters or maps. As she does so, she finds a young boy sitting on the side of the road. Rosaura begins to speak with him. The child sniffs, and we cannot understand his side of their conversation. Then, the boy leads her inside a humble building to a woman shivering on a pallet on the floor. Rosaura bends over the woman and says that she needs a doctor. She forces the boy and his older sister to leave the room and convinces a man with a caravan of horses to travel in a direction he had not planned to find a doctor. The anonymous male character may have trusted her because she was selflessly advocating for others, in line with expectations of women. The doctor arrives and tells the woman she is dying of smallpox. For this reason, he demands that she hand over her baby to Rosaura's care immediately. Although the dying woman is reluctant to do so, she eventually listens to the doctor. The woman may trust the teacher because of her *rebozo*, which, in addition to exemplifying modest dress, may remind the dying woman of a nun or call to mind a statue of the Virgin Mary. Rosaura's dress and actions liken her to a religious figure and allow her to facilitate the doctor's modern form of healing.

Rosaura also organizes a vaccination campaign. In the scheme of the film, her selfless womanhood and her use of religious objects in her campaign are crucial to her success. After she brought a doctor to Río Escondido, Rosaura gained some leverage with the townspeople. As García Riera claims, "Los Judas, los Herodes y los Pilatos no impedirán que esa encarnación del Poder Divino entre los hombres [es decir, Rosaura] cumpla su misión" (The Judases, Herods, and Pilates would not prevent this incarnation of Divine Power among men [that is, Rosaura] accomplish her mission) (*Historia* vol. 4 146). This affords Rosaura the power to work with both the local *cacique* and the local priest to conduct a campaign that would immunize everyone in town. Rosaura's behavior, which is similar to the Catholic and secular ideal of self-denying womanhood, is crucial to bringing people into her understanding of modernization. Moreover, on the day of the immunization campaign, Rosaura also uses a religious object: she rings the church bells to alert everyone and to ensure that the vaccinations occur. Like the quinine in *María Candelaria*, the actual usefulness of this vaccination is low (Dalton 120). Yet, in the fictional world the film represents, the people in the town will be better prepared for the future if they comply with the vaccination order. It is clear that they heed her because she embodies a religious ideal and because she adapts religious symbols for the post-revolutionary context.

Rosaura also establishes the local school. Part of the reason she is successful is because of the way the film likens her to religious leaders. This is a departure from the actual treatment of public school teachers in rural Mexico only a decade prior to the film's release (Kloppe-Santamaría 507–10). School were, as critic Susan Antebi reminds us, important sites for implementing revolutionary ideas of hygiene through a series of rules that were designed to improve society on a biological level (536–38). In other words, schools were a place where children's minds and bodies would be cleansed of old ideas and given new ones. According to critic Tierney, in *Río Escondido* the "school scenes evoke the socialist radical education of . . . the Cardenista period, which preceded it" (Tierney, *Emilio* 153). I propose that *Río Escondido* imbues this space with religious symbolism to make its revolutionary message relevant. One way it does so is through the architectural similarities between school and church. The school is a room with several rows of shared desks that face the front. There, the teacher, who in this case is the character Rosaura, stands and speaks from a raised platform. This is similar to the inside of a church where the congregation sits in pews facing a priest who stands behind a pulpit. The school further evokes a church in a scene where Rosaura takes attendance (see figure 1.4).

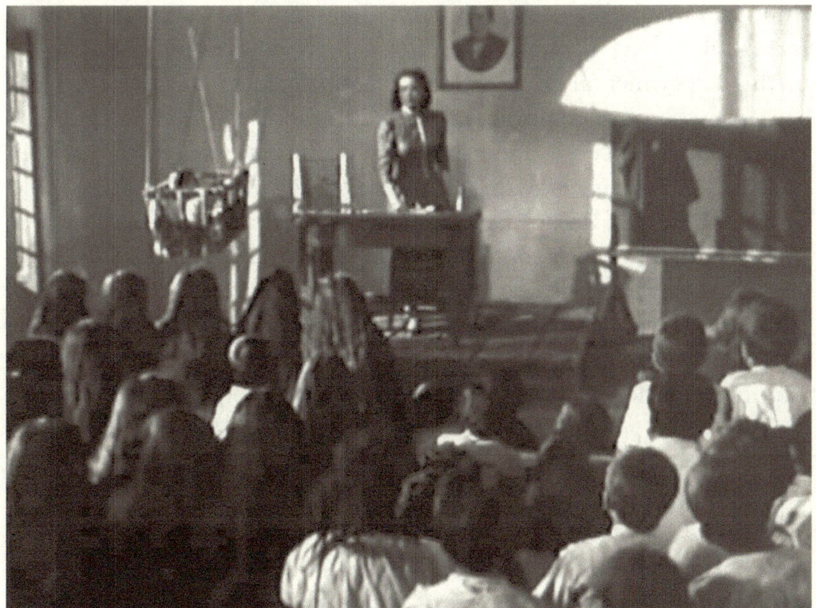

Figure 1.4. Rosaura teaches in *Río Escondido. Source*: *Río Escondido*, fair use.

The camera moves between her at her desk and her student's faces, and then displays her standing on a raised platform. The crib hangs from the ceiling in the upper left corner of the frame, with her desk in the middle. The light falls on her chair and makes it seem like there are candles on the table. This evokes an altar. When she gets up to stand, the film shows her wearing a dress with a high white collar that calls to mind priests' long black robes and white clerical collars. She is positioned just below and to the left of an image of Benito Juárez, which is in a similar position as images of saints or the Virgin would be in a Catholic Church. Other furniture is in the upper-right corner and the students' backs and heads occupy the rest of the frame, in the same spot as Catholic parishioners. The presence of the baby in the crib renders these parallels more significant. Rosaura is now the informal guardian of the three children whose mother died of smallpox and she has to look after the baby while she works. She places this youngest child in a crib in the front of the room, a space that is the same as a sanctuary lamp in a Catholic Church. This is a gilded candle holder that hangs from the ceiling and marks the presence of Jesus in a Catholic Church. This presence may protect the host, or the bread, after it has been blessed by a priest and becomes the real presence of Jesus's body, which people then consume during mass (Fray).[17] The host-like child could be holy or revolutionary. The infant is relevant in Catholic and revolutionary contexts; yet, rather than consecrating Jesus's body, in this experimental space of the school, Rosaura ensures that this baby and the other children who attend school will become Mexico's future. Rural Mexico is either holy, or revolutionary, or both. Later in the film, as Rosaura is dying, her words confirm that the child could be both. She tells the town's priest that she cannot leave the town of Río Escondido or her adopted children because "este niño es México y tengo que salvarlo" (this child is Mexico and I have to save him). This echoes her earlier interaction with the president, whose divine-like voice convinced Rosaura that she was to give this town the opportunity to join modern Mexico. She is effective within the plotline of the film and with its initial viewers because the film appropriates religious symbols to convey revolutionary messages.

Rosaura's speeches to the schoolchildren are another example of how her work as a teacher is effective because it draws on religious symbolism. In the school, she acts like a priest for the church of modernization. She encourages the children to become part of Mexico's future. The children will not ingest a host that she has transubstantiated; instead, they will metaphorically ingest her lessons and be transformed. In this way, the film echoes what Sánchez Prado has described as the utopian language popular in essays of the 1920s, which advocated for almost impossible ways for Mexico to achieve a better future ("El mestizaje" 384). At one point, Rosaura stands in front of a picture of Benito Juárez and admonishes her students to lift the "peso de ignorancia sobre ustedes" (weight of ignorance over you). She later tells them about Benito Juárez and his role in the project of improving the self and the nation. This speech is similar to a sermon, except that Juárez is the savior rather than Jesus. In her view, Juárez was an example of faith and patriotism who had overcome what she calls his rural "Indian" roots. This implies that they could do the same. She is only sympathetic to their Indigenous roots as long as she can bring them into the idea of *mexicanidad* (a stable understanding of Mexican identity) (Feder 252). This inclusion would force them to lose their unique cultural markers. Rosaura also tells her students to become good Mexicans, who understand their errors, as opposed to bad Mexicans who are poor and illiterate. This speech's parallels to religious rhetoric and her parallels to a priest make her message more powerful and palatable.

The final scenes of the film portray Rosaura's illness and death. She is loyal to the president until the end. The way these scenes visually liken her body to statues of saints in a Catholic Church makes her martyrdom for education even more potent. Rosaura's heart condition worsens, and she is no longer able to stand, let alone teach. She has sacrificed herself for others to such an extent that she succumbs to illness. The film shows a group of her former students as they crowd around her bedside and appear to be praying. She wears a white nightgown and her body is lit from a small window in the background. Her body appears similar to statues of the saints or of the Virgin that appear lying down in Catholic Churches. Rosaura has a tearful conversation with the doctor, who tells her, "Muy pronto te podrás liberarte" (You will soon be free). Rosaura responds, "Sabes que no es verdad" (You know that is not true), to which the doctor replies, "Te lo juro" (I swear it). Rosaura clearly does not believe him. So he adds, "Te lo juro por ti, no por Dios" (I swear it on your name, not God's). Rosaura's name is more powerful than God's in the town and in the film. This statement also increases the suggestion of Rosaura's sainthood. In her final act, she dictates a letter for the doctor to send to the president. The secular healer conveys Rosaura's dying wishes to the divine revolutionary father. This imbues the final moments of Rosaura's life with religious metaphors and makes her a secular saint.

Río Escondido presents few direct scenes of religious devotion in the popular or orthodox sense. Nevertheless, key moments remind us of the importance of Catholicism in Mexico in the 1940s, as they employ religious imagery or present very clear parallels to it. This includes the narrator in the opening scenes who gives divine implications to Rosaura's work in Río Escondido. Her vaccination campaign and her teaching are presented with religious overtones, which makes her work more understandable and more powerful. Only the saintly and almost martyred Rosaura can overtake rural bosses and priests and bring rural Mexico into revolutionary modernity.

EL SEMINARISTA

The final film I analyze in this chapter, *El seminarista*, was directed by Roberto Rodríguez, and portrays a young wealthy seminarian called Miguel. This role is played by Pedro Infante, one of Mexican film's most famous leading men. Miguel leaves seminary for his *hacienda* (ranch) in rural Mexico to recover from typhoid. Toño, a fellow seminarian, accompanies him as he recovers. Miguel and Toño live in Miguel's *hacienda* with Miguel's uncle, don Pancho. There, Miguel generally gets in the way of his uncle's relationships with women, teaches music at the local convent school for girls, and falls in love with a woman called Mercedes. Catholicism is central to the plot in *El seminarista*. I argue that in the film Catholic symbols and rhetoric put Miguel's version of masculinity in a positive light, particularly when compared to the behavior of other male characters in the film. These symbols are key to the way that the film endorses the secular ideal of a revolutionary family led by a benevolent patriarch with a selfless wife. The way the character Miguel adopts a gender role acceptable for men contrasts sharply with the flirtatiously malevolent Norberto, his fellow seminarian and aspirational *charro* Toño, and his uncle don Pancho, a quintessential *charro*.

The opening scenes establish a connection between Miguel's benevolence and humility and his vocation as a priest. Miguel and Toño arrive in town, and a servant comes to pick them up in a car.

When the car breaks down between the town and the *hacienda*, Miguel gallantly offers to fix it, in spite of the servant's protests. As soon as Toño and Miguel arrive at the *hacienda*, the film tells us that Miguel owns it but kindly allows his uncle to live there for free. Yet, Miguel's calling as a priest means that his uncle makes fun of him, telling Miguel that he has set out "trajes de hombre" (real men's clothes) in his room so that he can be a *charro*, part of what Pilcher reminds us was a "highly regulated performance of history and tradition" whose code of behavior was defined by "family values, loyalty, and bravery" (181).[18] Miguel's calling as a priest means that the *charro* makes fun of him. Yet, the seminarian's generosity, and willingness to assist others, confirms this positive impression.

Religious imagery reinforces Miguel's innate goodness in scenes that portray his work in the convent school. Miguel accepts the teaching position so that he will have something to do while he awaits his return to the seminary to prepare for the priesthood. This convent school is different from the rural school where Rosaura taught in *Río Escondido*. Miguel's classroom is full of Catholic religious imagery and the school's central courtyard includes statues of saints and the Virgin. The nun who introduces Miguel to his students explains that he will teach the girls "a superarse" (to better themselves). This reminds us of Rosaura's desire to better her students, which in turn would better the nation. Unlike Rosaura, however, he does not propagate a new national agenda. He simply provides a service to the town. The nun's statement offers a religious endorsement of this benevolent male leader.

Religious imagery is part of the way that the film represents Miguel's morally upright behavior at school, particularly towards his students. From the very first scene at the school it is clear that he garners significant attention from these girls and young women, who all ignore the fact that he is a seminarian. His students read racy novels and fall in love with him. The students express this in art and letters. At one point, a group of four girls sit on a bench in the courtyard. The young women's upper bodies fill the majority of a frame. The student on the far-right side of the screen draws a picture of Miguel. She then moves the image away from her to show it to her friends. An image of Miguel fills the screen. He appears in profile, wearing a blazer and tie, and there is a halo around his head (see figure 1.5). The film shows him teaching with regular men's clothing, rather than his seminarian's cassock, and so the drawing represents him in this way as well. The halo implies that

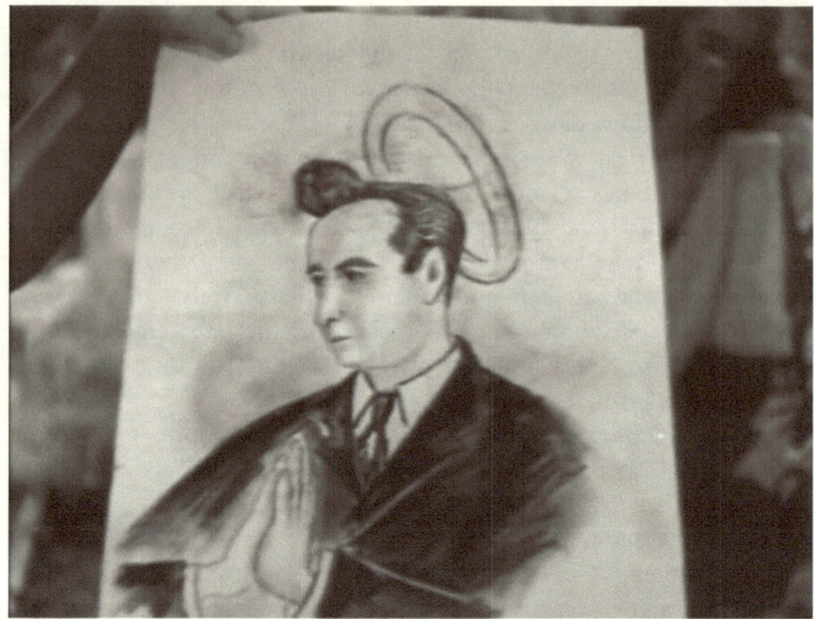

Figure 1.5. A student's drawing of Miguel's saintly face in *El seminarista*. *Source*: *El seminarista*, fair use.

he is a saint rather than a reluctant teacher. This quasi-holy image also foreshadows his interactions with his students. Another scene shows a classroom full of students waiting for him to arrive. They have left a stack of letters on his desk. Once Miguel arrives, he turns to the stack of papers and reads them aloud to the group. As he does so, he calls out the writers by name, as he can distinguish them by their handwriting and their perfume. He notices that one very young girl called "La Tucita," who was rescued from the steps of the convent, is particularly lovestruck.[19] Her letter fills the screen and shows the audience the words "Miguel es mi nobio [sic]" (Miguel is my boyfriend) in childish cursive. Miguel responds, "Eres mi novia" (You are my girlfriend) and picks her up. The scene concludes as Miguel tells the other students that they are young and full of hope. This implies that he will not marry any of them. The camera then shifts between him holding Tucita, the other girls' faces, and his face. Miguel explains that they are attracted to him because he is the only man around and that one day their true love will arrive. Miguel concludes with a Catholic truism: "Dios mismo y la naturaleza es amor" (God himself and nature are love). In this top-down scenario, Miguel is the one in charge. The way this character employs religious rhetoric in his conversations with students, and the drawing that likens him to a saint, make his appealing form of masculinity seem almost divinely ordained.

The film furthers the notion that the way Miguel performs masculinity is appropriate through his interactions with other characters. One male character is the urbane and sophisticated Norberto. He is engaged to one of Miguel's students, Mercedes, and is the regular client of an anonymous female sex worker. Norberto embodies what Pilcher calls an elegant *catrín* (fop) (162). This type of man was "libertino, oportunista, sin control de sus impulsos, desenfrenado en sus pasiones, infiel, sin escrúpulos, sin honor y sin moderación para ostentar lujos" (an opportunistic libertine, who could not control his impulses, unrestrained in his passions, unfaithful, without scruples, without honor, and flaunted any luxury he had) (Luna Elizarrarás 20). As a man without honor, he plans to give the dowry Mercedes would bring to their marriage to the sex worker. Miguel, who is already somewhat in love with Mercedes, chivalrously destroys Norberto's plans. Miguel tells Norberto that don Pancho is also one of the sex worker's clients and that don Pancho uses Miguel's money to give her the lifestyle that she wants. Once Norberto learns this, he shoots don Pancho, which leads to his eventual demise. In contrast with this violent conflict, Miguel persuades the sex worker to leave town. The film clearly prefers the benevolent Miguel to the flirtatious fop.

Religious imagery is a large part of the way that the film sympathetically portrays Miguel's patronizing relationship with Toño. Toño acts as Miguel's comedic foil and sidekick. In the beginning of the film, when a group of male characters insult Toño for being ugly and for being "tan redondito" (so round), Miguel comes to Toño's defense. Miguel also provides for Toño in a financial sense as he pays for his tuition in the seminary. This is contingent on Toño's behavior. At one point, Toño goes out with don Pancho and a group of *charros*. The next day, Toño cannot remember drinking or kissing women, but Miguel finds out that he had done both. Miguel wants Toño to become a priest with integrity and cannot abide by this behavior. Eventually, Miguel realizes that Toño was swayed by the charismatic don Pancho, and, in an act of charity that befits Miguel's role as benevolent patriarch, Miguel forgives him.

Miguel's profession as a seminarian is crucial to the way that he relates to his uncle. At the beginning of the film, don Pancho is a quintessential womanizer who spends significant amounts of time in a brothel, drinks heavily, and tries to convince others to behave like him, including Toño. Then, after Norberto shoots him, he lies on what he thinks is his deathbed, and changes (see figure 1.6). In this scene, a vulnerable don Pancho lies in a bed in the center-right of the frame. An ornate wooden headboard occupies much of the right two thirds of the frame. Miguel faces him, and his back occupies most of the left side of the foreground, with his back to the camera. Don Pancho raises his head from his pillow, and one of his arms is on top of his bedspread, covered in a bloody bandage. In a low gravelly voice, the now vulnerable don Pancho asks Miguel to hear his confession. The seminarian initially declines because he is not a priest. Don Pancho tells Miguel he wants this confession to be "de hombre a hombre" (man to man), not man to priest. The fact that the morally upright seminarian gives don Pancho peace after a deathbed confession with religious overtones rather than the formal ritual of last rites makes

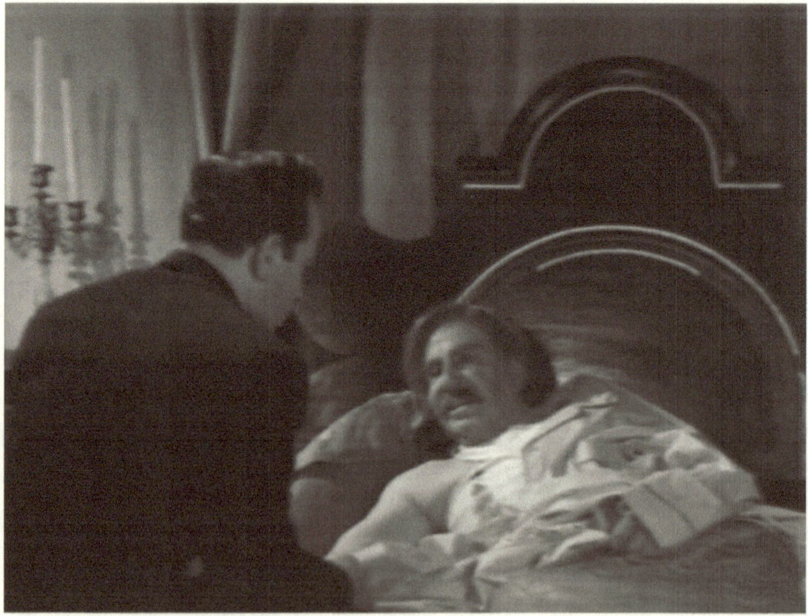

Figure 1.6. Miguel and Don Pancho on Don Pancho's deathbed in *El seminarista*. Source: *El seminarista*, fair use.

the scene plausible. This implies that don Pancho does not want to confess to a priest. Don Pancho claims he is remorseful, but he does not want Miguel to tell anyone about this remorse. Don Pancho recognizes that he is a *sinvergüenza* (shameless man). The camera turns to focus on Miguel, wearing a blazer and tie. Light shines behind his face and emotive music plays. This suggests a saintly appearance, as it evokes the student's drawing. Miguel states that "mi tío es un charrote honrado, generoso, valiente . . . que vive . . . sin pensar en mañana, algo jugador, bastante mujeriego y que se gasta todo en sus gustos" (my uncle is a great, honorable *charro*, generous, courageous . . . who lives . . . without thinking about tomorrow, gambles some, quite a womanizer, and he wastes everything on what he likes). As Miguel speaks, the camera shifts between Miguel's and don Pancho's faces, heightening the emotional impact of these words. Religious overtones in the scene strengthen Miguel's evident empathy for his uncle and put a positive spin on aspects of don Pancho's life that might merit criticism. These aspects of the scene reinforce the notion that Miguel, who dealt charitably with someone whose actions were selfish and may have harmed others, is an ideal male character.

Miguel's behavior leads to him winning a self-sacrificing wife, which is the ultimate prize for an honorable patriarch. In the scenes that show his developing relationship with Mercedes, orthodox interpretations of Catholicism are an obstacle. More popular understandings of religion make this possible. The first way that the film portrays the Catholic Church as an obstacle to their relationship is in a scene where Mercedes goes to the local Catholic Church and talks to the priest. He intuits that she wants to talk about Miguel. As she sits down, the camera shows a crucifix looming large behind her head. The camera then shifts between the seated Mercedes and the standing priest. This visually powerful position confirms the priest's role as religious authority. From there, he tells Mercedes to pray to overcome temptation. She is to kneel in front of the statue of Christ on the cross and ask for courage because "Miguel tiene vocación del sacerdocio" (Miguel has the vocation of priesthood). Miguel's own sense of vocation briefly confirms that the priest is right. Not long after that, the film shows Mercedes and Miguel at the school. Seated, Mercedes tells Miguel that she is going to become a nun. A standing Miguel, whose position on screen evokes the priest's position only moments before, listens and responds that they will see each other in heaven if not on earth. These two characters' religious vocations and the priest's pronouncements suggest that orthodox Catholicism is an obstacle to the two characters' love for one another. It is almost sufficient to destroy a happy ending.

In the final scenes at the school, religious language and the location itself show that characters can overcome orthodox Catholic obstacles. It also makes their reconciliation seem almost divinely ordained. Miguel goes to the convent on the day that he is supposed to return to the seminary. He wears boots, pants, and a shirt with a gun at his belt, inspired by *charros* like his uncle don Pancho or don Damián in *María Candelaria*. The film shows him entering the courtyard and then lands on his upper body in a traveling shot that shows him walking up to Mercedes. He kisses her and asks her if she really wants to be a nun. She responds, "Seré lo que tú quieres Miguel" (I will be what you wish, Miguel). Miguel responds that while God might punish him for forsaking his vocation, he does not care. The religious allusions in this scene make it seem as though the change of heart that has happened for both protagonists is ordained by God. As the film concludes, Toño observes that, through Miguel's marriage, society gained a good man and the Church lost a lousy priest.

Religious symbolism throughout the film, such as the painting of Miguel as a saint, gives a positive interpretation of Miguel's benevolence and self-denial, important features of the Mexican understanding of the benevolent patriarch. Religion marks Miguel's kindness towards Toño and his students and the way that he interacts with Norberto and don Pancho. It is also an important part of the film's portrayal of Mercedes, who was almost a nun, and instead became a devoted wife and mother. Their performance of gender roles, which conforms to roles within the ideal of the revolutionary family, is almost divinely ordained.

~

Golden Age films came out of a period of impressive cinematic production, facilitated by the country's economic growth. The ruling PRI party bolstered the film industry as a way to encourage certain perspectives among the general population that would align with its own. Catholic religious imagery was one way that these films communicated the need for revolutionary measures of health and education and the boundaries of acceptable behavior for men and women. Religious imagery is a crucial way films affirm women's ideal role as a helpmate who would be subservient to a husband who would imitate the revolutionary father and benevolent patriarch. In particular, religious imagery in *María Candelaria,* and expressions of popular religious devotion, illustrate the boundaries of acceptable behavior and the limits of male characters' ability to protect female characters. Then, in *Río Escondido,* I suggest that certain scenes portray Rosaura in ways that create visual parallels between the protagonist in the school and the priest in the church. This makes characters in the film sympathetic to public education, and most likely inspired a similar perspective in its initial audience. Finally, the religious imagery in *El seminarista* gives Miguel's performance of masculinity a stamp of approval and implies that it is the most desirable, as it is most aligned with the state's ideal of a revolutionary father. Attention to religious symbols and allusions in these films, then, expands our existing understanding of the films and the ways that they advanced certain ideas in their context of production.

CHAPTER TWO

CATHOLICISM AT ITS WIT'S END

Priests, Madams, and Sex Workers

In the previous chapter, we examined developments in the Mexican film industry during the Golden Age of Mexican film (1933–1964). This chapter studies films from the later part of the 1960s and the 1970s, another significant period of development for Mexico's cinematic milieu and of incredible changes in its political contexts. Films from this time period portray religion in different ways than films from the Golden Age. Religious imagery in these films, like those we examined in chapter 1, lends weight to the ways that the films engage with their contexts of production. This chapter analyzes three films from this type period: *El oficio más antiguo del mundo* (1970), *Las chicas malas del padre Méndez* (1970) and *Canoa: Memoria de un hecho vergonzoso* (1976).[1] Their representation of religious themes may seem innocuous. Yet, in spite of their potentially innocuous nature, these themes and related imagery are an important part of the way that these films work out contentious social and political issues, such as the state's relationship to the Catholic Church and acceptable gender roles for men and women.

Two of these films were aimed at a mass audience: *El oficio más antiguo del mundo* and *Las chicas malas del padre Méndez.* They are part of a broader group of popular films that referred to religion in some way. These include Julio Aldama's *Padre nuestro que estás en la tierra* (*Our Father Who Art on Earth*) (1971), Fernández Unsáin's *La guerra de las monjas* (*The War Between the Nuns*) (1970), Arturo Ripstein's *El Santo Oficio* (*Holy Orders*) (1973), and Jorge Fons's *Fe, esperanza y caridad* (*Faith, Hope and Charity*) (1972) (Estrada Romero 63; García Riera, *Historia* vol. 15 267–69).[2]

In the midst of this significant film production that related to religion, some of the films include a priest as a central figure. *El oficio*, *Las chicas malas*, and *Canoa* each represent one such religious leader. In each case, the priest character forms alliances with other powerful characters in order to negotiate their particular situation. The man who poses as a priest called Fr. Aurelio (Óscar Chávez) in *El oficio más antiguo del mundo* is recused by two sex workers (Jacqueline Andere and Maricruz Olivier) after he is injured in a car accident.[3] Their madam makes them stop working until he can recover because she wants to maintain appearances of devout Catholicism. After the supposed priest character gets better, he discloses that he was kicked out of seminary and is not even ordained. *Las chicas malas del padre Méndez*, for its part, fictionalizes the life of a priest called Fr. Juvencio Méndez (David Reynoso). This priest tries to rescue local sex workers from a brothel. In this process, he works with local nuns to create a home for these women and their children. The third film, *Canoa*, portrays a group of young men from the city of Puebla who travel to a small town, also in the state of Puebla, called San Miguel Canoa to go hiking. Due to rain, they have to spend the night in this small town rather than camping in the nearby mountains. The local priest, Fr. Meza (Enrique Lucero), believes that the young men are communists and so he encourages the townspeople to form a mob that ultimately assassinates them.

I propose that these films' representations of priests and their relationships with other leaders, such as madams, is analogous to the way religious and secular leaders behaved in their context of production. When the priest characters conform to government interests, I suggest that this parallels the way that the state and Catholic Church became closer in this time period, in part so that the Church would subordinate the people and encourage them to obey religious mores and secular ideals. The films also portray explicitly religious spaces like Catholic Churches, and spaces that are replete with religious imagery, symbols, and allusions, such as homes, meeting spaces for local peasant groups, a "rescue home" for sex workers, and a brothel.

These films were produced in the late 1960s and early 1970s, which was a period of upheaval in Mexico. One area of significant change was the Catholic religious context. Society was coming to terms with changes to the Catholic Church and gaining a clearer understanding of the extent of state violence against Mexican people. Most changes in the Catholic Church were associated with the Second Vatican Council (1962–1965), outlined in the introduction. There were several responses to these changes in Mexico. Some people wanted to further the Council's reforms, some were deeply unhappy and wanted to reverse the changes that had already been enacted, some were content with the changes, and still others pushed for radical change (Blancarte, *Historia* 238). Ultimately, most Catholic churches in Mexico adopted some of the Council's recommendations, and were open to some changes. At the same time, most official statements from the Catholic Church in Mexico were not so open as to recommend ideas adopted by liberation theologians, as Church leaders perceived them to be communist, and, as such, contrary to Catholic teaching.

The group that sought radical change was aligned with what we now call Latin American liberation theology, led by theologians such as Leonardo Boff and Gustavo Gutiérrez. They advocated for the idea that Jesus's message as revealed in the New Testament had a preferential option for the poor. Priests who followed these theologians encouraged Catholic people to read the Bible and to apply its message to their lived experiences of reality, particularly by participating in Comunidades Eclesiales de Base (Christian Base Communities) (CEB).[4] In Mexico, one of the most famous proponents of liberation theology was Samuel Ruiz, a bishop in the state of Chiapas, and another was Sergio Méndez Arceo, a bishop in the city of Cuernavaca in the state of Morelos.[5] Many conservative Catholics were virulently anti-communist (Muro González 548), and they objected to liberation theology because of its sociological and ideological stance, in other words, because of its close relationship to Marxism (Del Valle 261). This is because, as historian Roberto Blancarte explains, socialism was a subset of the already existing evil of liberalism for some sectors within the Catholic Church ("La doctrina" 23). For these reasons, the liberation theology movement was never as prominent in Mexico as in other parts of Latin America.

In spite of the fact that Mexico did not become a haven for leftist Catholicism, religious change did take root among Catholics in Mexico. *Las chicas malas del padre Méndez* and *Canoa*, for instance, portray Catholic religious services in the Spanish language, which shows some degree of acceptance of the changes associated with the Second Vatican Council. *Las chicas malas* and *El oficio más antiguo del mundo* both laud priests and nuns who interact with sex workers in a humane fashion. At the same time, these films also suggest that only a portion of the Council's reforms took root in Mexico, or at least in the Mexican popular imagination. The films portray the ritual of mass where, during the Eucharist, people kneel at the altar rail and the priest only distributes the host or the bread, demonstrating that churches in Mexico had not implemented the recommendations of the Second Vatical Council. *Canoa* includes a priest who represents those Catholics who were extremely unhappy with what they perceived as the radical changes proposed by the Second Vatican Council. The anti-communist Fr. Meza opposes a small group of local residents who have adopted some ideas from liberation theology and whose meetings remind us of the type of Bible study that would have taken place in Christian Base Communities. The films, then, reflect some of the changes in the global Catholic Church, and remind us that these changes led to ongoing tensions within Mexican Catholicism.

There was also significant political upheaval in the period surrounding the films' context of production. They were largely produced during President Echeverría's mandate and reflected his obsession with power and criticism of the Church. Essayist José Agustín for instance, observes that "Ejercer un poder como el del presidencialismo mexicano le gustó tanto que se le volvió adicción" (He liked occupying a role as powerful as that of the Mexican president so much that it became an addiction) (120). Addiction may be an overstatement, but the power that coalesced in this role was not. He sought to subordinate other entities and move towards a better future. Many of his speeches discussed the need to leave behind the "emisarios del pasado" (ambassadors from the past) such as the Catholic Church (Medina Torres 137–38). *Canoa*, which criticizes a Catholic leader, relates to these remarks. At the same time, the way that this film represents Fr. Meza's lust for power can be thought of as a criticism of the president himself.

Each of the films that I analyze in this chapter received direct or indirect state support. The state supported the cultural institutions that trained their directors, paid for their production, and subsidized the cinemas where the films would play for their audiences. Ignacio M. Sánchez Prado describes this tension between cinematic criticism of its context and the filmmakers' continued desire to receive public funding in the following way: for him, Mexican cinema of the 1970s "aparenta cierto grado de politización y conciencia social" (appears to have a certain degree of political and social consciousness) ("Alegorías"

51). As he goes on to explain, "Pese a ser financiado por el Estado, o quizá por recibir dicho financiamento . . . teoriza y figura la radical inexistencia de cualquier colectividad políticamente significativa" (In spite of being financed by the state, or perhaps because it received this funding . . . theorizes the radical lack of any politically meaningful collective) (51). Filmmakers wanted to continue to be able to secure public funding and may have therefore avoided representing significant confrontations to political power. That being said, I suggest that the religious imagery in the films is part of the way that they criticize the presidential administration and its policies.

Many films from this period refer directly or indirectly to the devastating losses of the 1960s, and, in particular, to the Tlatelolco massacre.[6] On October 2, 1968, ten days before the start of the Olympics in Mexico City, government snipers killed hundreds of students and other protestors in the Tlatelolco square in downtown Mexico City and injured or imprisoned at least one thousand more people. Tlatelolco was the first time that state violence had been enacted in such an obvious way in Mexico's capital against the middle classes, not just in rural areas or against marginalized groups of people (Long, *Fictions* 7). The 1971 Corpus Christi massacre continued this trajectory of state violence. On the feast of Corpus Christi on June 10, Los Halcones (The Falcons), an elite force trained by the CIA, killed students demonstrating in favor of greater democratic freedom for intellectuals and for a new form of autonomous government at the UNAM. It was another example of state violence enacted in the capital against a highly visible and sympathetic population.

These events influenced Mexico's cultural sphere. As critic Ryan F. Long's *Fictions of Totality* asserts, "such massive repression turned out to be impossible to conceal, let alone justify. It also impacted intellectuals (many of whom were also persecuted), who wrote about the violence" (7). It led to films such as Leoboldo López Arretche's well-known *El Grito* (1968). Its opening sequence presents "the sound of marching and then that of typewriters clacking. . . . [This] forecasts what is to come" (Steinberg 2). *Canoa* begins in the same way, juxtaposing scenes of a newsroom with images of soldiers marching. As brilliant critic Niamh Thornton observes, it takes 1968 "away from an urban setting into the countryside, thereby displacing this modern, urban clash and moving it so that it takes place against a backward rural space" (115). The fact that the central figure in this film is a priest takes the events outside of their context, and lends significant symbolic weight to the film's criticism of the way that Fr. Meza encourages the townspeople's violence.

The Mexican government, under the PRI political party, also attempted softer forms of control. It sought to bring Indigenous and rural people into its understanding of the Mexican nation through several government ministries, relationships with unions, and special programming.[7] The Secretaría de Reforma Agraria (Land Reform Bureau) (SRA) was in charge of land redistribution via the *ejido* system, the PRI party related to unions such as the Confederación Nacional Campesina (National Campesino Organization) (CNC), and the government's Instituto Nacional Indigenista (Indigenous Affairs Bureau) (INI) sponsored programs that worked towards health and education in Indigenous communities.[8] In this way, the government and its sole political party could position itself as a generous and benevolent protector of Mexico's Indigenous and rural people (Muñoz 124–25). Armed forces also attacked many people in rural areas throughout the 1970s.[9] They engaged in counterguerilla warfare against the Partido de los Pobres (Party of the Poor) in the state of Guerrero. Through paternalist programs and state violence, then, the Mexican government developed close and controlling relationships with Indigenous and rural people as it forced them into its view of the nation state.

Rural people pushed back against these changes with their own organizations and strategies. They developed a peasant group called the Central Campesina Independiente (Independent Peasant Organization) (CCI), which advocated for peasant interests outside of the CNC, the officially endorsed peasant union.[10] Gareth Williams notes that people engaged in guerrilla warfare as well: the Party of the Poor, for instance, attacked military convoys and installations in 1972 in order "to draw the state into open conflict" (165). The film *Canoa* represents characters who allude to those rural people who sought to create change outside of official structures through the CCI, and their participation in popular expressions of religion adds to my impression of the film's sympathetic view of the CCI and the Party of the Poor's rural activism.

Religious imagery in these films also demarcates the boundaries of acceptable and unacceptable behavior for male and female characters. In this way, these films also remind us that understandings of gender roles for men and women changed in the 1960s and 1970s. In the previous chapter, we saw how films held up certain behavior as acceptable for female characters because they participated in popular religious rituals or their behavior aligned with that of the Virgin Mary and her apparition in Mexico. Religious imagery also reinforced the notion that the acceptable role for men was as a benevolent patriarch. In the films from the 1960s and 1970s, religion emphasizes the validity of certain types of male behavior. For instance, it enhances the positive portrayal of Fr. Méndez, who believes that he is saving women from sex work in *Las chicas malas del padre Méndez*, and the negative impression of the anti-communist Fr. Meza in *Canoa*. Religious imagery also makes some female characters, like the madam in *Las chicas malas*, seem particularly evil, or other female characters, like the nuns in the same film, seem particularly selfless. Religious imagery, then, is a crucial part of the way that the films present acceptable and unacceptable versions of masculinity and femininity.

EL OFICIO MÁS ANTIGUO DEL MUNDO

El oficio más antiguo del mundo is about a man who is hit by a car and rescued by sex workers. They take him back to their brothel, where he recovers under the assumed identity of a Fr. Aurelio. The majority of the film takes place in this brothel, and the conflict centers around the fact that the madam has shut down the business while the priest is recovering, because she does not want to offend his sensibilities. A trilingual English, French, and Spanish advertising folder for the film summarizes the film in the following way:

> In a small country town, two prostitutes are having a wild night on the town, and on their way home, find a man who appears to be dead, but is only badly injured. They take him home and their life in their "house" changes drastically. Some of the girls tell their stories and receive religious instruction which changes their lives. (*El oficio* advertising folder)

Throughout the film, the false priest, Fr. Aurelio, cajoles the sex workers into living in a different way, as they talk about their lives with him. He is ultimately revealed as a hypocrite who was expelled from the Jesuit seminary for theft (Cima Films lines 646–47).

This comedic film has an atypical plotline, but does have a lot in common with other films from the time period. *El oficio* engages with political and religious themes, like other films by the reasonably well-known, although not famous, Luis Alcoriza.[11] *El oficio* is also part of Alcoriza's trajectory that includes other films about religious topics, such as his 1961 film *Tlayucan*, about a particular incarnation of the Virgin Mary (*Los que hicieron*). In addition to these religious topics, *El oficio* is part of a tradition of representing sex work on screen, which began with the 1932 cinematic adaptation of Francisco Gamboa's 1908 novel *Santa*, and continued with films like Arcady Boytler's 1934 *La mujer del puerto* (*The Woman of the Port*) and Ernesto Cortázar's 1949 *Callejera* (*Streetwalker*) (Hatfield 146). By the time *El oficio* was released, there was a new subgenre of popular B-movies. Films that dealt with sex work were called *ficheras*, a name that comes from the *fichas* (slips of paper) that a sex worker would receive in a bar each time a man would purchase a drink from her (de la Mora, *Cinemachismo* 110). All of these films, from the 1930s onwards, include elements of a formulaic story arc of "seduction, abandonment, descent into prostitution, and redemption" (de la Mora *Cinemachismo* 109). Alcoriza creates an atypical *fichera*, as it portrays a religious character who "descends" into the brothel. The fact that the priest does not succeed in redeeming anyone calls to mind other films from the time period, including those that represent religion.

The most powerful character in this cinematic universe is the madam, who is neither entirely good nor entirely bad. Religious imagery throughout the film, such as the madam and the sex workers' repeated mentions of Catholic devotion, and participation in popular religious rituals, confirms this ambiguous understanding of the powerful woman at the heart of the brothel. I suggest that the way she controls the brothel, and subordinates the priest, is analogous to the way that the president and the PRI seek to control Mexico. The initially positive portrayal of the liberal-minded false priest makes the fact that he is ultimately revealed as a fraud more disappointing. The way the film employs religious symbolism as it portrays him makes this point powerfully.

Religious symbols are part of the opening scenes of the film, where *El oficio* sets the stage for the events that follow. It opens with a still shot of white letters over a black background: "Los sucesos que verán ustedes en esta película se desarrollan en un país imaginario" (The events that you will see in this film take place in an imaginary country). Following this statement, the film presents shots of famous locations in Mexico City like the Metropolitan Cathedral. This foreshadows the religious elements of the shots in which the sex workers rescue a priest. Two sex workers, Graciela and Libertad, are in a car with men who appear to be their clients. One of them is driving, and almost runs over a man. The two sex workers then force their clients to drive them and the nearly dead man to their brothel, upending the typical rescue narrative. These short shots create a sense of the larger story within Mexico City, and the brief presence of a church foreshadows the role of Catholicism in the film's development

Once they arrive at the brothel, the film presents several scenes that illustrate divisions within Mexican society based on social class and sex. The way the film uncritically represents the priest's interactions with female characters and other characters of lower social classes implies acceptance of this hierarchy. The first shots of the brothel are close-ups of the madam (Gloria Marín) playing dominoes with men as they smoke. These characters call to mind critic Susan Dever's remarks about prostitution in Mexico in the 1950s. She observes that "real or metaphorical denizens of the night [were] wrapped in (faux) furs and dangling (faux) gems, admiring this wayward entrepreneur or that corrupt official, [and] were meant to covet more luxury for themselves and to inspire desire in others" (Dever 100).[12] Later scenes zoom out and show a large living room where some women lounge as they wait for clients and other women dance with the men that they hope will become their clients that evening. The sex workers are light-skinned, and their hair looks perfectly straight, meaning that they appear to be from a higher social class, since in Mexico social class is inextricably connected to color, and approximations of whiteness and European beauty are celebrated. We are given the impression of luxury, and that the setting is meant to inspire this desire in their wealthy clients. The clients conform to this interpretation, as they are light-skinned men. They smoke and drink in the brothel's main area, which is part of a home that is an illusion prepared entirely for their pleasure. The sex workers, madam, and clients occupy a privileged semi-public place in this brothel. Women serve men, men only see things that appeal to them, and even though a priest's presence closes down these nightly parties for some time, he does not end it in a permanent way.

In contrast with the madam, sex workers, clients, and priest, the butler and maid have darker skin. They occupy a much more precarious position, and in some ways, their position is similar to that of the sex workers. The butler and the maid wear uniforms that are common for servants in Mexico and the clients in the brothel routinely disregard them. For instance, after the brothel suspends its services, a group of clients show up at the door on two separate occasions. The first time, after showing a sex worker kicked out of her room to make way for a priest, the camera shifts to the butler standing to the right of the front door. The camera shows the back of his head and shoulders, following the butler's arm as he opens the door (see figure 2.1). A blond man tells the butler that he is rude for not letting him and his friends inside. He walks towards the butler and then both of their faces are visible in profile. The blond man claims that he and his friends should not be refused entry because they have money. The other two men's faces hover behind him. The butler yells at him and shoves him outside and slams the door in his face. The door is a barely viable barrier between the butler and these more powerful characters, who represent the outside world. The clients are willing to exert their gender- and class-based privilege over the butler and the sex workers. This same violent client reappears later and attacks one of the sex workers. He threatens her and tells her that

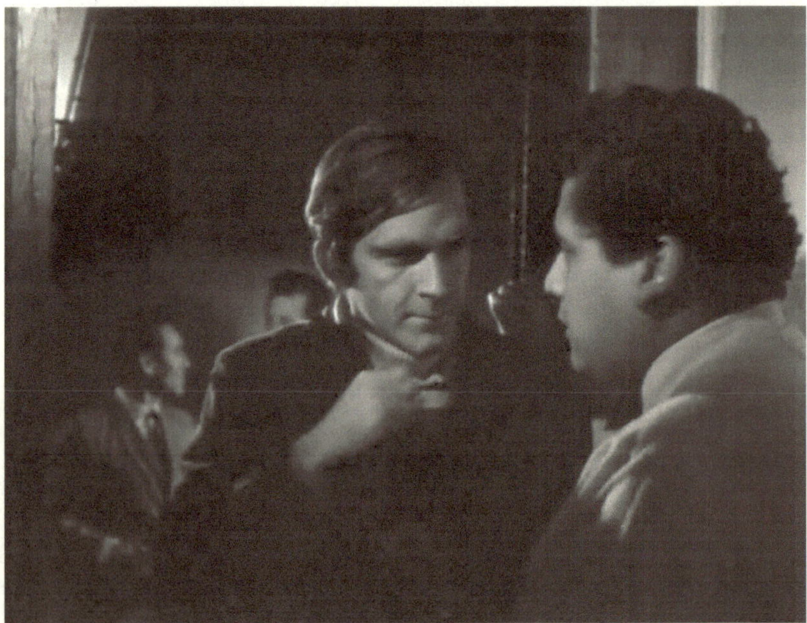

Figure 2.1. Upset clients in *El oficio más antiguo del mundo*. *Source: El oficio más antiguo del mundo*, fair use.

if the brothel remains closed, she will have no money to share with her family. This is a chilling reminder that she and her coworkers are doing a dangerous job to benefit others without recourse. In these scenes, we appreciate that the brothel is a space that evokes divisions in Mexico and highlights the precarity exacerbated by President Echeverría's economic policies. This is particularly evident for vulnerable groups whose existence depends on the whims of the wealthy and the powerful, and who, in this film, they serve almost without complaint.

The madam is the center of power in this divisive space. Gloria Marín, the actress who plays her, was a well-known star in the Mexican cinematic milieu. To understand these dynamics, I examine the actor's work and media coverage (Dyer 97). In this way, I follow the groundbreaking work of critic Olivia Cosentino in star studies and Mexican cinema ("Starring Mexico" 196).[13] In personal correspondence, Cosentino states that Marín was the daughter of famous Golden Age actor, Pedro Armendáriz, who played Lorenzo Rafael in *María Candelaria* ("Re: Star studies"). She had also reportedly been married to actor Jorge Negrete and producer Abel Salazar (Cosentino, "Re: Star studies"). This would have lent Marín influence in the filmmaking process, and likely affected her ability to cultivate a powerful persona on screen.

The madam in Alcoriza's film certainly behaves in ways that conform to these suppositions, and the way her influence is coupled with various mentions of Catholicism makes her seem more malevolent. The film implies that the sex workers have been brought to this brothel under difficult circumstances and now depend on the madam. This aligns with journalist Lydia Cacho's view of sex work in Mexico. In 2010, some four decades after the film was released, she published *Esclavas del poder: Un viaje al corazón de la trata sexual de mujeres y niñas en el mundo*, the most comprehensive analysis of sex work in Mexico to date. She explains that "casi el 60 por ciento de las personas en el ámbito de la prostitución ingresaron en ella entre los quince y los veintiún años, y lo hicieron bajo engaños, amenazas y coacción" (almost sixty percent of people in sex work began working at some point between fifteen and twenty-one years of age, and did so as a result of deceit, threats and coercion) (172). The film does not portray the madam's role in this process; nevertheless, several scenes imply that she exerts significant influence over the women who work for her. A breakfast scene, for example, begins with a traveling shot around a long dining room table where the madam sits at one end. All around her, the sex workers wear housecoats. Included are the sex workers who had rescued the priest, portrayed by well-known actresses Olivier and Andere. The madam sits in front of luxurious curtains, beautifully patterned wallpaper, and a china cabinet displaying fine silver. She tells the workers that since they are all Catholic, they will have to stop working while the priest is staying with them to recover. The madam imposes, and her subjects obey. Later on, the madam reiterates the message that "her girls" must do as she asks. They come into her bedroom and she inspects their clothes, hair, makeup, and bodies. This ensures that they reflect the image she would like her brothel to project to clients. After this inspection, she talks to the sex workers as she sits on a stool in front of an enormous mirror set atop a bureau full of lotions and perfumes. The sex workers move from their line of inspection in her doorway to face her (see figure 2.2). The camera displays their faces and the back of the madam's head in the mirror. It focuses on them to such an extent that it is as still as an image of a group of dolls, whose owner will dress and paint them as she sees fit. The madam tells them

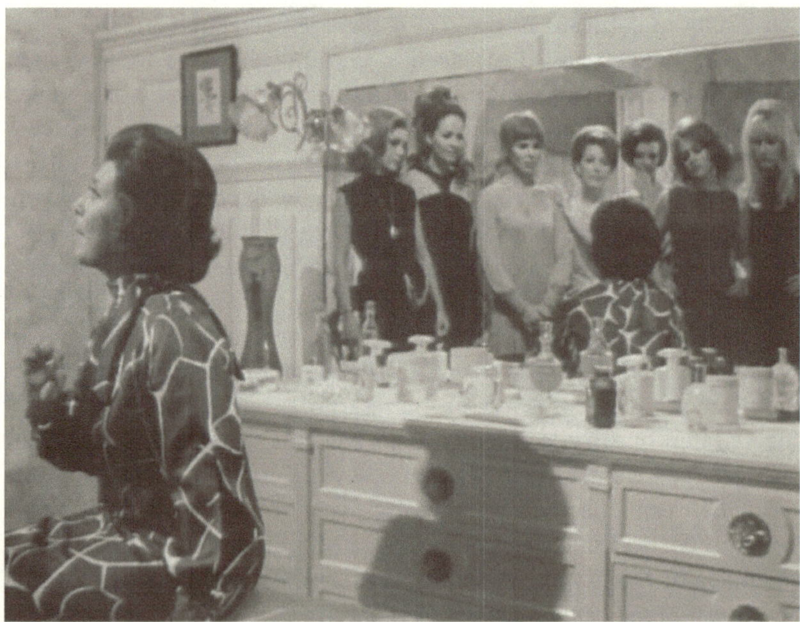

Figure 2.2. The madam's bureau and the sex workers in the mirror in *El oficio más antiguo del mundo*. *Source*: *El oficio más antiguo del mundo*, fair use.

to change into modest clothes and to take off their makeup. *El oficio* does not malign the madam for having encouraged other women to shift from their performance of Malinche to something more virginal. The priest encourages this change simply by his presence. In all of this, Catholicism emphasizes that the madam is a powerful figure whose virtue is above reproach, while the sex workers' virtue is not.

The film also shows how characters who represent different powerful entities negotiate with one another: the madam, the priest, and the doctor, representing political, religious, and medical power, respectively. The doctor and the madam, as power brokers, enforce discretion. The film first shows them interacting in the kitchen, after the injured priest has arrived at the brothel. The madam suggests that the butler call the doctor because he is discreet and would be able to confidentially deal with their situation. To prepare for his arrival, the madam chases the other clients out of the brothel. The doctor arrives under the cover of darkness and he converses with the madam in a dark courtyard. He walks forward, and she walks backwards, suggesting he temporarily exercises more power than she does. The madam, knowing her brothel is in a delicate position, reasserts herself as she makes a deal with him, so that he does not report her establishment to the authorities. The doctor also negotiates with the brothel; counselling the madam with ways to avoid attracting undue attention and likely securing some of the sex workers's attention for himself.

The priest's centrality to the plot in *El oficio* reiterates the profound importance of Catholicism for his fellow characters and the initial audience. The fact that he pretends to be a priest makes the fact that his presence deprives many women of their income that much worse. Indeed, as reviewer Francisco Sánchez observed at the time, "tiene que convertirse primero en delator, o sea, tiene que practicar el oficio de Judas, que si bien, no es el más antiguo, sin duda es uno de los más abyectos" (a failed seminarian needs to become a traitor, that is, he needs to play the role of Judas, which, if not the oldest profession, is undoubtedly the most abject) (7). The actor's career trajectory and the way that the priest interacts with other characters confirm the fact that the so-called Fr. Aurelio is untrustworthy.

The trajectory of Óscar Chávez, the actor who plays the priest, casts him as a somewhat untrustworthy character. Chávez was a famous singer in the 1960s and 1970s, and his first film was the cult classic *Los caifanes* (*The Outsiders*). Chávez's own music provided much of the soundtrack to that film, where he played a character called El Estilos, a working-class *caifán* (greaser). El Estilos's mix of bad boy looks and romantic sensitivity win over a woman called Paloma, who was to be married to another man from her community in the upper-middle-class neighborhood of Las Lomas in Mexico City (Cosentino, "Re: Star studies"). As *Los caifanes* was released shortly before *El oficio*, it set a precedent for Óscar Chávez playing a character with a complex past and charming but untrustworthy behavior.

Certain scenes in the film also present Chávez's body in a Christ-like way. This makes the fact that he was playing a false priest even more deceitful. In a few scenes, *El oficio* focuses on Chávez's aesthetically pleasing body. This injured body is not unlike statues of the bleeding Christ that are found in most Mexican Catholic churches. For instance, after the doctor examines him in his semi-dressed state, a group of prostitutes carry him upstairs on a sheet to a room belonging to one of the sex workers. There, this quasi-messianic figure directly impacts the life of one of the female characters in this film. The sex worker to whom the room belongs starts crying and packing her things so that the priest can recover there. As she packs, the film displays the crucifix on the wall beside her elaborately carved headboard, next to an image of a saint. There is also a small altar above her closet with images of saints and the Virgin surrounded by blinking Christmas tree lights. When she turns the lights on, it looks like an altar in a Catholic church or on the street, and its proximity to the injured Chávez calls to mind the statues of Jesus that emphasize his blood. These likenesses make the way that the film eventually reveals the priest's deception much worse.

The priest depends on the madam to maintain his position and so he pretends to be sympathetic to the sex workers. Early in the film, the madam goes into what is now his room and states that this is a pension for decent women—students, domestic workers, and so on. She states, "Todas son buenas muchachas, cristianas, eh, cristianas" (They are all good girls, Christian, eh, Christian). The priest responds by stating that he knows what this place is. From above, the camera focuses on the priest lying in bed, in a shot of his body that would be similar to an image of Christ. The priest adds, "No soy para juzgar . . . No hay nadie que no haya cometido errores" (I am not one to judge . . . There is no one who has not committed mistakes). The camera zooms out to display a crucifix on the wall above him as one of the sex workers kisses his hand. This type of sympathy calls to mind Chávez's career trajectory, which mixed romantic sincerity with bad boy behavior. It also reminds us of the way that then-president Echeverría used populist rhetoric to evoke other, more popular and populist presidents.

In the film, the priest acts like a benevolent representative of the Catholic Church as the sex workers tell him about their lives. This role as priest, coupled with representations of the characters' expressions of popular devotion, makes the priest character's actions seem more meaningful in the moment and more deceitful later on. Libertad inadvertently explains why her fellow sex workers opt to talk to him rather than with other priests: "¿Por qué no se arrepintieron con el padre de la iglesia? Porque es gordo y viejo. En cambio éste es un rorrazo, y en el fondo todos se han enamorado de él" (Why did I not confess with the priest in the church? Because he is fat and old. This priest is young, and ultimately everyone has fallen in love with him) (Cima Films line 612).[14] In one scene, the priest talks with another sex worker, Yolanda. The camera zooms in on him as he lies in a bed that fills up the entire screen. The camera then pans out and shows him lying down on the left-hand side of the bed. In this scene, the crucifix on the wall is now directly above the priest's head. Yolanda sits on a table to his right and leans over her hands as if in prayer. She wears a modest brown dress and her blonde hair is perfectly styled. The character, played by Isela Vega, was a new direction for this actress, who consciously constructed an image of herself as a tough and fierce woman with masculine qualities (de la Mora, "Tus pinches leyes" 248). At the same time, this role follows what critic de la Mora identifies as a tension within her work between sexual objectification and sexual agency ("Tus pinches leyes" 248–49). The camera follows the character Yolanda in a traveling shot as she walks around the room, telling the priest that her father would drink and hit her and her mother. It settles as she stops to face her altar, which has a sacred heart of Jesus, some angels, candles, and a Virgin Mary. There, Yolanda continues her story, about an uncle who hit her and eventually raped her, and how she then left their house to live in a convent. There, in this purportedly religious space, she met someone who got her the job in the brothel. This conforms to Cacho's observations that sex work is neither isolated nor hidden; rather, it is an industry where lawyers, bar owners, massage parlors, cantinas, and restaurants are all involved (173). She tells the priest that she hates it and that while she is working, she pretends that she is not there. The priest makes her feel better. In fact, later in *El oficio*, this character tells the other sex workers, "Platicar con él es como tener un baño pero por dentro" (Talking with him is like taking a bath, but for one's insides). One by one, the other girls tell him their own stories, which all include ways that men have taken advantage of them. The false priest displays empathy in each of these interactions. This benevolent representative of the Catholic Church sanctifies the brothel through these impromptu confessions.

The priest's relative liberalism and his willingness to empathize with the sex workers in the brothel does not last. He yells at one woman that of course her father drank too much, someone abused her, a boyfriend tricked her, and then she landed here. The priest blames the female characters for the consequences of their lived experiences of trauma. He tells them that they should not be content to be the playthings of so many men. They respond by saying that they can sell their bodies if they want to. In this way, the characters reenact what Cacho identifies as a key question in the debate about sex work: whether women can make choices in a cultural context that subjugates them (172). The priest's actions in these moments of confrontation mimic conservative elements of the Catholic Church. That he is ultimately revealed as a fraud suggests that the sex workers' position is the valid one.

This film portrays an unusual situation, that of a false priest shutting down a brothel, and exploits it to comedic effect. Moreover, *El oficio más antiguo del mundo* is part of a historical precedent in Mexico of using sex work on screen to offer social commentary in ways that conform to expectations of *ficheras* with religious overtones. Careful analysis of the religious imagery sheds light on the power dynamics in this environment. In the fictional universe of this *fichera*, religious imagery emphasizes the ways that the brothel mimics social stratification in Mexico. The madam exerts significant power, using sex workers as pawns in her own negotiations with the doctor and the priest. She asserts her power in many of the same troubling ways that political leaders exercised power in the film's context of production. Other scenes show that the false priest is a benevolent leader with whom the sex workers feel comfortable conversing, and so the fact that he is a false priest is more devastating. This points to the limits of sympathetic leaders and implies that weak or effeminate men are ineffective leaders. Within the world of the film, religious imagery, and the hypocrisy of the religious leader, demonstrate a clear preference for the madam's leadership style, similar to that of a benevolent patriarch.

LAS CHICAS MALAS DEL PADRE MÉNDEZ

Las chicas malas del padre Méndez is a *fichera*, part of the same subgenre of B-movies as *El oficio más antiguo del mundo*. It is one of many films directed by Fernández Unsáin, which, in the director's own words, filled movie theaters and made money for their producers (*José María Fernández Unsáin*). Critics have called it boring, and García Riera noted that it was Fernández Unsáin's most somber film (*Historia* vol. 14 291). It is based on a true story about a priest called Fr. Juvencio Méndez (David Reynoso) in the city of Uruapan, in the state of Michoacán.[15] A young and thoughtful priest decides that he is going to help the women of his town. During one of his regular debates with a local doctor about theology and ethics, the doctor challenges him to do something practical. So, he decides to rescue sex workers. The sex workers in question all work in a single brothel run by a madam, called doña Elvira (Beatriz Baz), and a pimp, called El Grillo (the cricket) (Claudio Obregón). Fr. Méndez and a group of nuns, led by Mother Rosa (Jacqueline Andere), challenge doña Elvira by creating a shelter for sex workers called the Instituto de Obras Sociales (Institute of Social Work). The film portrays Fr. Méndez as a leader who is improbably successful and acts in ways that benefit others. The religious imagery that is part of the way the film portrays this leader in a positive light means that the film presents the priest's paternalism and attachment to the traditional understandings of the role for women, where they can be rescued or can help the benevolent patriarch. This contrasts with the film's presentation of the pimp and the madam's false devotion to the Virgin of Guadalupe, which is presented alongside the negative way that they treat the priest and other characters in the film.

The film is set in Uruapan, in the state of Michoacán. This setting and its ties to key historical figures makes the priest's on-screen mission seem more credible. Michoacán has been considered the heart of Mexico. Indeed, during the 1930s, then-president Cárdenas encouraged tourism to the Pátzcuaro region of Michoacán. He also developed policies to ensure that his home state would be central to national myth-building as he encouraged artifacts from that state to be reimagined as national symbols (Jolly 21). The state of Michoacán was also important in the colonial period, when it was a site of the Inquisition. During the early part of that period Vasco de Quiroga became the first bishop of Michoacán (1535–1565). This bishop was so beloved he was often referred to as "tata," the affectionate term for a father. His relationship with the Inquisition is also significant, because Vasco de Quiroga was "known for his sometimes-violent authoritarianism as well as his Franciscan-like compassion for the native people" (Verástique xiii). He would also have been involved in arresting women for their supposedly immoral behavior. The state gained renewed importance during the film's context of production, and these allusions related Fr. Méndez to an important figure in Mexico's religious history, implying that he was right to rescue women from sex work.

This role of benevolent patriarch was a departure from the actor's previous roles. Immediately after the release of *Las chicas malas*, the actor David Reynoso starred in what Cosentino calls "the famous, scandalous, highly-seen *Sangre del enemigo* [1971] as a drunk and depressed 'jorobado' [hunchback] who loses his wife in an accident and then takes his stepdaughter as his wife. He is sexually impotent and there's lots of violence between the two of them because of his questioned masculinity" ("Re: Star studies"). On screen in *Las chicas malas*, there is no question about his masculinity. When Fr. Méndez decides to intervene in a local brothel, he puts on a disguise of a hat and tie and confidently walks into the local cantina. In what seems an unlikely turn of events, no one recognizes the priest. He first sidles up to one woman but when he explains that he wants to help her rather than pay her for her work, she responds, "Aquí no hay negocio . . . es una lástima. Parecías muy machito" (There is no business here . . . that's too bad. You looked very macho). This character describes the priest as very masculine, an appearance that predicts future success.

The allusions to biblical passages emphasize the importance of the priest's rescue project. In one sermon, for instance, Fr. Méndez reminds his detractors: "Recuerda la Magdalena . . . Dios personalmente la perdonó . . . llegó a ser santa" (Remember the Magdalen . . . God personally forgave her . . . she became a saint). This statement reflects a common conflation of the biblical character of Mary Magdalene with the woman who poured perfume on Jesus' feet, and the mistaken belief that both were sex workers, even though there is no textual evidence for this (see for example Matt. 26:6–7). The two characters were simply women who behaved in ways that may have been unconventional for their contexts. Yet, this misinterpretation of biblical texts likely connects the characters to the priest's addresses in mass, and might encourage them to stop judging sex workers. The priest continues to reference biblical texts to encourage people not to judge the women he intends to rescue. In another scene, a group of nuns ask him about the causes of sex work, and whether the women involved are sinners. In response, the priest quotes the biblical text that deals with a woman caught in adultery: "Let anyone among you who is without sin be the first to throw a stone at her" (John 8:7). This woman in the biblical text was likely in a very similar situation as the women in the brothel. These references to biblical texts are part of the way that Fr. Méndez gains authority and encourages others to adopt his vision.

The film's portrayal of a Catholic mass, in which the sex workers appear devout, and where the priest's homily admonishes people into kindness towards sex workers, is another effective way that the film promotes a sympathetic perspective towards these women. The sex workers are portrayed covering their hair throughout the entire service. This, much like the nuns in habits, was no longer required after the Second Vatican Council. It suggests that these characters were devout and morally upright. The priest's sermon admonishes his congregation: "Todos ustedes me dan asco y vergüenza, y del asco y vergüenza su dios, un dios falso que han fabricado para su propio provecho, porque el verdadero Dios, y el Dios en que creo no es venganza, es amor y no odio, es caridad y no negocio" (You make me sick and ashamed, and I am sick and ashamed of your god, a false god that you have created for your own gain, because the true God, and the God I believe in, is love not hate, is charity not business). In other words, the congregants who are not involved in sex work are hypocritical, because they insult the women even though after church they might be paying them for their work. He adds that to reach this God one needs to be clean on the inside and the outside, not just whitewashed. The idea of white-washing ties whiteness to purity and relates behavior to an unattainable physical goal and a certain level of wealth and the upper social classes. Fr. Méndez then encourages the congregation to imitate Christ: "Amen a su prójimo como aman a ustedes mismos" (Love your neighbor as yourself) (Mark 12:31). The priest practically bullies them into Christ-like behavior; the fact that he does so in his homily, in front of a group that includes seemingly devout sex workers, makes his perspective seem all that much more important.

The film also connects the priest to sainthood. Fr. Méndez realizes that he needs to rent space in order to rescue sex workers, and to acquire this space, he needs money. He sells a statue of St. Martin of Porres to pay the first month's rent for the facility. With the saint's help, the priest establishes his ministry in a relatively nondescript white building in Uruapan. He also collaborates with nuns, a group of women with an explicitly religious profession, to develop this project (see figure 2.3). In the scene that christens their building as the Instituto de Obras Sociales (Social Work Institute), the camera travels from a group of five nuns on the ground, to a nun on a ladder, to the priest holding the ladder. The group of nuns holds up a rope that is connected to the Institute's sign. It moves to show Fr. Méndez, holding the bottom of a ladder and facing the camera rather than looking up and ensuring the safety of the person on it, and finally, the camera continues upwards to show a young nun putting everything in place. She tells her mother superior, patiently waiting on the ground, "Madre Rosa, que mensa eres" (Mother Rosa, you are so smart). The priest's smile and posture suggest he is pleased with his work and with the women's assistance; together, these characters and their religious garb begin what the film presents as a worthy project.

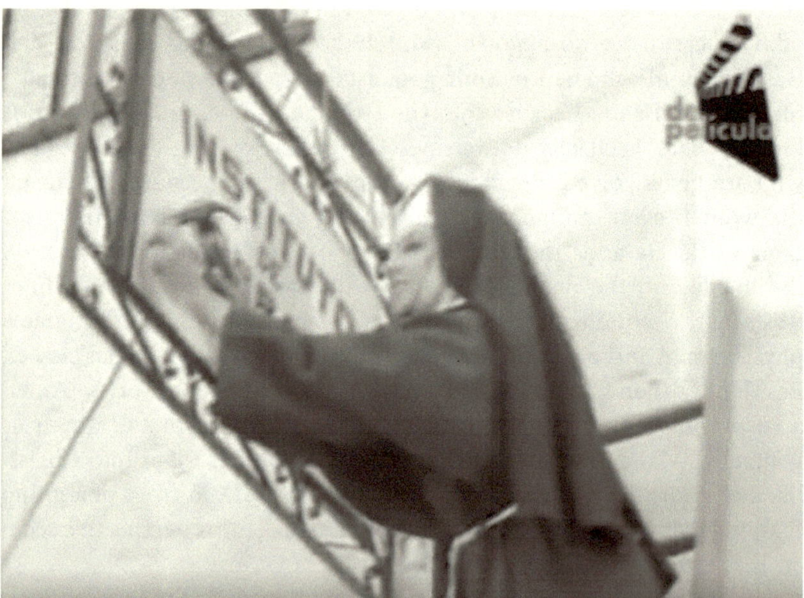

Figure 2.3. Setting up the Social Work Institute in *Las chicas malas del padre Méndez*. *Source*: *Las chicas malas del padre Méndez*, fair use.

Las chicas malas del padre Méndez imbues the priest's Social Work Institute and his attempt to rescue a sex worker called María with additional religious imagery in order to affirm his work. When the priest begins his mission, the film likens the priest to the Christian savior. The first character that Fr. Méndez rescues is a woman who was abandoned by her boyfriend after she became pregnant. This character, María, was metaphorically ruined after she could no longer conform to the virgin part of the Virgin-Malinche dichotomy. In accordance with the formula of a *fichera*, after seduction and abandonment, she descends into prostitution. This life involves dancing in a cantina, meeting men, and taking them back to a brothel. Once the priest finds her and convinces her to talk to him, María tells Fr. Méndez why she and the other characters engage in this type of work: "Por diferentes causas, todas tristes y sucias" (For different reasons, all sad and dirty). These stories echo those that the sex workers told the priest in *El oficio.* For some it was hunger, for others pregnancy, and for still more it was some other sin that prevented them from going to any decent home. Fr. Méndez extracts her from the cantina and brings her to his residence, where he tells her to take off her false hair and wash her face. He tells his mother—who is also his housekeeper—"Aquí se queda hasta que encuentre que hacer con ella" (She will stay here until I figure out what to do with her). The priest rescues her and brings her to a Catholic understanding of wholeness when María's ex-boyfriend reconciles with her and they get married in a Catholic church. Fr. Méndez bids her farewell as he performs the sacrament of marriage, officially welcoming her back to her faith. This likens the priest to the savior in the Christian tradition.

The film emphasizes Fr. Méndez's salvific qualities as the film progresses. Fr. Méndez initially allows the women to go to cantinas with him, but eventually decides that they should stay in the Institute building for their own protection. At one point, Mother Rosa (Jacqueline Andere) accompanies Fr. Méndez on a mission. The actress, who had played a sex worker in *El oficio*, now walks along a street towards the cantina to remove women from that work environment. In the cantina, a male character attempts to purchase sex from her. She says, "No soy mamacita soy madre" (I'm not a hot mamma, I'm a mother superior) and then runs away. After this altercation, the priest decides that the nuns will directly rescue women. They will focus on the appropriate traditional activities for nuns: teaching women and children and fundraising. Local people give them meat, milk, and other forms of assistance.

Thanks to this help, the nuns develop programs, such as sewing, cake making, and typing. Fr. Méndez gets credit because he performs the most visible part of this social work project, and the nuns make his savior-like rescue mission possible.

The film's portrayal of the priest and nuns' genuine religious devotion contrasts sharply with the false devotion of the people in charge of the brothel, doña Elvira and El Grillo. Like Fr. Méndez, they claim that they are helping women. After all, the brothel employs women when no one else will. Yet they do not pay them appropriately. The sex workers tell the priest that doña Elvira has three houses, and they have none. They call her a "mendiga vieja" (old beggar), an insult that implies she is taking their money. As it is directed towards a woman, it also includes an additional sense of offense, because women are usually thought to be more charitable than men; when women do not act in this stereotypical way, it can be more disappointing and lead to more extreme reactions. This couple's appearance on screen next to an image of the Virgin of Guadalupe confirms that they are reprehensible characters. The first time that film the shows them in the brothel's office, a room full of chairs with red patterned and textured wallpaper, they sit on separate chairs with an image of the Virgin between them. This enhances the perception of doña Elvira as an exotic evil woman. She has curly red hair, which is unusual in Mexico. This hair color has been associated with evil and hypersexual behavior. According to Laura Turner, St. Jerome thought that dyeing one's hair foreshadowed spending eternity in hell, and some traditions believe that Judas Iscariot, who betrayed Jesus, and Mary Magdalene, the disciple sometimes thought of as a sex worker, both had red hair.[16] Her eyeliner and clothing are designed to make her appear Asian, perhaps fulfilling a male fantasy of female submission. El Grillo, for his part, has an unappealing skinny moustache and slicked back hair. He encourages her plan to trap Fr. Méndez in a compromising position in the brothel. The camera zooms in from a scene of the two characters in their own chairs to focus on doña Elvira as she gets up and walks over to El Grillo to sit on his lap. They cement their plan to with a kiss (see figure 2.4).

As this plan develops, the redheaded doña Elvira is likened to the supposedly redheaded Judas Iscariot, the ultimate betrayer in the Christian tradition. She and El Grillo feign Catholic devotion as they attack the priest, and are very upset when the priest and nuns cut into

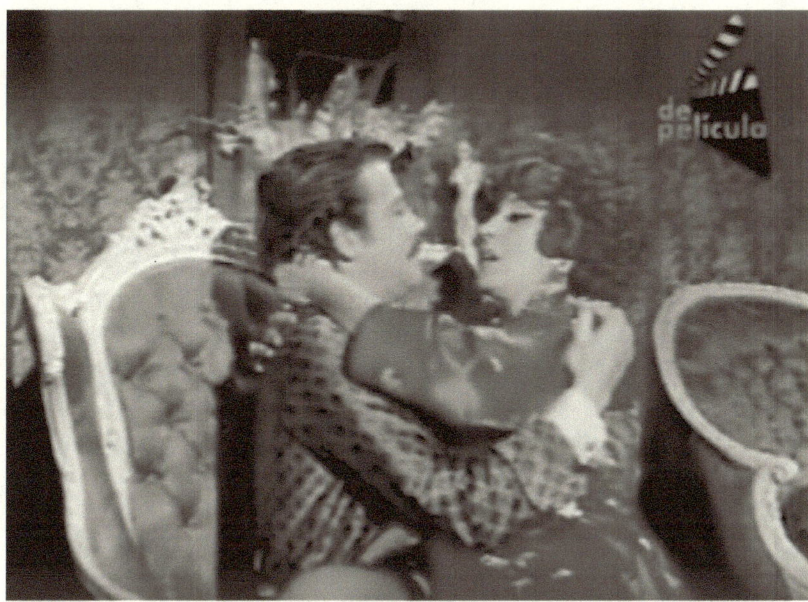

Figure 2.4. Doña Elvira and El Grillo in *Las chicas malas del padre Méndez*. *Source*: *Las chicas malas del padre Méndez*, fair use.

their earnings. In order to get back their lost profit, they take advantage of the priest's desire to protect women and children. Doña Elvira asks a young woman in the cantina to be a mole in his project. He takes her to the Institute, and then returns with her to the brothel to remove her belongings. While he is there, doña Elvira corners him. She tells him that she has realized she mistakenly employed some girls who are minors, which is inconvenient for her. Doña Elvira tells Fr. Méndez, "Ya ve padre, soy muy católica, por eso no quiero tener a las chiquillas" (You see, Father, I am very Catholic, and for this reason I don't want to have the very young girls). The way the film couples doña Elvira's purported religious devotion by returning to focus on a large image of the Virgin in Mexico in her office makes her seem even more corrupt. Out of nowhere, El Grillo appears with a drink for Fr. Méndez. He welcomes the priest with further false piety: "Que bien que estás en nuestra casa como amigo, padre" (How good it is to have you in our house as a friend, Father). Doña Elvira echoes this sentiment and adds that she will bring Fr. Méndez any young girl who comes to the brothel. Then, suddenly, there is unusual music and the screen blurs. The priest puts his hand on his forehead and a girl comes into the room and tries to comfort him. She then tells him, "Bésame padrecito" (Kiss me, Father). This seductive behavior uses a diminutive for the formal version of the word father—which when used in this way has sexual connotations. It may also allude to the fact that, in the universe of the film, some priests have frequented her brothel. It also refers to those men who would have enjoyed pretending to be priests; this is a line they would have appreciated. It likely made sense for the audience, as they could imagine either of those two situations. Another man appears out of nowhere. He takes advantage of the priest's drug-enhanced stupor and shock at doña Elvira's remarks to attack him. Once the priest realizes that he has been fooled, he manages to escape doña Elvira, El Grillo, and the attacker. The priest almost dies as a result. This further likens the priest to Jesus, who was crucified after he was betrayed. The way the film portrays doña Elvira and El Grillo's false piety and purported devotion to the Virgin throughout their interactions with the priest makes their attack even more reprehensible.

Las chicas malas is based on a heart-warming story that fairly predictably reinterprets a *fichera* to represent a priest and a group of nuns rescuing women from brothels. It employs religious imagery in order to emphasize the need for Fr. Méndez's project, and the evil nature of other characters in the film. Fr. Méndez is a leader who is successful in a way few leaders are in the film's context. The film's location, and the city in Michoacán it represents, parallel certain ideas about what it means to be Mexican and legitimizes Fr. Méndez's mission. The film employs common understandings of biblical ideas to encourage other characters in the film, as well as the audience, to sympathize with what it understands as the plight of sex workers. Moreover, it connects Fr. Méndez to sainthood and to ideas of salvation in the Christian tradition as he engages in his rescue mission. His collaboration with another group of explicitly religious characters, nuns, lends further credence to this positive understanding of his work. The way *Las chicas malas* represents the behavior of the priest and the nuns puts the priest in a favorable position when he meets the brothel's pimp and madam. These characters exhibit false piety, false respect for the priest's holy order, and false devotion to the Virgin, and the way they betray him only serves to confirm the importance of Fr. Méndez's rescue mission.

CANOA: MEMORIA DE UN HECHO VERGONZOSO

Canoa tells the story of Fr. Meza, who is a different type of priest that those in *El oficio más antiguo del mundo* and *Las chicas malas del padre Méndez*. He leads a town to massacre a group of university workers. This fictionalization of historical events was one several films Felipe Cazals made during this time period that dealt with historical or political events, to significant critical acclaim.[17] Other examples of Cazals's work from the period include *Aquellos años* in 1973, and *Las Poquianchis* and *El Apando* in 1976 (Leen 5; Sánchez Prado, "Alegorías" 51n4). *Canoa* represents an historical event, a massacre of a group of young men who worked at the Autonomous University of Puebla who decided to go hiking near the town of San Miguel Canoa, also in the state of Puebla. These young men were killed by the townspeople on September 14, 1968. The film represents what critic Miriam Haddu calls "the true accounts of a group of (apolitical) Universidad de Puebla employees who decide to go on a mountaineering expedition to a nearby dormant volcano known as La Malinche" (213). *Canoa* introduces us to them by printing their names along the bottom of the screen during the first few scenes of the film. The character Julián González Báez appears first, convincing his fellow workers to join his hiking trip. They remind Julián that the people in San Miguel Canoa are "bravos" (wild or rough). Julián tells them that he had a wonderful time when he climbed the mountain on two previous occasions. Ultimately, Ramón Calvario Gutiérrez, Roberto Rojano Aguirre, Miguel Flores Cruz, and Jesús Carillo Sánchez accompany him. It is raining heavily, so they cannot camp on the mountainside as they had planned. They have nowhere to stay for the night and the townspeople refuse to help them. Ultimately, Fr. Meza's rhetoric over loudspeakers persuades the townspeople to murder the university workers because they are communists, just like the medical students who had visited their town a few weeks before.

Cazals's film centers on the character of the priest, Fr. Meza, and portrays him in ways that are similar to then-president Gustavo Díaz Ordaz. In this way, it criticizes the Church for orchestrating the massacre in Puebla. It shows that the priest, in charge of the local church, colludes with municipal government to control the town and its people. The fact that the priest is a religious leader makes his actions seem more reprehensible and strengthens the film's implicit criticism of state action. The way the film portrays his ties to other forms of power stands in for direct criticism of secular political leaders in Mexico, as well as the Tlatelolco massacre that took place eight weeks later. The film's critical portrayal of the priest and orthodox Catholicism also contrasts sharply with the way the film presents a group of dissident peasants. On screen, CCI members' own forms of popular religious expression are part of the way they oppose the priest and act hospitably towards visitors to their town, which causes their eventual death.

Canoa encourages the audience to believe its version of events by presenting them in a documentary style with few special effects. The film begins with a series of black-and-white shots displaying the phrase, "Eso si sucedió" (This really happened), along with the date of the massacre. The sound of the telephone interrupts this initial information to show a newsroom. One journalist receives information over telegraph, and another types the story. A still image of a newspaper replaces the newsroom. Sounds of static in the background suggest that the film presents this information in real time. When the film moves to San Miguel Canoa, a "native informant" (Salvador Sánchez) introduces viewers to the town with descriptions of several scenes and asides throughout the film (Losada 63). The camerawork is straightforward. Cazals eschewed special effects, included only three panning types of shots and required "the use of traditional lenses—no tricks, none of the optical effects which were so popular back then" (West 16). These strategies encourage the audience to believe *Canoa* is truthfully portraying events.

The fact that the film appears believable is important, because it means that its direct criticism of the Catholic Church and indirect criticism of the Mexican government would also seem plausible. *Canoa* represents the events in San Miguel Canoa in ways that parallel the Tlatelolco massacre. Both massacres were orchestrated by anti-communist leaders, took place in public, and ended with the deaths of innocent people. In addition to portraying the massacre itself, the film highlights a priest, Fr. Meza, who dominates the town and whose behavior parallels that of then-president Díaz Ordaz, who dominated the country. Díaz Ordaz was, according to Felipe Cazals, "Torvo, aterrado; y al mismo tiempo colérico y peligroso" (Grim, terrified, and at the same time angry and dangerous) (García Tsao 138). The historical Fr. Meza's interactions with the film director confirm this impression. Prior to filming, Cazals and screenwriter Tomás Pérez Turrent went to the town of Canoa and met with its priest, Fr. Enrique Meza. Cazals and Pérez Turrent secretly recorded the conversation. Once Fr. Meza realized this, he placed a cardboard cutout of a gun on the table in front of Cazals and Pérez Turrent (Huerta Ortiz).[18] The priest's rabid anti-communism alludes to Díaz Ordaz, who had wanted to cleanse his country of communism (West 16). In the historical context:

> Días antes de la llegada de los montañistas, el sacerdote había lanzado un discurso inflamatorio: habló de "comunistas" que con su bandera "roja como el infierno, negra como el pecado" insultaban a dios y a la patria. Aseguraba que pronto llegarían a San Miguel a despojar a sus habitantes y a prohibir la religión.
>
> (A few days before the hikers arrived, the priest had given an inflammatory speech: he spoke about "communists" whose flag, which was "red like hell, black like sin" insulted God and the nation. He assured them that they [the communists] would soon arrive in San Miguel to dispossess its inhabitants and prohibit their religion.) (Solórzano)

Canoa reproduces the historical figure's anti-communism, furthering a parallel with President Díaz Ordaz. Critic Gustavo García notes that there were even physical similarities between the actor Enrique Lucero, the actor who portrays Fr. Meza, and the former president (293). The film presents events in ways that represent an historical figure and are analogous to the way the president created a massacre.

Fr. Meza's machinations are a key part of the film, and the fact that he is a religious leader makes his awful behavior seem even worse. The character on screen exhibits what Cazals called the "perfil, la actitud, la doblez, la marrullería, el caciquismo del padre Meza" (profile, attitude, tendencies, trickery and *caciquismo* of Fr. Meza) in the historical context (García Tsao 130). The film introduces him with a voice-over that states, "Como en todos los pueblos hay una iglesia" (As in every town, there is a church). This establishes the importance of the Catholic Church in the town. The narrator adds,

> También aquí el párroco ocupa un lugar importante en la organización social. Y su influencia es determinante en la vida del pueblo. Pero quizás sea difícil encontrar a un párroco

> tan particular. Llegó con su cocinera o ama de llaves a San Miguel de Canoa hace ocho años procedente de Aguatenpan en Puebla, de donde salió, dicen sus enemigos, ante las protestas de los habitantes por lo que llamaron sus abusos.
>
> (Here too the priest has an important place in local society. And his influence is decisive in the life of the village. But it would probably be difficult to find such a strange priest. He arrived in San Miguel Canoa with his cook or housekeeper eight years ago from Aguatenpan [Ahuatempan] in Puebla, which he left, according to his enemies, because of the protests of the inhabitants about what they term his abuses.) (Leen 11–12)[19]

The fact that the narrator claims it would be difficult to find such a priest implies that, elsewhere, priests are more normal. Indeed, the narrator's voice-over consistently uses the term *párroco* (parish priest) as opposed to the more common *cura* or *sacerdote* (priest), emphasizing Fr. Meza's relationship to his *parroquía* (parish) in San Miguel Canoa. The camerawork that introduces the priest confirms that what the narrator has said is true. The film introduces the priest and a group of men in a square in San Miguel Canoa. A building, painted blue, occupies the left side of the frame. An unpainted brick building and another faded blue structure are visible behind the group and a sliver of sky is present in the upper-side of the frame. The priest walks into the foreground and the film focuses on him and the baby goat that he is holding. A man brings some milk for the animal and a photographer in the left-hand side of the frame is ready to present this image of the priest to the world (see figure 2.5). This scene portrays Fr. Meza in a sympathetic way, as a character who looks after innocent animals. It also establishes the priest as the center of this group of men, and shows that others acquiesce to his needs, which is exactly the way that the film shows the priest relating to other people in the town.

He is, after all, the head of the church, the most powerful entity in San Miguel. The role of the Church in *Canoa* conforms to López-Vallejo y García's observations about the Catholic Church in Mexican film more broadly. For this critic, Mexican cinema showed that the Church was at once an

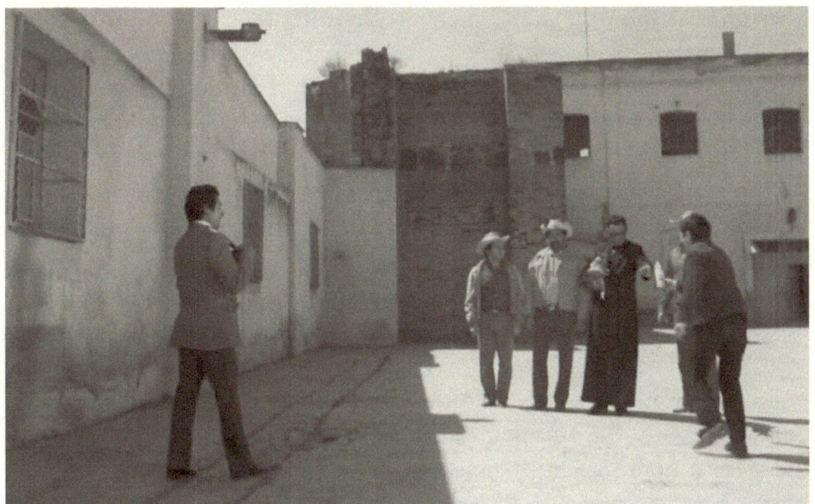

Figure 2.5. Fr. Meza in the town square in *Canoa*. *Source*: *Canoa*, fair use.

> institución sociopolítica, organización jerárquica, fundación autoritaria, estructura jurídica y forma de control ideológico, [y] aportaba al sistema socioeconómico que la gestó todo un variado catálogo de conductas a seguir, de obligaciones por atender y de exigencias por internar.
>
> (sociopolitical institution, hierarchical organization, authoritarian foundation, judicial structure and form of ideological control. It contributed to the socioeconomic system, which had created it [the Church] by giving it a code of behavior to follow, and obligations and demands to meet.) (119)

The opening shots of the church courtyard point to the power of the institutional Church. A scene is divided on a diagonal line where the foreground displays several buildings, including one cement wall with faded signs from a previous election. The tops of these buildings, from the bottom left to the top right, separate it from a huge blue and white church. In the small *zócalo*, a white gazebo matches the white municipal building. The blue-and-white flags that attach to the gazebo mirror the church's colors. This scene gains peaceful or pastoral overtones as the film shows men shepherding their sheep through the *zócalo* on their way to what we assume is the pasture. This establishes the church's prestigious role in the town, and in the events that the film will portray there.

The fictional Fr. Meza, the head of the church in the film, controls the political process, and relates to all branches of government active in San Miguel Canoa. This parallels the PRI political party's total control in Mexico. The narrator describes the priest's control and several scenes, including ones that insert images of song lyrics, confirm it. The narrator states that he selects *alcaldes* (mayors), *regidores* (members of town council), justices of the peace, as well as the treasurer for the boards for water and energy, and so on. The film also shows the priest colluding with the municipal bureaucracy when, relatively early in the film, a man in a suit states that his office likes the priest because he collects money on their behalf. The unnamed bureaucrat declares that the priest was instrumental in bringing light, water, the highway, and the telephone to San Miguel Canoa. The fact that he begins this list with the word light is significant. It evokes the beginning of the biblical book of Genesis, where God brought light to Earth (Gen. 1:3). This lends the priest some divine credibility. The narrator-informant corroborates the municipal official's remarks because he explains that town residents have to pay the priest for certain services: "Todo lo demás que cobra, si nomás cobra . . . Dice que es amigo de los meros chingones del gobierno" (He charges for everything else, and not only with money . . . It is said that he is a friend of the fucking big shots in the government). It follows that the priest "hace regir en sus fieles una mixtificación ideológica plena de postulados éticos que él mismo, previsor (¿o vidente?), santificaba y santifica" (creates an ideology among his followers that involves ethical positions that, in his wisdom and foresight (or prophesy?), had sanctified and could continue to sanctify) (López-Vallejo y García 119). In other words, he found ways to justify his ethnically questionable behavior to his followers. The narrator is unimpressed with the government's collusion and with the priest's willingness to do as he wishes with the people's money, as well as the implication that the priest may extract additional loyalty from them. Similarly, the mayor of San Miguel Canoa appreciates the priest's collaborations. He gestures as he compliments his own good works: "Ve las obras que estamos ejecutando. El padre nos ayuda. Quienes los atacan son los enemigos del progreso en nuestro pueblo"

(Look at the projects that we are doing. The priest helps us. Those who attack him are enemies of progress in our town). In one scene, *Canoa* captures the priest from below as he speaks to a group of boys who surround him. This suggests that the priest's actions and behavior will affect these children, and by extension, the town's future; it also poignantly emphasizes the priest's control of the townspeople through his connections with other entities.

Two scenes that present images of song lyrics confirm the way that Fr. Meza uses his role as the town's priest to collude with other powerful entities. At two points, the film shows still shots of lyrics from a book of *corridos*, which are a type of folk music whose ballads narrate historical events. Each time, the screen displays two yellowed pages from a songbook and reproduces what appears to be the spine of a book down the middle of the screen. The first of these *corridos*, "Historia de un curo impio" (The Story of an Impious Priest), describes a priest who held a mass on a Sunday in 1966, which was also election day. After mass, the priest locked the doors so that no one who had attended mass could vote. When the opposition won this election, he ordered people to attack their house and store:

> Fué [*sic*] un desastre tétrico en aquella vivienda,
> quebraron trastos, botellas y mucho comal;
> dejaron la casa como una molienda,
> por el elemento que hoy Gobierna.
>
> (That building was a horrible disaster
> they broke bottles and pans for frying tortillas
> it looked like they had ground the house down,
> [those from] the party that Governs today.)

This intervention in elections ended with significant violence and bloodshed. This *corrido* points to massive electoral fraud, collusion between the Catholic Church and a political party against a group of peasants, and presages the film's ending. The narrator-informant lends credibility to the inserted lyrics as he confirms that these events took place. The film later presents another *corrido*, titled "Nefasta división y odios" (Nefarious Division and Hatred), which describes the town of Canoa in great detail. It focuses on Fr. Meza's corruption and states that he had asked each family for so much money for a baptismal font that they suffered. Not only that, but he used the language of taxation rather than tithing, which suggests that he used state funds for a religious project. In this way, he was:

> violando nuestras Leyes de Reforma,
> y profanando la Ley de Dios;
> debiendo respetar en toda forma,
> a nuestra culta Religión así como las dos.
>
> (violating our reform laws,
> and making God's sacred law profane;
> requiring our respect regardless,
> to our holy religion and to him.)

The *corrido* observes here that the priest violates Mexican law and Catholic religious practice, and requires almost absolute devotion to his person. It concludes by stating that the town was corrupted by this "infiel; / dictador y usurpador de sotana, / que vino a perturbar como un Lucifer" (infidel; / dictator and usurper in a cassock / who came to disturb us like a Lucifer). This insults the priest, as it likens him to a Devil in priest's clothing. The insertion of both *corridos* adds to the film's criticism of the way the priest manipulated religion.

The film illustrates the priest's power with specific groups in multiple ways. He implicitly or explicitly controls members of his parish, as they seem interchangeable to him. This is especially true for female characters. Unlike Fr. Méndez, Fr. Meza is not even trying to be benevolent. At one point, the film shows a man and a woman who visit him while he is eating his lunch while his housekeeper watches. The camera focuses on the anonymous woman's face against a black background as she tells Fr. Meza that the activists put up a flag in the cathedral. The camera briefly shifts to show the priest sitting and eating, and then shows the woman's head and neck against a green wall and window as she says—in reference to the activists—"comunistas, hijos del diablo" (communists, children of the Devil). The camera pans out, and, in the background, the housekeeper is on the left side of the frame, the priest is on the right, and the unnamed woman stands, with her back to the camera, facing them, in the middle. In the bottom right corner of the foreground, a man hurriedly ties up parcels (see figure 2.6). The priest echoes her by calling them "atheists" and "enemies of

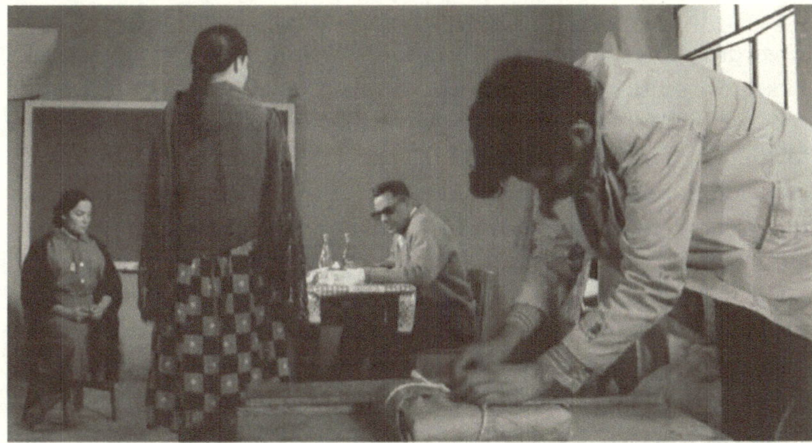

Figure 2.6. Anonymous women and Fr. Meza in *Canoa*. *Source*: *Canoa*, fair use.

God." The camera periodically moves back to the housekeeper, whose eyes are cast down and she plays with her hands. The housekeeper and the unnamed woman appear almost identical as when they speak, their heads and necks visible against a simple background. They are certainly interchangeable in front of the priest.

The priest's power extends to the townspeople as well, and the religious nature of his control makes it more malevolent. The film includes a native informant who describes the townspeople and their livelihood: "Cortan leña, hacen carbón . . . Unos son dueños . . . otros ya no más agarran" (They cut wood, make charcoal . . . Some own the land . . . others just take it). The fact that this semi-legal way to make charcoal is their primary source of income implies that most people in the town occupy a precarious economic situation. The priest seems to allow this behavior and threatens anyone who prevents his followers from earning money this way. The "informant" goes on to state, "Ni le decimos nada ya no les paramos porque matan" (We don't say anything or even stop them anymore because they will kill us). The priest has found ways for everyone in the town to bend to his wishes. In addition to these threats, the priest creates opportunities for people to be more active in the church. When the film first presents the church, the informant's voice-over explains that Fr. Meza had also started several congregations, which are groups of people within a parish devoted to a saint or specific cause. The priest would meet periodically with these congregations, and, in this way, gain more control in San Miguel Canoa. According to critic Niamh Thornton, the film presents "a grotesque image of country inhabitants as compliant followers of a corrupt and brutal church" (128). Haddu agrees with this assessment; for her, the town has a fanatical devotion to the priest, who manipulates the people based on "his own fears and prejudices" (214–15). The townspeople obey this fearful leader, thanks to his cajoling through the congregations, and his more violent threats.

The film portrays Fr. Meza in Catholic mass in ways that confirm his power in the universe of the film. *Canoa* films a mass from behind the altar, showing the church from the perspective of the priest or of the statues of the saints, where the townspeople appear to be interchangeable peons. It displays the altar, the table on which the elements will be placed for the Eucharist, the altar rail, and some candles. This angle also shows that the church is packed. Someone comes up the aisle and the priest and the sexton enter the sanctuary from a side door. The priest states, "Adoremos al señor" (Let us worship the Lord) to the congregation, and the mass begins. During the mass, he speaks in Spanish and faces his congregation. So, in spite of his conservative leanings, he follows some of the reforms of the Second Vatican Council. Yet as he never looks directly at any other character, as if they are part of the masses that he can control.

The priest's control extends to the townspeople's interactions with visitors as well. The characters who live in San Miguel Canoa fail to give the hikers shelter. In light of the heavy rain, Julián and the other hikers first ask a local shop owner where they might be able to stay. He tells them to ask the mayor, and they decide instead to ask at the church. Once they arrive at the priest's home, they ask the priest's housekeeper for shelter. This female character, under the priest's control, claims that there is no room. When Julián insists that they are simply looking for shelter, and asks, "¿Acá eso es malo?" (Is it wrong to ask that here?). This is ironic, considering that Christianity is based on the life of a person whose parents begged for shelter for his mother to give birth to him (Luke 2:6). In the film, Fr. Meza is so powerful that he has convinced his congregation, and by extension, the town of San Miguel Canoa, that it is Christian to deny the humanity of others.

The lone group of people who the priest cannot control demonstrate a completely different kind of behavior. Their expression of popular religious devotion counters Catholic orthodoxy and strengthens the way that they oppose Fr. Meza's accumulation of power in the town and his collusion with local government. This cinematic representation alludes to *campesinos* fed up with the false promises of government-associated agencies, including the CNC, the INI, and the government's corrupt relationships with *ejido* leaders. The group of dissident characters in the film refer to real historical figures who joined groups like the CCI, which they believed was a democratic alternative to state-funded structures (Sepúlveda 17). This group of dissatisfied men and women appear on several occasions. The first time, the film shows a room where six men and one woman sit in a dark room around a table. The men all have moustaches, cowboy hats, and red bandanas. The film focuses on the face of one of these male characters, who is much older than the rest. His wrinkles and withered bandana around his neck evoke the lengthy struggle for justice in this town and in Mexico. Their leader, a character called Lucas García, speaks. After a quick glimpse of the countryside through a window, the film returns to the room to focus on Lucas (see figure 2.7). There are religious and secular images on the walls behind him, including an altar that centers around images of the Virgin and Jesus Christ which, in this case, appear to be the Virgin of Guadalupe, the Virgin of the Immaculate Conception, and the Divine Child Jesus. There are also images of important Mexican

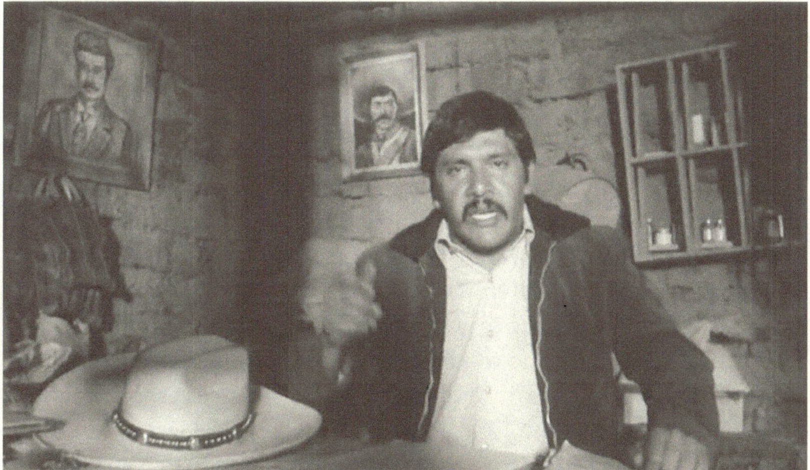

Figure 2.7. Lucas García and posters of Ricardo Flores Magón and Emiliano Zapata in *Canoa*. *Source*: *Canoa*, fair use.

leaders on the walls, including one of the revolutionary hero Emiliano Zapata, and another who may be the anarchist leader Ricardo Flores Magón. This implies that the characters in this room have attempted to model themselves after these figures, particularly since several of them wear blue shirts, the same color as the shirt that Zapata wears in the picture on the wall. The fact that the image of the man on the left is not clear means that the film could tie these characters to general ideas of communism and anarchism. These connections to Catholicism and the left lend the group credibility.

The film is so rich with religious overtones that this group's interactions with the hikers can be thought of in a religious sense as well. They were the only ones to extend hospitality towards the visitors, acting in line with Christian teaching about loving one's neighbor (Mark 12:31) and being kind to strangers, as they could be angels (Hebrews 13:2). This group also dies for their willingness to host the hikers, a sacrifice that is similar to the Christian understanding of Jesus's death on the cross as he laid down his life for his friends (John 15:13). The fact that the characters who belong to the CCI behave in a way one might expect to be based on Catholic ideals lends their position moral weight.

It also makes the way the priest encourages the town's hatred towards visitors seem even more reprehensible. The way the film includes religious rhetoric and religious spaces as part of mob violence is chilling. The townspeople first gather in the store and the priest sends them an emissary: his housekeeper. The same character who had denied the hikers a place to stay for the night tells the group gathered in the store: "Dios nos hará de ayudar" (God will help us). Her words suggest that the town understands its actions were divinely ordained. They agree, stating that by the next day people will have died. The film shifts to portray a group of male and female characters gathering in the church's courtyard. This space, with clear religious overtones, is strewn with light. The church's white façade pops behind the people wearing dark clothes. The camera shifts to the *zocalo*, where a larger mob has gathered. Even though they are not in an explicitly religious space, they use religious rhetoric to justify their murderous actions. The mob chants, "cristianismo sí, comunismo no" (Christianity yes, communism no) as it breaks in to the CCI house and kills Lucas García. The film's portrayal of violence ends with the echoes of the mob's chants. It then shifts to portray a Catholic religious ritual that confirms that the priest orchestrated the events: a mass shown from the church's entry door, so that it portrays the parishioners' backs, the exact opposite perspective used for the earlier mass in the film. Religious imagery bookends this bloodshed, which, in the film, is understood to take place thanks to God's help, using Christian rhetoric, with an outdoor space next to the church playing a key role.

The film emphasizes the priest's evil through the way that it represents his attempts to distance himself from the events. In a scene towards the end of the film, Fr. Meza wears a suit and tie rather than a clerical collar and robe. He confirms what had occurred but claims that he could not have done anything because he was sick that day. He also claims that cooks in the church were the ones who had denied the hikers a place to stay for the night. The priest adds that perhaps it was the men's fault for not clarifying that they were workers. He says, "El sentimiento católico de esta gente es muy profundo, muy arraigado" (The people's Catholic beliefs are very deep, very profound). He, as the center of power in Canoa, the town, and the film, could not possibly have been at fault. So he blames the victims for their own deaths. The juxtaposition of these statements proves that for this priest and in this film, Catholicism is the antithesis of the left.

The film's simple camerawork and documentary style both highlight the way a very powerful priest could convince otherwise ordinary townspeople to murder innocent people from outside their community. The way the film portrays the priest's manipulation of his role as a Catholic religious leader, and his manipulation of Catholic rhetoric, in order to ally himself with other powerful figures and to control the people is chilling. The characters affiliated with the CCI appear to engage in popular forms of religious expression and to behave in ways that would conform to Catholic understandings of the Christian religious ideals of loving one's neighbor. The fact that they refuse to obey the most powerful character, on screen and in the town, means that the townspeople eventually murder them and the hikers that they host. This film clearly cautions against powerful religious leaders and orthodox Catholicism, as well as the president and the broader Mexican context to which they allude.

~

Canoa, along with *El oficio* and *Las chicas malas*, alludes to significant changes in Mexican society, including changes in the Catholic Church and acceptable gender roles for men and for women. Each of these films portrays a Catholic religious leader or someone who would like to be one. Their qualities vary. *El oficio más antiguo del mundo* portrays the false Fr. Aurelio, who puts on a mask of liberalism as he attempts to model sympathetic behavior towards a group of sex workers. He is quashed by the madam's authority and his own lies. *Las chicas malas del padre Méndez,* for its part, celebrates a priest who seeks to help his community by fashioning himself as the sole rescuer of vulnerable women. In *Canoa,* Fr. Méndez closely adopts the anti-communist line of the Catholic Church, and his authoritarian power goes too far: he makes his peons put his opposition to death. By paying attention to the role of priests in this sample of Mexican films from the 1970s, we see three different representations of religious leaders. These portrayals offer a damning verdict on Mexico's religious, political, and social context, and the possibilities for long-term change.

CHAPTER THREE

COMPLEX RELIGIOUS EXPRESSION WITHOUT REDEMPTION

Catholicism, Syncretism, and Judaism

Films from the 1970s represented Catholic priests as they critically engaged with their social and political context. Mexico changed in the ensuing decades in a process some political scientists describe as democratization.[1] As Mexican society changed, so too did Mexican films; however, they continued to represent elements of Catholicism, as well as aspects of other religions.[2] I focus on three films from this period: *Ángel de fuego* (1992), *Novia que te vea* (1994) and *El crimen del padre Amaro* (2002). I argue that the films' representations of religion, via troubling religious figures, perverted religious spaces, and frightening religious imagery, are their social and political context, particularly in establishing acceptable boundaries for gender roles for men and women in the 1990s and 2000s. Moreover, their disturbing imagery is analogous to a context with widespread social disintegration where there is no possibility of redemption.

This context of political, social, and economic crisis relates to the type of neoliberalism that prevailed in Mexico from the 1980s onwards. During this time, the Mexican government's concerns were no longer solely regarding the legitimate use of force against its population or maintaining control over its territory. Instead, it needed to maintain legitimacy in a consistently worsening economy. In 1982, for instance, the Mexican government attempted to deal with the fallout of the international oil crisis, which devastated its economy. Mexico received loans from international lenders, experienced hyperinflation, and eventually reissued its currency. These changes were most significant for people who were already marginalized and from the lower social classes.

Alongside of issues, the PRI political party continued to hold power on a federal level. It manipulated the electoral system to encourage the population to cast votes in its favor and made promises for social development that it did not keep.[3] President Carlos Salinas de Gortari (1988–1994) won the 1988 election, for instance, by claiming that his administration would stabilize the country. His government did enact programs that were supposed to improve the lives of everyday Mexicans. These programs included Solidaridad (Solidarity), which was an umbrella social program, and Programa de Apoyos Directos al Campo (PROCAMPO) (Direct Aid for Campesinos), which was specifically directed at rural Mexico. "The[se] programs provided the financial support for ambitious projects that included the building of new schools, hospitals and drainage systems for the benefit of Mexico's marginalized communities" (Haddu 146n136). The government did not recognize its own role in creating the problems that affected the most marginalized people. In critic Elissa Rashkin's words, the Salinas regime "hoped to clean up the Federal District through increased regulation . . . [but] it did little to address the problems that had created the mess in the first place" (213). The government's corruption, "ill management and wasteful planning . . . meant that many of these projects were never fully completed" (Haddu 146n136). The PRI political party claimed to meet people's needs. The programs that it developed succeeded only in making promises, not in delivering results.

Mexico was also marked by the effects of trade liberalization, which led to significant instability throughout the country, extensive internal migration to Mexico's border with the US, and an increase in crime. Alongside the loans that Mexico received in the wake of the 1982 oil crash, various industries began making agreements for free trade with their counterparts in the US. By the time NAFTA came into effect in 1994, free trade extended to all sectors. Yet, as some scholars observe, because of these preexisting agreements, NAFTA was more rhetorical than practical (Haber et al. 75). In spite of this observation, NAFTA certainly stimulated foreign direct investment along the Mexico-US border (Haber et al. 77, 93). NAFTA was also cited as a cause for the

Zapatista uprising in Chiapas, which created further instability throughout Mexico.[4] This trade policy is also a reason for an uptick in violent crime, especially against women in border cities. Mass urbanization combined with the economic crisis and a frail jail system created a violent reality for many (MacLaird 64). Many in Mexico's capital were unhappy with these changes. A widely cited newspaper column by Carlos Bonfil states that Mexico City was "una ciudad al borde del naufragio y del colapso moral" (a city on the edge of a shipwreck and moral collapse) ("Las ciudades"). This vivid imagery reminds us that Mexico City is literally sinking because of ecological destruction. In his view, this city experienced "una modernidad que sólo ofrece la proliferación de la injusticia social, la corrupción política y la vida prostibularia" (a modernity that only offers the proliferation of social injustice, political corruption and a life of prostitution) ("Las ciudades"). The misogynist allusion to sex work suggests that Mexico opened itself up to foreign investment for temporary gain at the cost of long-term success. In these ways, and in others, economic policy brought about significant insecurity and instability for many people in Mexico.

Film financing also changed in this period, and these reforms in cultural policy led to the production of new types of films. Misha MacLaird's *Aesthetics and Politics in the Mexican Film Industry* explains that neoliberal privatization policies in the 1980s and 1990s also applied to the cultural sector. As we saw in the introductory chapter, the government created new agencies for cultural production, dissolved unions, sold its chain of movie theatres and its television station. The government also changed quotas for Mexican films that had to be shown in Mexican movie theatres and deregulated ticket prices, and so film was more accessible to wealthier people, who were now watching more films sponsored by the private sector and by studios in the US.

The films I analyze in this chapter were not initially blockbusters, and it is unlikely they were conceived of with these new multiplexes in mind. They were all, however, produced with the new model of film funding, that is, the co-production model, which responded to public and private interests. *Ángel de fuego* received funds primarily from IMCINE, producer Leon Constantiner, and director Dana Rotberg (Arredondo, "Dana" 169). Similarly, *Novia que te vea* was produced by FOPROCINE, one of IMCINE's funding programs, independent investors, including members of Mexico City's Jewish community, and Guita Schyfter's company, Arte Nuevo (Arredondo, "Guita" 52).

El crimen del padre Amaro was also financed in part by FOPROCINE. An additional portion of funding came from Alfredo Ripstein (Merino and García Estrada 112; Soutar 110). Later, once the Catholic Church's censorship led to it becoming a blockbuster, *El crimen* received further financing for improved distribution.

Ángel de fuego, *Novia que te vea*, and *El crimen del padre Amaro* also represent several aesthetic tendencies from the era: adaptation, being set in a home, and the impossibility of redemption. Remakes and nostalgia are key parts of this era's cinema, and so, for critic Sánchez Prado, adaptation is common (*Screening* 26). Indeed, *Novia que te vea* and *El crimen del padre Amaro* are adaptations of novels. Most of the cinematic version of *Novia que te vea* takes place in the 1960s, not long after the 1950s, the same time period in which the novel was set. *El crimen*, for its part, is a double adaptation. It takes place in its context of production, the late twentieth century, instead of the nineteenth century represented in the novel the film adapts. There is often no redemption in films from this period either (Sánchez Prado, *Screening* 110). *Ángel de fuego*, for instance, represents depraved parts of the human experience, including incest, and it ends with a circus tent going up in flames. Similarly, *El crimen del padre Amaro* shows religious disturbances, like a woman giving the host (or communion wafer) to her cats, and a priest taking advantage of a young woman and forcing her to have an abortion that eventually kills her. In addition to these tendencies, Schaefer has proposed that "the economic and cultural agendas of end-of-the-twentieth-century modernization (in the guise of a global neoliberal agenda) are constructed and deployed in the bathrooms, foyers, and private studies of Mexican households in films" (31). *Novia que te vea*, for example, has multiple scenes in its protagonists' homes.

Women directors also received greater recognition in Mexico during this time period. Noted feminist Ilana Dann Luna highlights that the 1990s were the decade of change in Mexican cinema and she situates female directors and feminist strategies within that understanding, even if the directors do not self-identify as feminists (Luna 3).[5] These include María Novaro, who directed *Danzón* (1991), Guita Schyfter, who directed *Novia que te vea*, and Dana Rotberg, who directed *Ángel de fuego*. When their works center female characters, it is within a patriarchal culture. These films and others from the 1990s "address the imaginaries of all spectators, [and] offer women a vehicle for looking at themselves in society, not just as objects of someone else's vision" (Schaefer 53). In other words, women in the audience will see truthful representations of their lived experiences in film. Schaefer continues, arguing that this "entails the aesthetic (cinematic) and economic empowerment [of women] related to the production of the image" (53). They explore topics pertinent to women's lives, which represents a departure from previous decades of film production. At the same time, these films were not necessarily aimed at changing society, nor were they directed by women who sought to do so. These representations suggest changing understandings of gender roles, especially for women, in Mexico. They are products of the deregulation of the cultural industry that included a changing context for film financing, changing laws for the percentage of Mexican films displayed in cinemas, and changing ticket prices and locations of movie theatres.

ÁNGEL DE FUEGO

Ángel de fuego was released in 1992 and portrays a girl, Alma (Evangelina Sosa), who is a trapeze artist in a circus.[6] Throughout the film, religious symbols illuminate the characters' precarious economic situations and set boundaries for acceptable expressions of masculinity and femininity. The characters' precarity relates to marginalization in the film's context of production of the late 1980s and early 1990s, which is also the context the film represents.

In the film, the protagonist becomes pregnant via an incestuous relationship with her father, Renato (Alejandro Parodi). The film suggests that Alma is in love with him (Lahr-Vivaz 81). After he dies, a pregnant Alma leaves the circus and eventually joins a traveling group of puppeteers who put on Christian religious performances in poor neighborhoods. This group is led by a character called Refugio (Lilia Aragón), who is accompanied by her son, Sacramento (Roberto Sosa) and another boy, Noé (Noé Montealegre). Sacramento invites Alma into their family. Then, in what Sánchez Prado calls a "twisted attempt to 'redeem' her," Refugio convinces Alma to engage in a purification ritual, which causes her to have a miscarriage (*Screening* 123). After these experiences, Alma returns to the circus for a final performance, burning the tent to the ground. *Ángel de fuego* "no permite ningún tipo de concesiones para volverlo más agradable o fácilmente digerible" (does not concede to the audience in any way, to make itself more agreeable or easier to digest) (Carro 10). There is no redemption on screen, much less in the circus.

The film's director, Dana Rotberg (1960–present), has had a circuitous career that did not begin in filmmaking. This broader perspective is part of why her films draw on and represent diverse aspects of Mexican culture and society. In 1992, she told journalist Susan López Aranda (8) that her interest in film only began after she got a job at the Cineteca, an institution in Mexico City that promotes film culture with film screenings, a research library, and other resources. After taking this job, she began filmmaking. She then pursued filmmaking at the CCC, which, as mentioned in the introduction, is a school that focuses on the mechanics of filmmaking rather than its theory or history (Haddu 117; Arredondo, "Dana" 167). Over the course of Rotberg's study there, she directed several films. Her first documentary, *Elvira Luz Cruz, pena maxima* (*Elvira Luz Cruz, Maximum Sentence*) (1985), won an Ariel award that same year (Haddu 117). After this incredible beginning to her career, "In 1989, Rotberg directed her first feature film, *Intimidad / Intimacy* (1989) which participated at the Berlin, San Sebastian, Sundance, and Toyko Film Festivals" (Haddu 117). This trajectory laid the groundwork for *Ángel de fuego.*

Ángel de fuego was Rotberg's second feature film and has been widely acclaimed by critics. She was the director and, together with Omar Alain Rodrigo, the screenwriter. Both are credited for it but, according to journalist Nelson Carro, Rotberg took one part of Rodrigo's script, the character of a girl playing with fire, and adapted it completely (7–8). "To date it has been Rotberg's most successful project, opening the Directors Fortnight at Cannes in 1993, and then going on to participate in more than seventy film festivals worldwide" (Haddu 117). It won awards for best film and set design at the New Latin American Film Festival in Havana (1993), best film at the Latino Film Festival in New York (1993), and best actress at the International Film Festival in Porto, Portugal (1994). It was also presented at the International Festival in London (1992), International Festival in Tokyo (1992), Toronto International Film Festival (1992), Sundance (1993), and the International Film Festival in Sidney (1993). It was nominated for 17 Ariel awards in Mexico and won the Best Spanish American Film from the American Society of Film Editors (ACE) (Arredondo, "Dana" 169). *Ángel de fuego* was so successful that it was eventually purchased by Columbia Pictures (Rashkin 202).

The film reflects Rotberg's multiple artistic influences. The most significant, and certainly the most relevant for the analysis I am undertaking in this monograph, was the fact that Rotberg had collaborated with Felipe Cazals on a number of projects (Rotberg, "A Malena" 187). *Ángel de fuego* is similar to his film *Canoa*, as they both display limited character development, a single character's desire for power and control, and take place in unadorned and often dusty spaces. Other critics, like the brilliant Elissa Rashkin, highlight other influences. She claims that *Ángel de fuego* shares themes of depravity and a lack of redemption with Alejandro Jodorowsky's *Santa Sangre* (*Holy Blood*) (1989) and that is indebted to Luis Buñuel's *Los olvidados* (*The Young and the Damned*) (1950), especially in the way that that film demythologized *mexicanidad* (Rashkin 201–2). Other critics suggest that Rotberg's film hearkens to the Golden Age *arrabal* genre, which is a term "in Mexican Spanish [that] signifies 'ghetto' in English" (Haddu 144n107).[7] The way that *Ángel de fuego* portrays communities living in poverty, like the puppet show audiences who live in concrete houses with tin roofs, reflects this genre. Rotberg's work, then, was a product of her experience as well as a number of artistic and cinematic influences.

Rotberg's work portrays the devastation experienced by marginalized communities in the late 1980s and early 1990s. Critics have recognized the significance of this imagery, which is present from the opening scenes of the film. As the film's storyline develops, religious symbols underline the devastation the most marginalized characters experience. The film conveys the problems associated with economic and political developments in this time period through almost exclusively unsettling images. This has led some critics to "accuse Rotberg of crafting an exotic, unrealistic spectacle of Third World misery" (Rashkin 202). Regardless of whether or not this spectacle was realistic, its social criticism was evident to most reviewers and film critics. Sophia McClennen observes that the film is a highly allegorical critique of society (87). A 1993 review in the newspaper *El Universal* understood the film in a more literal sense, as it celebrated the film's truthful portrayal of marginalized people in Mexico: "Sin ser panfletaria, la realizadora propone una visión entre asombrada y paradójica de un México de enormes contradicciones y pobreza que ningún milagro económico ha podido eliminar" (Without being propaganda, the director develops a paradoxical vision of Mexico, with enormous contradictions and poverty that no economic miracle had been able to eliminate) (Ortega Mendoza 3). Rashkin adds that:

> *Angel de fuego* can be read as a radical critique of this situation, placing the most marginalized Mexicans at the center of a narrative whose moral and theological themes never mask or supersede the social reality in which the story takes place. The nation—that mythic unified entity presumed to be on the triumphant verge of First World Status—is absent, its place is filled by garbage. (196)

This allusion to garbage is integral to the absent possibility of redemption in this film, and to the possibility of changing the Mexican political and economic situation.

The opening scenes of the film evoke the economic marginalization characters experience throughout the film, the idea that the most marginalized people are often on display, and that whatever actions they may take to remedy their situation are always insufficient. The credits, white text on black background, appear in silence. The film then slowly starts playing the sounds of the city. A siren quickly supersedes all other sounds. Then, after the opening credits end, the circus appears. On the left-hand side of the frame, there is a barely visible tent with some lights on top that spills over into the right-hand side of the frame. It dwarfs a trailer, which is barely visible in the right-hand side of the frame (see figure 3.1). This creates a sense of malevolence, as the sounds of what is supposed to be jovial music mix with barking dogs and sustained sirens. As the camera moves closer to the tent, the scene reflects economic disadvantage as it shows the worn-down circus sign and a woman closing up the ticket booth. The camera jumps to the tent, pans across the screen, and shows a person peering in the side of the tent. It moves to the inside of the tent as if through this person's perspective and shows the protagonist Alma performing. The camera cuts again, this time to an audience of four people. One of them is a middle-aged and middle-class woman wearing dark sunglasses, as if in disguise. It is later revealed that she is Alma's biological mother.[8] Alma is doing her part for the circus; the roles she and her mother play in this performance are an allegory of Mexico's failure to address their surroundings. While Alma's experience is unusual, it could stand in for the experiences of other marginalized people and communities in this context. Indeed, critic Maricruz Castro Ricalde adds that in this film "[se] visibiliza la violencia física, psicológica y simbólica sobre los habitantes que viven en los márgenes del orden ciudadano, a través de la

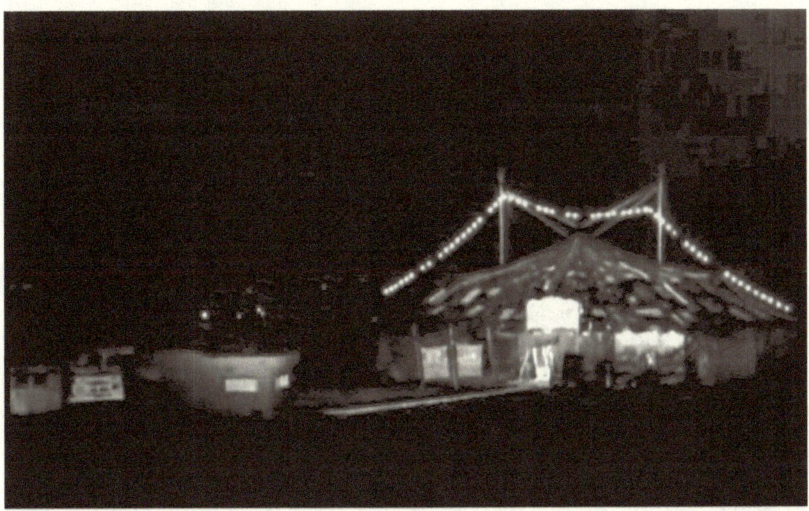

Figure 3.1. Opening scene and circus tent in *Ángel de fuego*. *Source*: *Ángel de fuego*, fair use.

historia de una adolescente que encarna muchas de las contradicciones engendradas por el sistema económico vigente" (the physical, psychological, and symbolic violence against people who live at the margins of the social order become visible, through the story of an adolescent who embodies many of the contradictions that are the result of the current economic system) (113). As we know, neoliberal policies that preceded the free trade programs of the 1990s worsened these contradictions. The opening scenes of this film, then, present stark contrasts between silence and noise, words and images, forced happiness and the fact that hardly anyone wants to visit a traveling circus. The representation of the lived experience under neoliberalism is a brutal one.

On screen, patriarchal relationships between male and female characters compound their marginalization, especially for women. We observe representations of patriarchal gender norms in the negative portrayal of feminized male characters and the fact that female characters are often in conflict with one another. There are also problematic relationships between men and women on screen, especially between Alma and her father. The film ridicules feminized male characters. One of them, Rito (Salvador Sánchez), is Orientalized, in that he wears a turban, a lot of makeup to highlight his eyes so they appear mysterious, and red lips contrast with the heavy layer of foundation that evens and perhaps darkens his skin tone. He is also in a relationship with another male character, called Lidio. This places them outside of social norms and diminishes their masculinity and authority on screen. Other characters do not listen to Rito or take him seriously, and he is not able to participate in what Irwin would call the contests of wit that prove one's masculinity in Mexico. The sole somewhat powerful male character in the circus is the announcer who introduces performers. His voice clearly directs their actions. Yet, on screen, a female character easily overshadows him because she collects money from the audience. He also walks happily arm in arm with another man, a male homosocial behavior that alludes to homosexuality. This further diminishes his power. These characters do not embody the *charro* behavior we saw earlier, nor do they upend that stereotype in creative ways, as we saw in some films from the 1970s. In this phase of filmmaking and the corresponding political and social context, men of lower social classes have limited power. It is clear that, in this film, social capital relates to gender but depends on a variety of factors.

The film also portrays relationships between women in troubling ways. The competition between the female characters in the circus community for what they perceive as the right kind of male affection and approval complies with the patriarchal myth of scarcity. The woman who counts money, for example, tells Alma that she knows what Alma is doing, and we are to understand that this is in reference to Alma's relationship with her father. The ticket-taker also reminds the other women not to take their makeup off at the end of the show, because they will have to work later. This implies that they are also sex workers who make more money for the circus after the men are done working. These other female performers echo the ticket-taker's behavior towards Alma, gossiping about her as if her experience of incest were her fault. In light of this behavior, after her father dies, Alma is despondent (see figure 3.2). She leaves the circus, carrying a small suitcase. A long shot captures her walking with her back to the camera. The dirty circus tent, held up by fraying ropes, is in the background, and contrasts with bright green grass in the background. The camera focuses on the tent even after she has left the frame, which highlights the sense of despair. Although this suggests that she is off to a better future, her solitary journey is a powerful example of the mistreatment of women in *Ángel de fuego*. Alma is left alone to fend for herself in a context

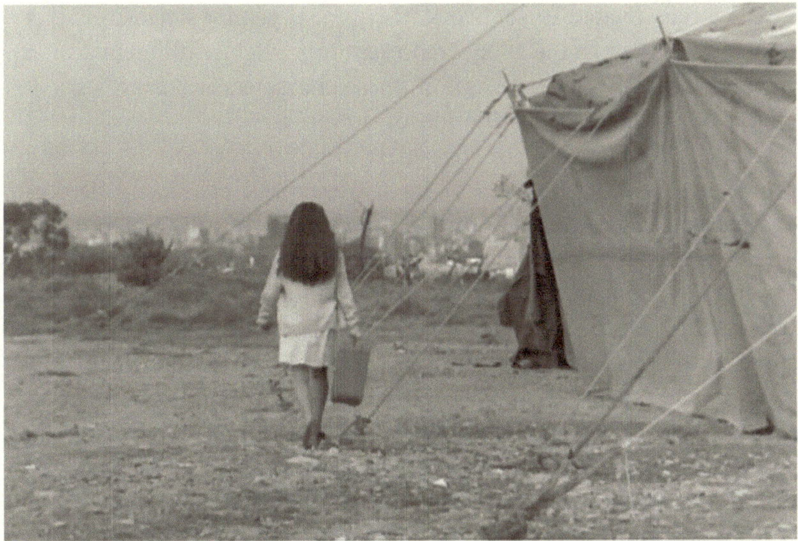

Figure 3.2. Alma leaves the circus in *Ángel de fuego*. *Source*: *Ángel de fuego*, fair use.

where women compete with one another for minimal power, which they then use to exploit others for the benefit of an unseen (and likely male) more powerful circus owner.

These relationships occur against the backdrop of the most significant representation of patriarchal gender norms in the film: the abusive relationship between Alma and her father.[9] As Rashkin argues, "the otherness of the circus allows for a visual poignancy that enhances the emotional quality of the narrative and . . . facilitates the treatment of taboo subjects, particularly incest" (207). An early scene shows the relationship in which he abuses her and fathers her child.[10] Alma kisses him in a way that appears voluntary. For her, the incestuous relationship was an expression of love. This behavior conforms to the experiences of many victims of sexualized violence, particularly those of childhood sexual abuse. These children are usually groomed from an early age and often feel empathy for their perpetrators, and may blame themselves if the perpetrator receives charges or other consequences for his actions.[11] These scenes occur within a context where no character has solidarity for another, and where slightly more powerful characters exploit more vulnerable characters, be it through incest or economic exploitation in the circus related to sex work. Patriarchal gender norms on screen may have shifted in the 1990s, representing a slightly different context. In this world without redemption, these characters still experience the effects of an unequal distribution of power.

Religious imagery on screen is a significant part of the film's representations of the lives of its marginalized characters, Refugio, Sacramento, and Alma. Unique interpretations of religious rituals on screen make the leader, Refugio, seem more malevolent, and Alma's experience of purification more damning and Sacramento's death more tragic. Much of this religious imagery is drawn from Rotberg's understanding of the Jewish tradition. In an interview with Susana López Aranda, she explained that her upbringing was a fusion of Judaism and the Mexican tradition, and that her current religion is best described as pagan-Jewish-Mexican (9).[12] Her form of religious expression takes important symbols and stories from multiple origins. Haddu adds that "the depiction of religion in *Angel de fuego*, although influenced by key Judaic beliefs, is multiple in forms, articulating the syncretic nature of Mexico's spiritual belief system" (117).[13] Rather than syncretism that would tie the Virgin de Guadalupe to the goddess Tonantzin, however, this film presents rituals and performances based on Genesis and Exodus in the Hebrew Bible alongside Catholic rituals—like confession—that are common in Mexico. Rotberg has also stated that Biblical stories in Hebrew were a big influence on her. In her view, "es una maravilla como mundo fantástico, como mundo narrativo, es alucinante" (if we consider it as a fantastic world, it is a marvel, and if we consider it a narrative world, it is amazing) (López Aranda 8). She discusses the fact that the film was motivated by questioning a God who, as in various Biblical examples, required faithful people to sacrifice someone or something innocent (López Aranda 8). This combines stories from the Hebrew Bible, such as Abraham sacrificing Isaac (Gen. 22:1–18), with the Christian interpretation of Jesus's crucifixion as the ultimate sacrifice. This theme is present throughout the film, such as Refugio's purification ritual for Alma. These scenes also evoke the way that millions of marginalized people sacrifice their bodies and lives for a system that does not ever appear to redeem them.

The primary religious space on screen that refers to Rotberg's multiple religious heritages and questions about sacrifice is the puppet show, which heightens the way Refugio welcomes Alma initially and eventually condemns her. On screen, after Alma leaves the circus, the film shows her in a market. She has now changed from her sensible-looking skirt and cardigan to her circus outfit, performing in traffic to earn money. In addition to these performances, she stops in front of a shrine to the Virgin, and, in a long almost-still shot, chats with a group of plainly dressed young men in front of a decaying grey brick building. In each place, her fire-red outfit stands out. A deep voice interrupts this bleak scene, announcing: "Dios prometió a su pueblo . . ." (God promised God's people . . .). She walks towards this voice. The camera stays still until Alma leaves the frame, and then it zooms out to show her movement in space, traveling more slowly than she does. This suggests both that Alma is eager to see what the noise might mean, and that her situation drags her down and prevents her from realizing meaningful change. The camera shows Alma in profile as she walks towards the edge of a bus that also has a stage. It then cuts to show marionettes on this stage as they tell a biblical story. Alma is likely drawn to this space because of its performative aspect, which would have reminded her of the circus. As McClennen states, "the circus and the religious group are not different; they offer fantasy and illusion as distractions from the horror of everyday life" (85). This form of religious expression is a fusion of Christian beliefs and Mexican culture. The puppets evoke *alebrijes* (large statues of animals made of papier-mâché) and other types of popular art sculptures, and the performance calls to mind the medieval Catholic tradition of morality plays for audiences who were largely illiterate. This religious symbolism makes the play seem more interesting at first, and adds a dramatic flair to Refugio, the older female leader of the marionette group, and her hospitality.

The film presents Refugio in ways that allude to Catholic religious rituals and beliefs that emphasize this character's positive qualities. The characters' names are significant—although they are all possible names in Mexico, it is worth commenting on them because of their obvious connections with the events portrayed in *Ángel de fuego*. Refugio, which means Refuge, is presented as a complex and caring figure, whose world of the puppet show and workshop shelters Alma as she deals with her pregnancy. She first appears on screen at the end of the performance in smoke and fire. She kneels on the left-hand side of the stage, occupying almost half of the space on screen (see figure 3.3). The film employs religious imagery that calls to mind the Catholic Church, which emphasizes Refugio's power. One way it does so is by costuming her in a purple robe. Although worn and faded, her robe still calls to

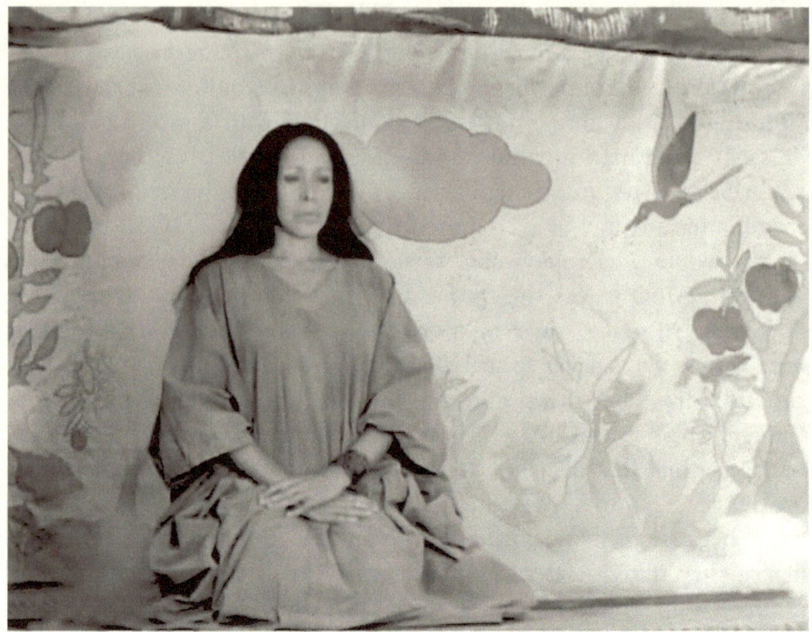

Figure 3.3. Refugio appears in smoke in *Ángel de fuego*. *Source*: *Ángel de fuego*, fair use.

mind the fact that, for Catholics, purple is the color of penitence, and that it is worn by priests during the seasons of Lent and Advent. In this scene, moreover, Refugio's eyes are half-closed. The camera stays fixed on her and Alma appears in the bottom of the frame, and we realize that she has walked up to Refugio. Refugio leans over, strokes Alma's face, and tells her audience that there is a place for everyone in God's kingdom. Her son Sacramento's name means "sacrament" and refers to the most important rituals of the Catholic Church. Yet, on screen, this character does not participate in these rituals, which are to confirm and deepen Catholic people's connection to God: baptism, Eucharist, confirmation, reconciliation (confession), holy orders, marriage, and anointing of the sick (last rites). According to critic Castro Ricalde, Sacramento's behavior facilitates Alma's inclusion into his community, which may be a type of sacrament (116). Perhaps he intuits that Alma, whose name means soul, could provide something his family lacks. He comes closest to realizing the potential for sanctification towards the end of the film when he dies by suicide to compensate for his sins (Castro Ricalde 116). Noé, a child previously adopted by Refugio, may allude to the Biblical character who built an ark to save his family from floods (Gen. 6–7). The cinematic character guards the workshop where Alma and Sacramento interact, and so he lives out some of the characteristics of his namesake. These names form part of a film where every element has meaning and is a key component of how the film portrays Refugio in a positive light.

Refugio's religious practice is more complex, as it blends existing and emerging forms of religion in Mexico. The ways that the film portrays these practices gives Refugio's power divine connections. Refugio's religious practice, as performed by her theater company Mensajeros de la Nueva Alianza (Missionaries of the New Alliance), refers to biblical and theological ideas that are pre-contact and Pentecostal, rather than Catholic or Jewish. As Castro Ricalde states, "representan la voz no convencional del catolicismo mexicano que mezcla prácticas y creencias propias de esa religión con otras de corte pagano de raíces prehispánicas" (they represent the unconventional voice of Mexican Catholicism that mixed practices and beliefs from this religion with pagan practices and pre-Hispanic roots) (122). I would add that the representation of these religious practices alludes to the growth of Pentecostalism and other forms of Protestantism in Mexico and elsewhere in Latin America in the 1980s and 1990s. These groups increased to such an extent that, in 1992, Mexico passed new laws governing religion. These laws allowed non-Catholic religious celebrations to take place outside of homes and public places of worship. Congress was allowed to regulate religious expression and proselytizing in public, but it could not prohibit it (Saldaña Serrano 286n1).[14] *Ángel de fuego* refers to these groups through the theater company's name. "El nombre mismo de la compañía, los Mensajeros de la Nueva Alianza, indica ese tránsito permanente que se autoexcluye de las entidades reglamentadas en el marco de la sociedad y, en cambio, se inscribe en un orden superior: el de los vasallos de la divinidad" (The name of the company, Missionaries of the New Alliance, indicates its permanent mobility that automatically excludes it from the entities that regulate society, and, in turn, inscribes it in a superior order, as a vassal [and servant] of the Divine) (Castro Ricalde 115–16). The film emphasizes the traveling theater company's particular relationship to the divine in a scene where Refugio consecrates a new location for her puppet show. She walks on sandy ground in front of dilapidated buildings, scattering something that appears to be grain, likely to symbolize growth. Sacramento and Noé are close behind her, and Alma follows the other three characters at a slight distance. The camera moves more slowly than the characters and it stops when Refugio scatters grain in a circle. The other characters also stop, and appear like timeless statues, as the mountains and the blue sky visually dominate the scene. Once this stage of the ritual has been completed, Refugio walks over to a now-kneeling Sacramento and covers his hair with her hands. The children then leave the consecrated ground and Refugio sets up an altar. The spontaneous nature of this religious ritual reminds viewers and critics of charismatic and Pentecostal practices, which involve the direct intervention of a divine spirit into the human experience. This suggests that Refugio's entire project is the result of some otherworldly connections.

The religious imagery in the altar itself gives an unsettling overtone to these religious rituals (see figure 3.4). It is a modest table, covered in lace with two red prayer candles and a cylinder wrapped in gold. This is similar to how a Torah would be protected and presented in a synagogue. Alma brings Refugio a framed image of the Virgin of the Immaculate Conception and a small model of a cathedral to add to

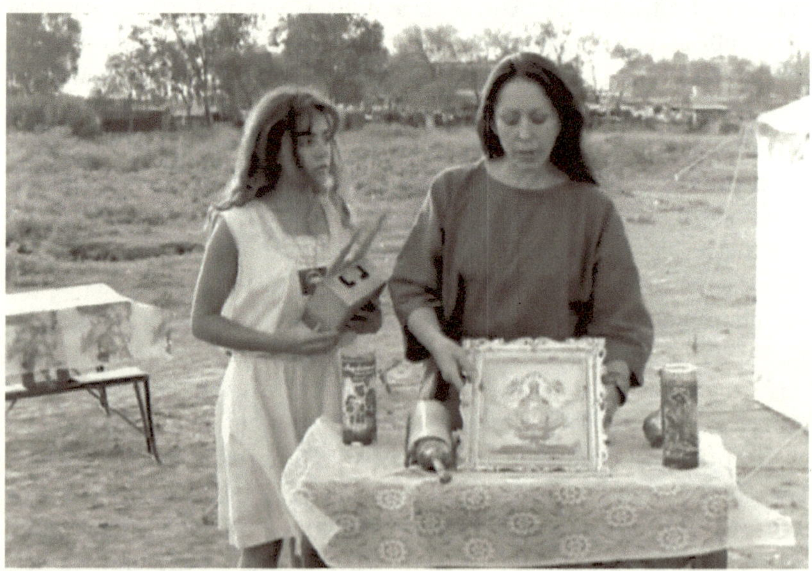

Figure 3.4. Alma and Refugio at Refugio's altar in *Ángel de fuego*. *Source: Ángel de fuego*, fair use.

the altar. This image of the Virgin, often represented with a halo of stars around her head, can be considered an apocalyptic virgin. Critic Patricia Saldarriaga explains that, when the Virgin is represented with sun, moon, or stars, her image calls to mind the end times (237). This imagery evokes a description of a woman in the biblical book of Revelation, "clothed with the sun, with the moon under her feet, and on her head a crown of twelve stars" (Rev. 12:1). It also employs symbols rooted in Catholicism such, as the apocalyptic Virgin and the placement of objects common in other religious communities. This foreshadows Refugio's later cruel behavior towards Alma and implies that participation in Refugio's rituals might assist in bringing about the end times.

Refugio then devises a purification ritual that employs Catholic religious rhetoric and centers on this altar. The ritual almost kills the younger character, which makes it even more terrifying. At one point, Refugio tells Alma that her body is sinful and must be purified. This implies that Alma's experience of incest was her fault, and that Refugio believes that she can rescue Alma. This is in line with the symbolism of purity discussed earlier in relation to Refugio's purple robes. In this improvised ritual, Refugio makes Alma stand in a small clearing inside of a circle of stones and then of fire. Her arms are outstretched for what seems like an endless amount of time. The camera circles around Alma as she crouches in this inhospitable circle of fire. Refugio bathes her and then makes her sleep naked outside in the cold. The next morning, a sacrificed goat appears on the altar, flanked by white candles (see figure 3.5). The film then zooms out to show that Alma warms herself with a quilt a few feet away. The goat symbolizes a sacrifice made for Alma, so that she could be purified. This is in line with the Biblical story of Abraham and Isaac, where Abraham is about to sacrifice Isaac, but a ram appears and saves Isaac at the last minute from death (Gen. 22:13). Refugio's ritual leads Alma to have a miscarriage, an experience also marked by blood. This ritual evokes Catholic ideas of purity, and a story in the Hebrew Bible, as it confirms Refugio's chilling level of power in this domain.

The film also perverts Catholic rituals in the scenes that confirm Refugio's power in her relationship with her own child. In addition to forcing Sacramento to participate in the puppet show, Refugio subjects Sacramento to strange rituals. She anoints Sacramento as a prophet as part of her religious vision. She engraves designs in his back with a knife, and then covers his naked body with oil. This perverts the

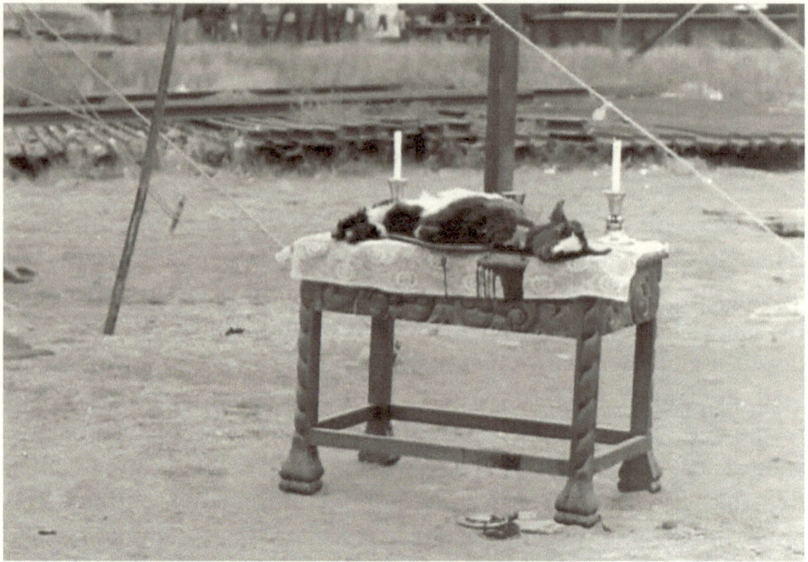

Figure 3.5. The goat on the altar in *Ángel de fuego*. *Source*: *Ángel de fuego*, fair use.

way that oil is used in the rites of extreme unction, colloquially called last rites. As critic Traci Roberts-Camps states, in the film "Refugio explains that Sacramento will be thankful later as she was to her father for doing the same to her . . . there is a cycle of abuse and self-abuse passed on from parent to child" (17n9). Later in the film, Sacramento stands with his back to the camera in the workshop. We see the words his mother had engraved on his back, and, in light of the seemingly fresh marks, we as viewers conclude that he enacts his mother's style of cruelty towards himself. Sacramento "mortif[ies] himself with napes tied tightly to his back to the point where we can see blood streaming down his back" (Roberts-Camps 10). The way the film presents a distorted understanding of Catholic religious rituals confirms the malevolent nature of Refugio's power in the film.

Ángel de fuego continues, eventually showing Sacramento's death. It portrays his death by suicide in ways that evoke the imagery of a crucified Christ, which justifies his actions. Before he dies, Alma takes advantage of him. She sneaks into the workshop where Refugio makes her puppets to speak with Sacramento. The camera follows Alma as she walks back and forth and tells him that, since her purification ritual, she has felt empty. This character finally stops in front of Sacramento. In a relatively still shot, the camera focuses on the two characters' bodies as they come together, and then the camera slowly lowers as Sacramento kneels in front of Alma. They embrace and the scene ends. The film cuts away from these characters, and then briefly returns to film a naked Alma, implying that she and Sacramento have had sex. The way that the film portrays Sacramento's response to his perceived sin is by likening him to a crucified Christ. In a powerful still, Sacramento stands behind an indoor altar. There is a cup, two candles, and a bloody scroll on this lace-covered table. He then pokes his body with a knife, and the camera leaves the room. It returns to the workshop as Refugio finds Sacramento bent over a table in the workshop with his wrists slit. This quasi-crucifixion imitates Refugio's behavior towards Sacramento, and redeems his death, even though it was caused by suicide.

This film presents a series of troubling relationships between male and female characters in a circus at the margins of Mexican society. Refugio's traveling puppet show initially seems like a positive change for Alma. The film consistently portrays its central characters, Refugio, Sacramento, and Noé, participating in religious rituals, and it likens their actions to well-known biblical stories and to Catholic religious rituals. In some ways, this puts its characters in a positive light, particularly in the way Refugio is willing to rescue Alma. At the same time, the film includes religious imagery and ideas as it portrays her inventing a cruel purification ritual for Alma, which eventually leads to the younger woman having a miscarriage. The scenes that portray Refugio abusing her son so that he will act in ways that comply with her perspective are also replete with religious imagery, even when she is not there to influence him. These ideas are central to his eventual death.

The film was produced under new film rules and a new regime for film funding. Its religious elements, particularly in its portrayal of the puppet show, strengthen the film's central idea: that there is no escape from the world on screen. I extend this cinematic portrayal to suggest that there is no way out of the negative effects of changing economic policy in Mexico or distorted relationships of any kind between people. When Alma finally sets fire to the circus tent, it is a destructive—not purifying—act.

NOVIA QUE TE VEA

Guita Schyfter's *Novia que te vea* was released not long after *Ángel de fuego* and, on the surface, the films have very little in common. Schyfter's work adapts Rosa Nissán's novel, also called *Novia que te vea*, and tells a coming-of-age story largely set in 1962, right before then-US President Kennedy visited Mexico.[15] A character called Oshinica Matarasco (Claudette Maillé), from a Sephardic Jewish background, narrates the majority of the film, starting with her grandparents' arrival in Mexico in the earlier part of the twentieth century, and then touches on her childhood in the Sephardic community in Mexico City in the 1940s and 1950s, and her life as a young woman who became familiar with the outside world in the 1960s. At that time, Oshi meets Rifke Groman (Maya Mishalska), whose life has involved more contact with the rest of Mexico beyond her Ashkenazi community. Rifke invites Oshi to participate in her Zionist socialist youth group, and the two date men and eventually find husbands. Other characters in the film bring up important questions of belonging within the Jewish community, such as the role of the then-recently created State of Israel for Jewish people, the role of Jewish people in Mexico, and how to commemorate the Holocaust. *Novia que te vea* is profoundly marked by Jewish history, tradition, and religious practice. Its portrayal of these multiple historical contexts, as well as questions of identity and belonging in two Jewish communities, is crucial to the way that the film engages with the 1990s, the decade in which it was produced, as well as the multiple historical contexts that it represents.

Schyfter is a well-known director in Mexico, and, like Rotberg, had a unique career trajectory that connected pedagogy and public engagement with filmmaking. She was born in Costa Rica, but the majority of her education and training occurred in Mexico. Schyfter studied psychology at the UNAM, and, after graduation, directed programming for *telesecundarias* (televised secondary schools, grades 7–9) for the SEP, and produced videos for the SEP and the national archives (AGN) ("Currículum"). This experience of creating films for educational purposes to engage the public is evident in *Novia que te vea*, which educated the Mexican public about Judaism. It was a huge change from previous decades, where, as critic Guadalupe Pérez-Anzaldo affirms, "there are few examples in Mexican literature of addressing the Jewish subject, and in these cases, they have been based mostly on representing cultural stereotypes" (45).[16] Schyfter's film, and the novel on which it was based, were released in a context of increasing Mexican cultural production about Jewish people, by Jewish people, in Mexico.[17] Schyfter and Nissán counter prevailing stereotypes, along with work by Sabina Berman, Gloria Girvetz, Ethel Krauze, Sara Levi-Calderón, Myriam Moscona, Angelina Muñiz-Huberman, Sara Sefchovich, and Esther Seligson (Luna 123). Schyfter's film thus connects her experience in creating media for educational purposes as it represents Jewish characters, and themes relevant to the Jewish community.

Novia que te vea, as a film that adapts a novel, aligns with a popular tendency in 1990s film. Some critics have even called it a cinematic *midrash*, referring to the Jewish rabbinical tradition of retelling stories from biblical texts using contemporary examples so that they will make sense for a new audience (Mennell 53). Adaptation may also be a feminist strategy. Critic Luna argues that this is the case because adaptation is "a tool for gender subversion, a strategy that could be deployed to multiply meaning and critique the existing symbolic order of things, not as a singulative act, but as a reconditioning repetition" (xvii). That is, for Luna, when women filmmakers adapt existing works, they repeat some of their core themes and symbols, and rebel, challenge, or recast others. Schyfter's film clearly expands Nissán's portrayal of Oshi and the Sephardic Jewish community, as it includes the Ashkenazi community and Rifke's life. This character is likely based on a minor character called Tzivia in Nissán's novel (Silva Martínez). According to some reports, Schyfter simply incorporated Nissán's idea into an existing script (Ríos Alfaro); yet, interviews with Rosa Nissán suggest that she, Schyfter, and Schyfter's husband, the screenwriter Hugo Hiriart, wrote the script together (Silva Martínez).[18] The fact that the film represents the 1960s, a tumultuous decade in Mexico, rather than the 1950s may also make it more interesting or relevant for its audience in the 1990s. In any case, the cinematic version of *Novia que te vea* calls to mind a Jewish rabbinical tradition as it expands the novel and represents two Jewish communities on screen.

The film represents multiple time periods, which relate to important moments in the Jewish experience in Mexico. In this way, the film also critically engages with the period in which it was produced. In each period represented, the film mentions some element of anti-Semitism. The narrator begins her account in the present, around 1981, and over the course of the film she narrates her grandparents' arrival in Mexico in 1927, her childhood in the 1950s, and her young adulthood in the 1960s. Her grandparents migrated to Mexico because they were fleeing religious persecution in what is now Turkey. The narrator adds that, when they arrive, they are able to speak Spanish even centuries after they had been expelled from Spain. These grandparents were obviously not expelled in 1492; however, that they speak Ladino, a language related to Spanish, all these centuries later; it is clear that these events continue to define their Sephardic Jewish community.[19] The film's representation of Oshi's childhood and young adulthood also include many of the protagonist's experiences of discrimination. The multiple time periods in *Novia que te vea* relate to aspects of Jewish history in Mexico. The film presents them alongside one another, and we can think of them as analogous to the Mexican people's multiple lived realities in the 1990s. During that decade, Mexican people experienced the unequal effects of economic development and prosperity associated with deregulation for trade purposes, foreign direct investment along the Mexico-US border, and internal rebellion, particularly in Chiapas. People of different backgrounds thus lived in very different but simultaneous realities.

The way the film shifts in time to portray the Jewish experience in Mexico also relies heavily on memory, another important tendency in the film's context of production. The 1994 Zapatista uprising, for instance, was rooted in the Maya understanding of history that blurs time and event, in a unique combination of history and memory (Benjamin 417–19). The film also draws heavily on memory, rather than written history, as it moves between these multiple time periods and the community's ongoing lived experience of discrimination. As Mennell observes, the film uses the "cámara lenta para establecer una sensación de atemporalidad y una cualidad a la vez onírica y mitológica/legendaria" (slow motion to establish a sense of timelessness and something like a dream or myth/legend) (56). Memory, even if it is unreliable, is important in the film. This time is biblical and cyclical. The scenes that introduce Oshi's grandparents, for instance, relate her family to the Bible. The camera slowly pans over a series of photographs of Oshi's ancestors. She states, "cuando era niña creía que estas fotos eran de la Biblia" (when I was a child, I thought these photos were from the Bible) and later adds "de alguna manera son" (in a certain sense, they are). The reference to a biblical time reminds us that the Jewish community is rooted in these stories and relates to the sense of cyclical time in the film. The end of the film repeats these phrases: "Cuando era niña creía que estas fotos eran de la biblia. . . . De alguna manera lo son. ¿por qué no?" (When I was a child, I thought these photos were from the Bible. . . . In a certain sense, they are. Why wouldn't they be?). Oshi adds the rhetorical question "¿por qué no?" as if daring her audience on screen, the character Rifke, and the film's audience to challenge her. She lends weight to that the way she tells certain parts of the Jewish experience in Mexico by referring to the Bible. The repetition of certain phrases, and accompanying camerawork, relate the questions of cyclical time and memory to ongoing discussions of temporality in the years surrounding the film's production.

The film also explores the question of how Jewish people might belong in Mexico. The way the film presents the widespread idea that Judaism is not Mexican enough implies a close relationship between Mexican identity and Catholicism. Catholic ideas continued to be powerful, even in a period when fewer Mexicans expressed Catholic beliefs (on the census) than in prior decades. Indeed, in the film, both characters struggle to find their place in the broader context, maintaining "their ethnic consciousness while participating in *mexicanidad*" (Alfaro-Velcamp 280). At one point, the film presents an adult Rifke meditating on this idea in conversation with the adult Oshi:

> Yo quería pertenecer. Decir nosotros esto, nosotros lo otro. Nosotros. Creía que tenía que elegir entre lo judío y lo demás. Pero no puedes elegir; te quedas en el limbo; no estás aquí no estás allá; no estás, punto. Era como estar en una fiesta a que nadie me había invitado, sentía vergüenza, como si todos me miraran y me dijeran tú no eres de aquí.
>
> (I wanted to belong. To say us this, us that. Us. I thought that I had to choose between that which was Jewish and everything else. But you can't choose. You remain in limbo. You are neither here nor there. You simply aren't. It was like being at a party I hadn't been invited to, I was ashamed, as if everyone were looking at me and saying, you are not from here.)

Rifke's remarks reflect how difficult it is for the Jewish community to be included in the Mexican imagination, and, by extension, in any understanding of Mexican identity.

I suggest that the emphasis on the characters' Jewish identity and corresponding lack of belonging illuminates what Rifke describes as limbo, and reminds viewers that cultural Catholicism is part of belonging in Mexico. Oshi's childhood visit to the cathedral, Rifke's childhood experience of Christmas, and both young women's experience of a Passion Play, a theatrical representation of the week leading up to Jesus's crucifixion, present a tension between Judaism and Mexican identity. The adult Oshi moves from her family's story to introduce the audience to her childhood in the 1950s. She meditates on her sense of belonging in childhood, stating that she felt as though she swam in two waters and that the limits between them were imprecise. As she speaks, the film shows a child Oshi, with her family's maid and another woman. They get their picture taken in front of a cardboard model of the Metropolitan Cathedral in the *zócalo* in downtown Mexico City. The friend says to the maid, "no sé como trabajas para judíos . . . el dinero se va como agua, quien sabe por qué" (I don't know how you work for Jews . . . the money goes like water, who knows why). This female character employs anti-Semitic tropes to contest negative attitudes middle- and upper-class people have towards their Indigenous descendant domestic workers.[20] Then, the maid and her friend go into the cathedral to pray. Oshi stands nearby as they pray. The film shows other parts of the church sanctuary, including a statue of the crucified Christ. Candles flicker in the background. The camera moves from their faces to focus on the statue, and its bleeding side and feet become apparent (see figure 3.6). Critic Luna adds that "Oshinica is torn between being Mexican and being Jewish and innocently believes that she can overcome her otherness by ritualizing her behavior to perform Mexicanness as she understands it" (134). Oshinica cannot perform Mexicanness by simply accepting this scenario. Instead, she looks at the statue of Christ and remarks, "qué bárbaro, mira nada más como lo dejaron" (how awful, look how they left him). She then walks up to her family's maid who is kneeling at the altar rail. The woman's brown *rebozo* blends in with the dark wood paneling behind her and the brown altar rail in front of her. Oshi's red hair, yellow dress, and flickering orange, likely from candles behind her, add light to the scene. As the maid strokes Oshi's face, Oshi says, mostly to herself, that she hopes no one knows that she is Jewish and asks the maid not to tell anyone. The camera then cuts to the women praying at the rail and crossing themselves, as if they had not heard what Oshi had said. They

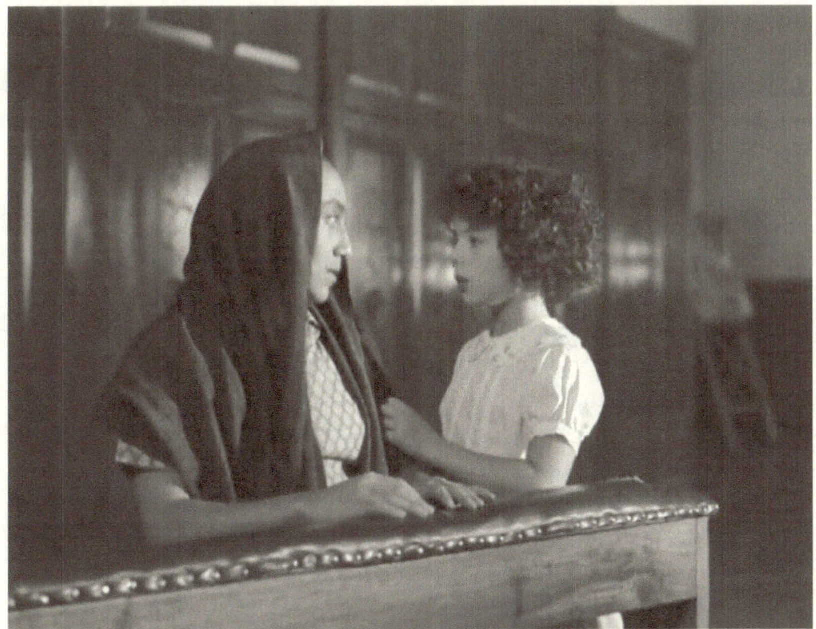

Figure 3.6. Oshi in the Metropolitan Cathedral in *Novia que te vea*. *Source*: *Novia que te vea*, fair use.

do not engage critically with their religious symbol in the way the child does. Moreover, the way they ignore her could be analogous to the experience of the Jewish community in Mexico. Oshi could enter the church and kneel at the railing, but she could not be part of it; the Jewish community could not enter Mexico either. Thus, the film suggests that, for most Mexicans, the performance of Catholicism is a key component of identity, and by extension, Judaism does not belong. Rifke had a similar childhood experience of her Judaism invalidating her Mexican identity. The film portrays her younger years, including a scene where she yells at her parents because they do not have crèche for Christmas. She screams, "El niño Dios sí existe" (The child God does exist) and runs out of the apartment to a nearby park. As children, they experienced tension without a complete understanding of the implications of their experiences.

A scene that presents a university-age Oshi and Rifke at a Passion Play confirms the close connection between Catholicism and Mexican identity. They travel from Mexico City to Malinalco, in the state of

Mexico, with Rifke's boyfriend Saavedra and his friends. They plan to take advantage of their holiday for Holy Week, between Palm Sunday and Easter, and to watch a Passion Play. One evening, they gather under the *portales* (walkways with arches and pillars) that surround the *zócalo* in Malinalco. They see a man on horseback riding through the square and yelling. Oshi turns to the person next to her to find out what is happening. She tells Oshi that "son los judíos. Andan buscando a nuestro Señor para matarlo" (they are the Jews. They are looking for our Lord to kill him). Oshi responds, "¿Los judíos?" (The Jewish people?). She and Rifke comment on this clear example of anti-Semitism with their friends, and their friends assure them that it is not related to prejudice towards Jewish people in their present. The camera focuses on Rifke and Oshi as they stand in a corner, now separate from the others. Oshi is uncomfortable and Rifke is irritated. Oshi adds, "Todo el antisemitismo empieza con la idea de que los judíos matamos a Cristo" (All anti-Semitism starts with the idea that Jewish people killed Christ). Saavedra and his friends do not understand why this play would be a problem. They participate in rituals that are part of Holy Week, the most important week in the Catholic religious calendar, and for many Mexican people. Yet, they are only welcomed into this religious and cultural event if they do not ask too many questions or emphasize their Jewish identity. If they do, they will not be allowed in. This experience, together with those that the film shows in Oshi and Rifke's childhoods, strongly suggests that Catholicism is integral to Mexican identity. It seems that, while the government had expanded its understanding of religion in the film's context of production, society, both in the contexts the film represents and the context in which it was produced, does not.

Novia que te vea also presents several examples of ways that characters attempt to graft themselves into Mexican identity without needing to change their religious and cultural identity. These include scenes where Rifke claims space for herself in Mexico by rhetorically connecting Jewish communities to Mexico's Indigenous groups, Rifke's uncle Meyer invents a personal religious and national ritual and Rifke and Oshi participate in a Zionist youth group that connects Judaism to international socialism.

Rifke claims space in Mexico by drawing parallels between Jewish and Indigenous people, without engaging with the experience of Indigenous people in the twentieth century. Rifke begins to establish this connection as a university student. In an almost entirely dark scene that represents a history or archaeology class, Rifke looks at slides about Mexican history and the professor explains that Mexico is a nation of immigrants, from the Aztecs onwards. This sows the seed for Rifke to think of Jewish people as heirs of the Aztecs. In this way, she also inherits decades of Mexican intellectual work that employed the idea of Indigenous people as part of their discussion of Mexican identity. This includes *indigenismo*, the intellectual movement that understands Indigenous people in largely simplistic ways, as if they were part of the past rather than the present. Intellectuals also understood Indigenous people as part of what Pedro Ángel Palou calls hegemonic *mestizo* identity, an idea of racial mixture that required Indigenous participation even as it erased their cultural specificity (15). In this scene at university, then, Rifke finds her own place within the Mexican intellectual sphere, and finds a way to expand their ideas to create a place for Jewish people in Mexican identity. Earlier in the film, but later in time, Rifke develops this Jewish-Indigenous connection in a dinner at her boyfriend Saavedra's parents' home.[21] Rifke and Saavedra drive to his parents' home and an older Rifke narrates the events. A shot from above captures the younger Rifke walking inside with Saavedra. The camera then switches to the dining room table. A servant brings in food, including pork. The camera then zooms out and shows six people around a table: Saavedra and Rifke, Saavedra's parents, and a journalist friend of Saavedra's father and the journalist's wife. The older male characters ask Rifke questions. As they do so, Saavedra's politician father hispanizes Rifke's name by calling her Rebeca, and the journalist asks Rifke how many Jewish people live in Mexico. She ignores the father's misnaming and tells the journalist about 40,000. He replies, "¿Estás segura? Creía que había como dos millones" (Are you sure? I thought there were about two million). After a brief pause, he adds: "Parecen más. Están en todas partes. Pero no se integran" (It seems like there are more. They are everywhere. But they do not integrate). The camera focuses on each character's face as they speak and shows that Rifke glares at the journalist and Saavedra asks him if this integration would be into "la gran familia mexicana" (the great Mexican family). Rifke recovers by stating that there are many cultural minorities in this family in addition to Jewish people, such as the Indigenous Otomi, Huichol, and Nahua people. She also argues that minorities enrich a country, like salt. Rifke tries to integrate herself and her religious and cultural group into a broader understanding of Mexico via her knowledge of its pre-Hispanic history (Rashkin 151). This meal "demonstrate[s] a multiplicity of ways to espouse anti-Semitism, either through ignorance or prejudice and malice" (Luna 160). Rifke is not Mexican enough, even if she is willing to reinterpret her Jewish heritage or refashion it to be akin to an Indigenous group.

The film also presents a unique ritual that integrates Judaism with Mexican identity. Rifke's Uncle Meyer (Leslie Hoffman) attempts to integrate these two strands of his identity on his own terms. He refuses to engage in Jewish religious practice, not even attending the synagogue to commemorate his parents' Yahrzeits, the anniversaries of their deaths. He also disagrees with Rifke's father (Nathan Grinberg) about Zionism, and what was, in the context the film represents, the newly create State of Israel. As Meyer asserts, Israel does not solve the problem of anti-Semitism, nor does it resolve divisions within the Jewish community. This anti-Zionist, and anti-Israel, position isolates him from both his religious community and from his family. It gives him space to integrate into Mexico—inasmuch as he will let himself integrate anywhere. Meyer's "performance of [Holocaust] survivor's guilt . . . is significant because it explains both his mistrust of Zionism and his unwillingness, or inability, to fully assimilate into his new Mexican homeland despite his gratitude at being received there. The Yiddish [he speaks] carries with it the weight of the Holocaust and the memory of great cultural loss and collective trauma" (Luna 151). As part of the way this character deals with his trauma, each year he places a large floral arrangement with the Star of David in the middle at the Ángel de la Independencia (Angel of Independence). This landmark statue, located in a rotunda near downtown Mexico City, commemorates Mexico's nineteenth-century independence (see figure 3.7).

The film shows this ritual after Meyer has driven with Rifke and her family to the Ángel. Rifke's father is in the middle of the frame, next to the wreath, and Meyer is further to the right. The arrangement, with white flowers in the middle and red roses around the edges, is of a size and scope that would normally be used for a funeral arrangement, and which today can be purchased in a market not far from the Ángel. This arrangement is different than these funeral flowers, as a faintly blue-colored Star of David has been added to the sea of white flowers, implying an almost-reluctant integration of Judaism into Mexico. Rifke, her sister, and her mother stand in a group next to her father on the left-hand side of the frame, which leaves Meyer alone.

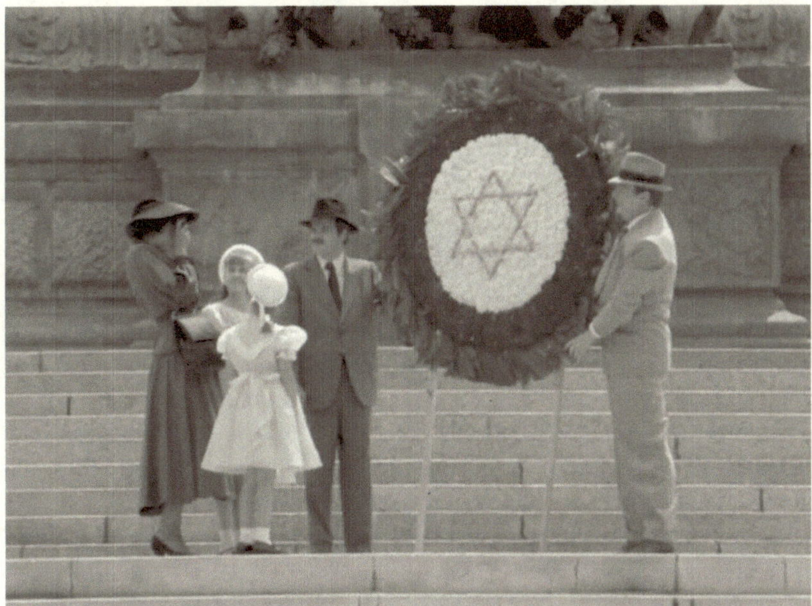

Figure 3.7. Meyer and Rifke's family at the Ángel in *Novia que te vea*. *Source*: *Novia que te vea*, fair use.

Rifke and her sister face one another, wearing matching dresses and hats, and their mother, Meyer's sister, is featured in profile, taking a picture of Meyer and of the wreath. Even though his family accompanies him, the characters' positions on screen make it clear that the ritual is primarily for Meyer. In this way, the film implies that the character is grateful to be alive, to be Jewish, and to be in Mexico. The individual ritual was a way for this character to make sense of his surroundings in the face of unimaginable loss. It also reminds us that social problems were increasingly framed as individual choices in the film's context of production, the 1990s, and that this tendency began as early as the neoliberal policies of the 1970s. Individual rituals were the only way to make sense of this context.

Another way that characters attempt to integrate Judaism into Mexico is through Zionist socialism, an understanding of socialism that integrated it with Jewish history and religious ideals. *Novia que te vea* introduces Zionism by representing the character Rifke in several iterations of an annual play about Jewish history. This play spans events like the heroic Warsaw ghetto fighters and shows gratitude for Israel, a "patria donde crecer" (homeland in which we can grow). The film connects this type of Zionism to the broader socialist movement, as it portrays Rifke's participation in a youth group the film calls the Shomer. Critic Stephanie Pridgeon explains that this was a cinematic representation of the Hashomer Hatzair, the socialist Zionist youth group with chapters throughout Latin America (101). Rifke invites Oshi to join her to celebrate Hanukkah there. A character called Jacobo lights candles on a menorah shaped like a Star of David. He says that the final candle is "para la libertad de todos los pueblos" (for the liberty of all people). Pridgeon highlights the fact that men continue to control this space, even though it is supposed to be revolutionary (102–3). In a slightly later scene, Rifke tells Saavedra that the socialism she had learned in the Shomer made it easy for her to be sympathetic to other communist causes, like in Cuba. The film thus ties the Shomer to communist and socialist movements throughout Latin America. This representation of Jewish socialism, then, is one example the film gives of how Jewish people may struggle to be considered Mexican, while it also provides an avenue for integration.

Guita Schyfter's *Novia que te vea* is a film that comes from an era of increased recognition of female filmmakers and Jewish writers and artists in Mexico's cultural sphere. Its portrayal of two young Jewish women is noteworthy as it represents both Sephardic and Ashkenazi communities. The way the film represents these minority communities, with strong religious and cultural features, leads to an analogous contemplation of similar questions in the film's context of production, the 1990s. Its discussion of memory, identity, and belonging relates to the role of Indigenous people in Mexico, particularly in the context of the Zapatista uprising; the role of memory, especially in women's storytelling as a feature of women's ongoing and overlooked contributions to Mexican cultural production; the role of Jewish people in Mexico, and their attempts to negotiate integration into Mexico; and the role of socialism and communism in Mexico, which was gaining greater traction at the time.

EL CRIMEN DEL PADRE AMARO

El crimen del padre Amaro, like *Novia que te vea*, adapts a novel. Unlike that film, which represented multiple Jewish communities, and

Ángel de fuego, which represented a unique form of Christianity, *El crimen* portrays recognizable forms of Catholicism. It centers around a priest, Fr. Amaro (Gael García Bernal), who is sent to the small town of Los Reyes in the fictional state of Aldama after he graduates from seminary. There, he is to work under an experienced older priest, Fr. Benito (Sancho Gracia). Upon his arrival in Los Reyes, the film presents multiple examples of corruption in the local church. Fr. Benito, for instance, has a long-time female companion, defying the Catholic norm of celibate priests, and launders money via the church's alms baskets to fund a new hospital building. Fr. Amaro is no stranger to corruption either. He abuses Amelia (Ana Claudia Talancón), a young woman in his parish. When she becomes pregnant, he forces her to have an illegal abortion, and she dies as a result. In addition to presenting these priests' morally and ethically problematic behavior, the film portrays Fr. Benito in conversation with other local priests with different perspectives on Catholicism. One of these characters, Fr. Natalio (Damián Alcazar), for example, works in a rural community and his work there is deeply influenced with liberation theology. The representatives of the Catholic Church in this film denounce corruption in the Catholic Church and allude to changes in the Mexican context in the film's context of production.

The film draws directly on several sources as it criticizes the Church. It adapts José María Eça de Queirós's 1875 Portuguese novel, titled *O Crime do padre Amaro* (*El crimen del padre Amaro*), a novel that portrayed a young priest, Fr. Amaro, who was sent to a rural area. That literary Fr. Amaro immediately noted that the priest who was assigned to be his superior had a female companion. Following his boss's behavior, Fr. Amaro developed a relationship with a young parishioner.[22] She became pregnant and died after giving birth. The younger priest then arranged for his child to be killed as well (Ortigão 131).[23] The 2002 film included most of these elements. Indeed, critics have noted that while the contexts of the novel and film differ, both condemn the Church (see for example Brescia 186). The film also reflects tropes found in other nineteenth and early twentieth century novels and films. These include other novels by Eça de Quierós, which dealt with religion, such as *El primo Basilio* (1878), *El mandarín* (1880), *Los Maya* (1880), *La ciudad y los siervos* (1901), *Alves y compañía* (1925), and *Prosas bárbaras* (1896) (Viñas 6). The Mexican director Carlos de Nájera's 1934 cinematic adaptation of one of Eça de Quierós' novels,

El primo Basilio, also influenced the cinematic representation of *El crimen del padre Amaro* (Viñas 6). The priests on screen remind us of characters in Cazals's *Canoa*: Fr. Benito's collusion with the local government communists evokes Fr. Meza, and Fr. Natalio's liberation theology leanings call to mind Lucas García and the CCI community in the film *Canoa*. While neither he nor Fr. Amaro is as anti-communist like Fr. Meza, all three priests on screen are deeply invested in power. This is no surprise, given that *Canoa*'s director, Felipe Cazals, was involved with the production of *El crimen* and his work undoubtedly influenced Carrera.[24] The twenty-first century film thus adapts a nineteenth century novel and the way it presents its characters' roles as Catholic leaders powerfully criticizes institutional religion and the surrounding political context.

El crimen del padre Amaro attracted a lot of attention when it was released because it did not shy away from controversy, which ultimately led to box office success and a number of important awards. The US Conference of Catholic Bishops condemned the film and in Mexico, a group called Pro-Vida even sued the Mexican government for financing the film, with the goal of preventing its release and distribution (Yarri; Soutar 109–15).[25] In light of this controversy, the film's director and producer made a small concession. They postponed its release by one week so that it would be released a week after—rather than during—a papal visit to Mexico. The film's posters warned that the film contained controversial content (Soutar 112). In spite of these compromises, clergy remained critical of the film. It has been stated that priests in the state of Puebla would stand outside of movie theatres to see which of their parishioners were going to watch *El crimen*.[26] The controversy was part of why it was so successful. MacLaird states that the media attention around its release meant that, when it was released, *El crimen del padre Amaro* had the second highest number of ticket sales in Mexican film history (59). Carrera's film also won national and international awards, such as best screenplay at the Havana Film Festival (2002); best music and actor at the Guadalajara Film Festival (2003); best film award at the ACE film festival in New York (2003); and a total of eight Ariels awards in 2003 (López Ramírez; Marshall 100). It was even nominated for best foreign film in the Golden Globes and Oscars in 2003 (Brescia 184; MacLaird 93). This controversial film was a success by every measure.

The film presents three priests who exercise power in different ways, in contrast to a female character, Dionisia (Luisa Huertas), who leads a unique popular expression of religion. This symbolizes the diffuse nature of power in the film's context of production. By 2002, when the film was released, Mexico that has experienced almost a decade of the effects of NAFTA. In this phase of neoliberalism, there is not a single locus of power, nor is there a single character who could represent it. The older priest Fr. Benito is analogous to traditional methods of holding on to power and negotiating with other entities, no matter how corrupt, to maintain it, and the younger, good-looking (but no less corrupt) Fr. Amaro aligns with the Partido de Acción Nacional's (National Action Party) (PAN) claims of reform without any evidence that their reforms fundamentally changed Mexico. Fr. Natalio, for his part, reminds viewers of the hopes that many had in a leftist expression of Catholicism and the emergence of a left-leaning political party on a national scale, the Partido Revolucionario Democrático (Democratic Revolutionary Party) (PRD).[27] Dionisia's failure to leave the Catholic paradigm for her rituals suggests that, in spite of many changes in Mexico, there is no option outside of existing structures that would lead to a better future.

The conflicts between the priests are analogous to criticisms of the Catholic Church, and, by extension, Mexico's political system. This builds on the work of several critics, who articulate that the central problems in this film are tied to characters that represent the Catholic Church. Most significantly, Elena Lahr-Vivaz synthesized the film as a national allegory where the Church is a synecdoche for the nation (102). Similarly, MacLaird claims that the film represents the "ethical deadlock of a failed state legal system based on the Church's failed moral infrastructure" (97). The legal system is like the Church's failed moral infrastructure: the powerful know that the hypocrisy embedded in these systems serves them. In 2002, critic Juan María Naveja analyzed the film for the newspaper *Milenio*'s cultural section. He suggested that the priests in the film were like PAN politicians. The priests in the film take *narcolimosnas* (alms money from drug cartels), fight guerrilla uprisings, sexually abuse congregants, are complicit in abortion, and act in sacrilegious ways (36). He implies that this portrayal of priests is not unlike the presidents from the PAN party (2000–2012). Indeed, the film centers on what he calls "un auténtico coctel explosivo para una relación que se suponía unida por ideas, valores y principios: la que vinculaba al Partido Acción Nacional con la Iglesia católica" (an authentically explosive cocktail about a relationship that was united by ideas, values and principles: that which connected the National Action Party to the Catholic Church) (Naveja 36). In other words, the PAN political party and the Catholic Church were united by a perversion of the same stated values. That same year, an article by the film's screenwriter, Vicente Leñero, condemned the Catholic hierarchy. Leñero, a well-known Mexican author whose work often included Catholic themes or characters, criticized the church on this occasion by likening it to the Mexican government: "Carrera [el director] entendió muy bien que el problema del [personaje] Padre Amaro no es, al fin de cuentas, un problema sexual. Es un problema político. Un problema de poder" (Carrera [the director] understood that Fr. Amaro's problema was not, in the end, a sexual problem. It is a political problem. A problem of power) ("Unión").[28] The film's portrayal of rape, then, is analogous to problems in the political sphere and other problems that relate to power, regardless of political party. A year later, Jesuit priest Luis García Orso reviewed the many crimes in the film for a journal affiliated with ITESO, a Jesuit university in Guadalajara. They include *caciquismo*, that is, ongoing allegiance to rural strongmen; corruption; drug trafficking; the arrogant use of power; and illegal abortion ("*El crimen*" 105). These crimes allude to other elements of Mexican society, particularly the hypocritical relationship between the conservative PAN party and the Catholic Church. The ways that the film portrays these figures, then, can be understood as a criticism of other social elements. The Catholic Church does not live up to its goals. The Mexican government does not either.

In the film, Fr. Benito is a parish priest in charge of the local church and one of the more powerful characters in the town of Los Reyes. The film represents his relationships with a group of junior priests, his lover Augustina, the local drug cartel, and the local mayor, which illustrate this character's lack of moral compass. He is also the oldest priest on screen, and, as a *gachupín* (derogatory term for Spaniard), he may be of Spanish descent, which evokes older forms of power, like the Spanish colonizers and the PRI political party.

The way the film represents Fr. Benito's monthly meetings reminds us of the PRI's attempts to hold onto power in the twenty-first century, even after losing the presidency to the PAN in 2000, the way all institutions desperately try to hold on to power in any context (see figure 3.8). The priests meet in a room with couches and armchairs, surrounded by tables, lamps, and bookshelves. A framed image of then-Pope John

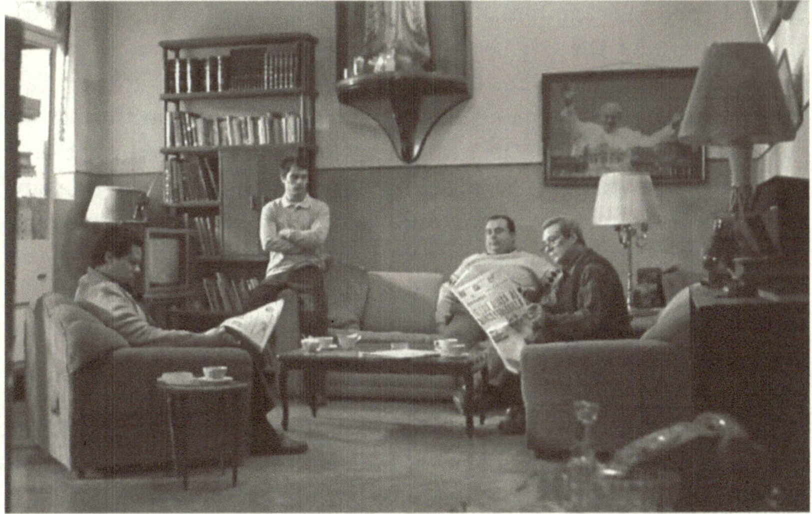

Figure 3.8. Priests in a meeting in *El crimen del padre Amaro*. *Source: El crimen del padre Amaro*, fair use.

Paul II with his arms outspread, superimposed over the Basilica of the Virgin of Guadalupe in Mexico City, oversees their meeting. This image of the now-canonized Pope is in the upper right-hand side of the frame, and from the upper middle, candles flicker at the base of a statue of a saint. It is as if these figures bless their discussions and suggest that some priests behave in ways condoned by the Catholic Church and others do not. When the first meeting ends in an argument between Frs. Benito and Natalio, the film sympathizes with Fr. Natalio over Fr. Benito. Then, Fr. Natalio misses a second meeting. Amaro and two other junior priests wonder aloud whether the accusations against Fr. Natalio are true and if Fr. Benito really receives money from cartel leader Chato Aguilar. In the frame, Fr. Benito sits under one edge of the poster of Pope John Paul II, so the Pope's outstretched arms appear to be blessing Fr. Benito in particular. Along with this perceived blessing, Fr. Benito unsuccessfully tries to change their discussion and justify the fact that he launders money through the offering plate. Fr. Benito claims that God can cleanse anything, and so through divine means bad money can become good. The sound of a phone ringing interrupts his speech. When Fr. Benito gets up to answer it, the film moves on. Fr. Benito struggles to maintain power in this situation; not even the image of a beloved Pope can help him. This implies that, while traditional powers like Fr. Benito or the PRI use newer methods, like alliances with drug cartels, to maintain power, it will not lead to long-term success.

The film furthers its negative portrayal of Fr. Benito through its portrayal of his relationship with a female character called Augustina (Angélica Aragón). This relationship's deep power imbalance means that fellow townspeople call Augustina *la sanjuanera* rather than by her name, which some critics argue is a name that alludes to her role as the priest's housekeeper and his lover (Marshall 102). Fr. Benito finally realizes that he has placed her in a vulnerable position when he has a heart attack near the midway point in the film. In a moving scene, the camera remains fixed on him in bed and he apologizes to Augustina in raspy voice. This scene evokes don Pancho's near-death experience and his confession to the not-priest Miguel in *El seminarista*. Like don Pancho, Fr. Benito does not confess to a priest nor does he receive the sacrament of extreme unction. After he apologizes, Augustina reminds him that he was there for her when her husband left her. He still feels badly because, as he states, "Te convertí en la puta del cura" (I turned you into the priest's whore). She gazes at him adoringly as he adds, "Por ese amor voy a ir al infierno" (For that, I will go to hell). The film shows her moving from her chair to lie on top of his covers to stroke his hair. Fr. Benito approached her when she was in a vulnerable position and, by offering her some assistance at that time, he was able to maintain control over her for many years to come. This is similar to the way that the PRI extracted loyalty from marginalized sectors of the Mexican population by providing minimal assistance to them in the film's context via rural and urban development programs that never fulfilled their promises.

The film also points to Fr. Benito's questionable morals through the relationships between the priest and members of the local drug cartel. Early in the film, Fr. Benito goes to cartel leader Chato Aguilar's *hacienda* to perform a private baptism ceremony. One of Aguilar's men chauffeurs him to this estate on suspiciously well-maintained highways and a short distance on a dirt road. Once they arrive at the gate of the *hacienda*, a guard approaches the car. Fr. Benito rolls down his window (see figure 3.9). In this scene, the chauffer's rosary hangs from the rearview mirror and divides the frame in half. The left-hand side of the frame displays the priest's head, clerical collar, and black robes and the right-hand side displays the guard's reflection in the window. The combination of

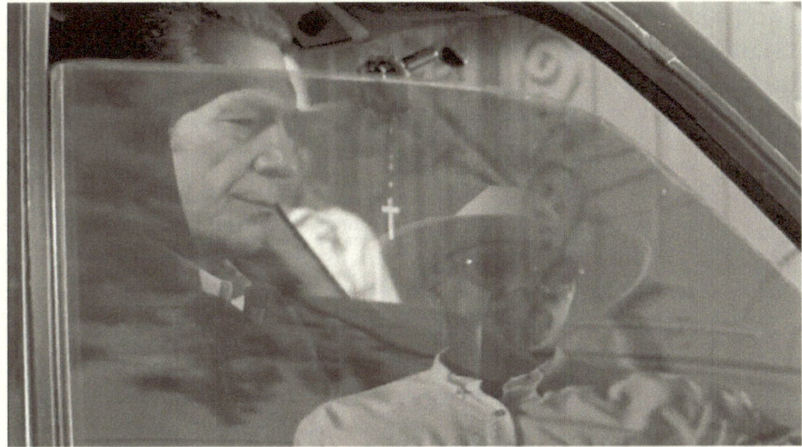

Figure 3.9. Fr. Benito and a guard at Chato Aguilar's *hacienda* in *El crimen del padre Amaro*. *Source*: *El crimen del padre Amaro*, fair use.

the rosary, which is a popular expression of devotion approved by the Catholic hierarchy, the priest, who represents this hierarchy itself, and the well-dressed guard is jarring. Then, the two characters interact. Fr. Benito makes the sign of the cross, blessing the guard, as he says the word *tiburón* (shark), which may be a password. Knowing the guard's nickname could mean that the priest is familiar with the guard, and by extension, the cartel. Once he is inside the *hacienda*, Fr. Benito talks with Chato Aguilar about the peso-dollar exchange rate. This suggests that he has laundered money for Aguilar by converting his contributions to the church to US dollars. Then the priest baptizes a new member of Aguilar's extended family. A photographer takes pictures, which are inserted into the film as black-and-white photographs. *El crimen* goes on to show an anonymous man killing Aguilar's photographer during the baptism. Later, when Fr. Benito is ill, his illicit lover Augustina calls Chato Aguilar to save him. Aguilar's strongmen carry Fr. Benito to a helicopter that airlifts the priest to Mexico City. The cartel props up the dinosaur priest. These controversial scenes illustrate clear collusion between the Catholic Church and the cartel.

The film confirms Fr. Benito's corruption in its subsequent scenes. Off screen, the character who killed Aguilar's photographer gives the roll of film that captured the baptism to a young male character called Rubén (Andrés Molina).[29] He is Amelia's boyfriend and the son of the newspaper owner, and so he uses these photographs and the research that his father had already conducted to write and publish a story about the local priest. Rather than owning up to his mistakes, Fr. Benito conspires with his bishop to erase this negative reporting. The bishop calls the mayor and demands that he assume responsibility for the money laundering. The mayor, who was playing dominoes with his friends, reflects, "No hay peor política que la negra" (Church politics are worse than other [politics]). This phrase was inspired by a conversation that the screenwriter Leñero and his wife Estela had had with the left-leaning bishop of Cuernavaca, Sergio Méndez Arceo, a position he held from 1953 to 1983.[30] Leñero retells the conversation in *Proceso*: "Cuando don Sergio niño comunicó a su padre su decisión de entrar al seminario, el padre de don Sergio niño refunfuñó: 'Acuérdate siempre de lo que te voy a decir, hijo. No hay peor política que la negra' " (When don Sergio told his father that he wanted to go to the seminary, his father said: "Son, always remember what I will tell you. There is no politics worse than the Church's") ("Unión"). Fr. Benito and the bishop's behavior in the film confirms the truth of this statement, that the politics in the Catholic Church are more nefarious than those in other spheres. Fr. Benito's questionable alliances with the drug cartel remind us of the PRI's model of powerbroking, using any available powerful figures to maintain their status.

Fr. Amaro illustrates another aspect of the problematic nature of priestly authority, and the film's portrayal of his hypocrisy evokes the way the PAN political party wielded power. In some ways, casting Gael García Bernal as Fr. Amaro chillingly foreshadows the legacy of President Enrique Peña Nieto (2012–2018). Peña Nieto was a good-looking president, and Fr. Amaro is so good-looking that if he were in a parish some would call him "Father What-a-Waste." In fact, the actor's good looks have led culture critic Daniela Cabrera from *Remezcla* to coin the term *Gaelindura*. This and the fact that he belonged to the transnational star circuit—even before he was well-known in Hollywood—helped the film's distribution (Tierney et al. 170, 172). We also recall that Peña Nieto's first wife, Mónica Pretilini, died under mysterious circumstances in 2007. He then married telenovela star Angélica Rivera in 2010 (The Reliable Source). The priest's behavior towards his purported love interest is no less suspect. Peña Nieto also held a number of roles in the government of the state of Mexico around the time the film was the produced. He was the Secretario de Finanzas (2000–2002), then a state-level representative (2003°2005) and finally its governor (2005–2011). During this time period, Mexico state became more violent, in part because of an increasingly militarized police force. Fr. Amaro's behavior and the actor's star power call to mind some aspects of Peña Nieto's persona.

Fr. Amaro's hypocrisy becomes clear in the film's portrayal of his relationship with Amelia. This relationship relates to the general abuse of power in the Catholic Church:

> En el momento en que el joven sacerdote [Amaro] avizora un futuro político dentro de la organización eclesiástica, cuando la ambición lo tienta con más furor que el cuerpo de su chiquilla, el cándido pecado sexual del Padre Amaro—fácilmente superable y perdonable—se convierte en un dardo de fuego que lo lanza directamente al crimen. Crimen no entendido como asesinato sino como unión adúltera con el poder.
>
> (When the young priest [Amaro] glimpses a political future within the ecclesiastical organization, when ambition tempts him even more than the young girl's body, Fr. Amaro's clear sexual sin—which could be overcome and forgiven—turns into a flaming dart that throws him straight at the crime. Crime understood not as assassination; rather, as an adulterous union with power.) (Leñero, "Unión")

While Leñero underestimates the problem of clergy sexual abuse, he does correctly observe that the crimes in the film are a metonymy for the Catholic Church's ties to power. Aleksandra Jablonska Zaborowska's article provides an important corrective to this, as she relates this film's representation of the problematic nature of power in Mexico to abuses of power by the Catholic hierarchy, including clergy sexual abuse (120–22). These remarks shed light on the fact that Fr. Amaro, and priests like him, look like a new type of leader and call to mind the promise of a new political party. Underneath, however, they are just as bad as older priests like Fr. Benito. Younger priests, bureaucrats, and politicians often simply serve to bring about cosmetic change.

The film suggests that Fr. Amaro is desperate for power through the way he manipulates religious spaces. This underscores the corrupt nature of his actions. Early in the film, Fr. Amaro waits in the confessional booth for his congregants. The camera focuses on his face behind the lattice work. First, the mayor's wife Amparo (Verónica Langer) goes to confession. When she is done, she crosses herself. She then opens the priest's side of the booth to give Fr. Amaro an envelope full of cash. Then, Amelia enters the booth. The camera first shows Amelia's face through the lattice work, then Fr. Amaro's, and then shows the two characters' faces together. The prescribed ritual immediately goes awry. She discloses that she is sensual, that she touches herself, and that she is very intense. Amaro assures her that "la sensualidad no es ningún pecado" (sensuality is not a sin). She elaborates, saying she thinks of Jesus as she touches herself. The camera shows Amaro's face in profile, as he confirms that this is a sin. The camera abruptly cuts away from his face and the scene ends. In the confessional booth, Amelia, like Catholics in the world outside of the film, submits to the priest. With regards to another confessional booth on screen, in the television show *Fleabag*, critic Shannon Keating observes that "the momentary power difference between the two of them is made breathtakingly explicit . . . Fleabag [the female character] relinquishes all her autonomy in exchange for the euphoria of submission." The confessional booth in *El crimen* presents a similar dynamic.

In a second scene in the confessional, Amelia attempts to subvert the dynamic of submission embedded in the sacrament of confession. This time, Amelia tells Fr. Amaro that he knows her sins, but that she does not know his. But he responds in a way that allows him to maintain control: "Dios nos bendice a través de este amor" (God blesses us through this love). In spite of this blessing, he adds: "Tenemos que tener cuidado. La gente no entendería" (We need to be careful. People would not understand). In this way, Fr. Amaro justifies his behavior and attempts to prevent Amelia from disclosing their relationship to anyone else. This behavior is typical of an abuser; he makes a vulnerable person feel special and forces her to maintain secrecy (Bancroft 243–45). The film shows this character perverting Catholic sacraments to accomplish his goals. The film also portrays Fr. Amaro manipulating Amelia in the church building. From the door, Amelia walks into the church and kneels to pray. The camera shows Amelia's face, then Dionisia's face, then the faces on statues of the Virgin Mary and Jesus. This establishes that Amelia is not alone. Then the camera returns to Amelia's back, where a hand touches her shoulder. Amaro asks her if she is crying about her boyfriend, Rubén. The camera moves to show Amelia's face, which is full of tears. She says no, that it is not about him. Lights—candles out of focus—flicker in the background and Amaro kisses her. The camera, which had continued to shift between their faces, stops as they kiss. For a moment, it frames Jesus's face above their heads. Amelia runs out of the church and Fr. Amaro remains in a pew. The fact that their first kiss on screen is in a church highlights his ethically questionable behavior, and the religiously imbued space clarifies the way Fr. Amaro abuses his power.

To further this relationship, he also exploits other, less powerful characters. In these interactions, he quotes the Bible and likens Amelia to the Virgin Mary, which makes his actions seem even more perverse. Fr. Amaro manipulates Martín (Gastón Melo), the *sacristán* (sexton), and Martín's daughter, Getsemaní (Blanca Loaria), a girl with developmental disabilities. He tells Martín that he is preparing Amelia in secret to be a nun and that he will need to use Martín's house for these classes. While he is there training Amelia, he explains that Amelia will also teach Getsemaní the catechism. This girls' name refers to the garden of Gethsemane, where Jesus was betrayed by his disciples (Mark 4:32–50). This adds a level of religious condemnation to Amaro's machinations. As Joseph Cunneen states, it is "hard to sympathize with Fr. Amaro's careful planning of his tryst with Amelia in a shack inhabited by the mentally handicapped daughter of one of Fr. Benito's assistants" (19). This is an understatement. While he is there, Fr. Amaro seduces Amelia by reciting: "Your hair is like a flock of goats moving down the slopes of Gilead . . . As a lily among brambles, so is my love among maidens . . . Your lips are like a crimson thread" (Song 6:5b, 2:2, 4:3a). He tells her this these passages, which come from the Song of Solomon, are from the Holy Book. Then he begins to undress her. The camera rotates around them and he continues to quote the Bible: "Your two breasts are like two fawns, twins of a gazelle, that feed among the lilies" (Song 4:5). He discusses the joint of her thighs, her lips, and her tongue, as he continues to quote biblical texts. These verses, part of what is colloquially considered the sexiest part of the Bible, were undoubtedly provocative for viewers, and part of the way that Fr. Amaro manipulated Catholic religious texts for his own gain. A few minutes later, Fr. Amaro covers Amelia with a cloak that evokes the Virgin Mary and tells her, "Eres más hermosa que la Virgen" (You are more beautiful than the Virgin). This was reportedly the most controversial part of the film. Amelia would no longer be a virgin after these scenes, let alone pure enough to be thought of as more beautiful than the Virgin. These scenes employ sacred texts and religious figures to illustrate the extent to which Fr. Amaro manipulates other characters.

The film also shows that Fr. Amaro retaliates against the same marginalized characters after Fr. Benito realizes what he is doing and confronts him. This emphasizes Fr. Amaro's desire to maintain power at any cost. In one scene, Fr. Amaro dismisses Martín, after the *sacristan* tells Fr. Benito what he suspects is going on. The now-unemployed Martín and his daughter become homeless, as his home in the sacristy was provided as part of his position. In a heartbreaking scene, the film shows Martín placing his daughter on a bed in the back of his horse-drawn cart. The camera then zooms in on Getsemaní and shows her holding a paper, which says "Come and follow" with an image of Jesus, which she may have received from Amelia during a brief Catechism class. The camera zooms out and Martín walks off the screen to go to the front of the cart and drive away. As Leñero sorrowfully pronounced in an interview: "Me duele este regreso de mi Iglesia a la penumbra preconciliar" (My Church's return to the pre-Council darkness hurts me) ("Unión"). It seems that on screen, as in the context of production, the Catholic Church has not applied any significant reforms associated with the Second Vatican Council, and thus it has simply maintained the figurative darkness associated with pre-Council Catholicism. In this system, Fr. Amaro manipulates other characters to get what he wants. This means that some, like Martín and Getsemaní, are left homeless. The way *El crimen* employs religious imagery in the scene in which these characters leave the town of Los Reyes emphasizes that Fr. Amaro's actions have devastated them. Moreover, this harsh judgment of a power-hungry young priest could be extended to other politicians in early twenty-first century Mexico.

The portrayal of Fr. Natalio, on the other hand, is one of a very ethical priest. His behavior contrasts with Frs. Benito and Amaro and alludes to the leftist wing of the Church, which was inspired by the possibilities of the Second Vatican Council. His presence in the film connects to other parts of the screenwriter's oeuvre, which present a vision of Catholicism that can be reformed. Lahr-Vivaz believes he alludes to the Zapatistas (107). While the Zapatistas were part of the context in which the film was produced, I believe Fr. Natalio alludes to liberation theology and perhaps to politicians from the left-leaning PRD.

Fr. Natalio's commitment to the gospel implies that the other priests in the film are not committed to it. This is evident in scenes that portray him with other priests. Fr. Benito accuses Fr. Natalio of being aligned with liberation theology and of helping *guerrilleros*. Fr. Natalio responds by bringing up Fr. Benito's relationship with Chato Aguilar, at a time when cartels were becoming recognized as a powerful force in Mexico. Fr. Natalio reminds his superior that the cartel forces peasants to plant poppies, conscripting them into the drug trade. He adds that Chato Aguilar launders money through donations for Fr. Benito's building campaign for a hospital. This criticism leads Fr. Benito to retaliate via the bishop and Amaro, drawing on the conservative wing of the Church and its ongoing anti-communist rhetoric.

Fr. Natalio receives Fr. Amaro in his community on two occasions. These scenes portray Fr. Natalio's commitment to his community, which makes Fr. Amaro's thirst for power become even more apparent. Martín drives Fr. Amaro to Natalio's rural parish. The film emphasizes its isolation as it gives multiple shots of the back of the car moving slowly on a dirt road, as well as brief shots of the truck's wheels in the dirt. Amaro and Martín arrive in the middle of a construction scene. In a traveling shot of a group of men, Fr. Natalio is indistinguishable from his parishioners. His role as priest here contrasts sharply with the same actor's role as a corrupt PRI governor in the film *Ley de herodes* (1999), whose script was also written by Leñero and which was released only three years before. In *El crimen,* Fr. Amaro confronts Fr. Natalio and they leave the group. The film shows the men in Natalio's humble abode as they drink coffee and the camera goes from one man's face to the other. The lighting shows Fr. Natalio's sweat and dirt, and we notice his simple bed in the background. This contrasts with Fr. Amaro, who wears a suit with a clerical collar, and presents a letter to Fr. Natalio from the bishop. The pristine white envelope contains a letter that tells the radical priest to scale back his work with *guerrilleros*, or he will be sent to be a priest at a convent. Fr. Natalio responds to Amaro by telling him that at least he follows the letter of the gospel and obeys God and the people. Natalio's behavior contrasts with Amaro's willingness to obey the Catholic hierarchy.

This culminates in a scene where Amaro tells Natalio that he cannot be a priest anymore. Critic Bonfil characterizes this interaction as one where Amaro's behavior is reprehensible, through "el hostigamiento y la excomunión a un cura disidente, el padre Natalio (un Damián Alcazar notable), que evangélicamente hace suya la causa de los pobres" (the harrassment and excommunication of a dissident priest, Fr. Natalio (notably played by Damián Alcazar), who evangelically makes the cause of the poor his own) ("El crimen"). In line with Bonfil's observations, Fr. Amaro interrupts a funeral as he enters Natalio's open-air worship space from the back. His dark-colored shirt contrasts with the palm trees that surround him and with the *campesinos*'s white shirts. The deceased man, Lucas, was of such modest means that he does not have a coffin. His name reminds us of Lucas García, the CCI leader in Cazals's *Canoa*, as well as the name of the narrator in one of Leñero's novels with religious imagery, *El evangelio de Lucas Gavilán*. He is instead wrapped in a white shroud and surrounded by candles. An altar to the Virgin of Guadalupe is somewhat visible above the man's head. The mourners pray the Litany of the Blessed Virgin Mary, also called the Litany of Loreto, in a call and response with Fr. Natalio ("Letanías lauretanas"). The people are expressing religious faith under the guidance of a leader who is in solidarity with them. Amaro destroys this community because he follows the bishop's orders. The camera follows Natalio as he walks through the mourners to stand with Amaro and then shows their faces and the mourners' backs as they leave the space. Natalio explains to Amaro that Lucas was found dead in a canyon, likely killed by cartel members. He believes that the assassins are allied with the municipal guards, a local police force. Amaro suggests that Natalio contact the authorities. Natalio responds by explaining that "aquí las cosas se arreglan de otra manera" (here we resolve things in a different way). He realizes who is responsible for this man's death: the cartel that killed him, and the state that is either directly allied with the cartel or tacitly approving of them as it refuses to prosecute its leaders.[31] This implies that Fr. Natalio has a better understanding of how power works, and it is perhaps for this reason that he is less likely to abuse it. Fr. Amaro disagrees, because for him, all unofficial methods of resolving problems are morally equivalent. He asks what Fr. Natalio thinks of abortion. Fr. Natalio responds that they do not have that problem in his parish, implying that Fr. Natalio does not abuse power in such a way that familiarity with abortion providers is required. Amaro then gives Natalio the letter. Natalio says he will stay as another *campesino*: "Elegí este camino. ¿Y tú?" (I chose this path. What about you?). His allusion to the path reminds viewers that there are people like Fr. Natalio, committed to his community, in multiple historical periods. Fr. Natalio also refers to leftist leaders in the film's context of production, in the way that the PRD gained power through coalitions with other left-leaning parties.

A morally ambiguous character called Dionisia controls female-led expressions of religious belief in *El crimen*. Her religious practices contrast with the way all of these priests express Catholicism.[32] The film juxtaposes her with Fr. Amaro from the beginning of the film. He travels to the town by bus, arrives in the *zócalo*, and walks to the church building. The camera, which is situated at or near the altar at the front of the church, shows Fr. Amaro as he enters. Dionisia's off-key voice sings, "Bendito, bendito, bendito sea Dios" (Blessed, blessed, blessed be the Lord) in the background. It is as if her voice, singing a song typically used for services outside of daily mass, welcomes Fr. Amaro to his new position. Later, when Fr. Amaro celebrates mass for the first time, Dionisia takes money from the collection plate rather than adding to it. After this, Dionisia participates in the Eucharist in her own way. The camera shows other parishioners' heads and shoulders as they walk up one by one to the altar rail and kneel. They open their mouths so that the priest can place the host in their mouths for them to receive. Dionisia also walks up to the rail and kneels. She takes the host, but rather than ingesting it, she keeps it in her mouth. She returns to her seat and places it in a missal, which is a book that contains the texts used in Catholic mass throughout the year. Dionisia remarks to Amelia's boyfriend, who is sitting in front of her, "Amelia le gusta el nuevo cura" (Amelia likes the new priest). After the mass, Dionisia gives the host to her cats, calling it their medicine. In spite of her own interpretation of communion, Dionisia does not extend this liberal view of the Eucharist to other characters. In fact, she yells at a group of kids in the church courtyard because they are eating left-over wafers, which may or may not have been sanctified, and putting *cajeta* (caramel-flavored spread) on them to make them worth eating. Subverting Catholic rituals is acceptable, as long as it is done her way. The film furthers the sense that her religious practice is a cruel one in a scene where Dionisia tries to give the sacrament to Getsemaní, the girl with disabilities. Dionisia goes to Martín's home when he is not there and enters Getsemaní's bedroom. There, she sits on top of the vulnerable young woman and forces the host down her throat. Getsemaní cries until Martín returns. He throws Dionisia off his daughter and forces her to leave. Later on, Dionisia leads an attack on the home of the newspaper publisher, where she and other local women stone the home and the men, calling them heretics. They were not, in fact, heretics; they simply published articles that criticized Fr. Benito's relationship with Chato Aguilar and the drug cartel. The film's misogynist portrayal of Dionisia's alternative religious practice emphasizes her cruelty in a way that the film does not emphasize Fr. Amaro's. At the same time, the film shows that her problematic expression of religious belief depends on those sacraments celebrated by priests recognized by the Catholic Church. Thus, Dionisia's actions suggest that there are no real alternatives to Catholicism, or redemption within its framework.

Dionisia and her religious practice are crucial to the film's climactic point. When Fr. Amaro decides to terminate Amelia's pregnancy, he visits Dionisia's home, which is also the sanctuary for her unique religious expression. The scene begins with him in profile walking in front of a building in the semi-darkness. Then, the priest turns a corner and the film shows his back as he walks on unpaved streets with water running down them. Once Fr. Amaro arrives at Dionisia's home, and the camera pans out to show vegetation in parts of the foreground and background, and a young girl walking down the dirt road carrying a pot. Water runs off the bottom left-hand side of the screen. In this scene of evident economic poverty, Fr. Amaro stands in front of a door, next to a ladder and junk that may be sold so that Dionisia can earn some money. Her home is made of unpainted cinder blocks, with a tin roof, and a wooden door closes off her courtyard in the right side of the frame (see figure 3.10). He opens the door to the courtyard, which is the only door in this ramshackle home. The cinder-block shelter has plastic tarps in lieu of a second door and is full of cats and dolls. Ominous music plays as Dionisia enters the frame and welcomes him to her "iglesia particular" (own particular church). It includes dolls that she calls Saint Joseph, Saint Anthony, and Virgin of Guadalupe. The camera does not show these figures directly. It does settle briefly on some dolls adorned in blue robes that evoke some incarnations of the Virgin, such as the Immaculate Consumption, the Ascension of the Virgin, and *La Milagrosa* (the Miraculous Virgin). Fr. Amaro dances around the question of abortion by asking for a doctor: "Uno de esos qué . . . trae niños al mundo" (One of those who . . . brings children into the world). She responds, "Usted lo que quiere es un aborto padrecito" (What you need, little Father, is an abortion). This is the same terminology doña Elvira used in *Las chicas malas del*

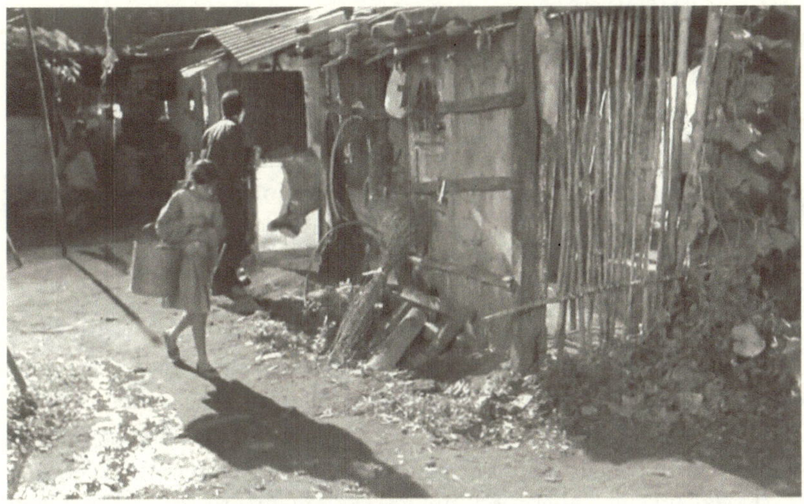

Figure 3.10. Fr. Amaro arrives at Dionisia's home in *El crimen del padre Amaro*. *Source*: *El crimen del padre Amaro*, fair use.

padre Méndez when she and El Grillo tried to drug Fr. Méndez. As Fr. Amaro is not as morally upright as Fr. Méndez, he gives Dionisia some money, and she responds, "Falta mucho . . . pero lo arreglamos" (That's not enough . . . but we will figure it out). Dionisia comes to the confessional to confirm the details, telling him to bring twice the money he had brought before and meet her on Friday at 2 a.m. He returns a cloth to the division between priest and parishioner in the confessional and the scene ends. Dionisia seems like she could be a redeemable character, but ultimately, she is just as problematic as Frs. Benito and Amaro, albeit in different ways. This figure does not bring about love; rather, she facilitates the removal of evidence. Her abilities, much like her religious rituals, depend on the Catholic Church.

In this film, Fr. Benito is predictable, like the PRI. On screen, he maintains stability through relationships with the mayor, his wife, and the local cartel leader, not unlike the party. His negotiations also parallel the conditions of film production in Mexico in the 1990s, where neoliberal policies led to different groups being able to exercise power, and thus, further negotiations between entities that held power. Fr. Amaro represents corruption and selfishness and evokes the PAN's hypocrisy, as well as foreshadowing the presidency of Enrique Peña

Nieto. Fr. Natalio's solidarity with peasants and his integrity implies that leftism may still be relevant in Mexico. Faithful Catholics on film use religious rituals to make meaning out of senseless death; yet, it is clear that the church hierarchy was never for them—and neither was the political system as a whole. Dionisia's religious practice is so dependent on the Catholic Church that it does not offer a true alternative.

~

El crimen, as well as *Novia que te vea* and *Ángel de fuego*, represent a distinct phase of Mexican history and film production; in spite of their different aesthetics and ways of reaching their audiences, they continued to employ religious imagery, which is, as I have shown, part of their social and political criticism. This imagery was so powerful—or at least recognizable—that the filmmakers were able to receive financing from the Mexican government and private sources, and, in the case of *El crimen del padre Amaro*, box office success. They also represent religious express beyond Catholicism. *Novia que te vea* represents multiple Jewish communities and expressions of Jewish cultural and religious identity, and *Ángel de fuego* reinterprets Catholicism and evangelicalism and combines them with influences from the Jewish tradition in Refugio's traveling puppet show. *El crimen del padre Amaro*, for its part, portrays various forms of Catholicism that are led by priests, alongside Dionisia's religious practices, which also relate to the Catholic Church. Each film also presents troubling relationships between men and women and among groups of women, suggesting that, in spite of an increased role for women in Mexican cultural production, patriarchal gender relationships are still the norm. The films allude to the breakdown of Mexican society under trade liberalization and deregulation, compounded by decades of crisis. Many of the characters in *Ángel de fuego* and *El crimen* allude to economically marginalized people, and characters in all three films struggle to belong. The films deal with questions of identity as it pertains to cultural and religious groups, as well as indigeneity. There is, ultimately, no redemption in any of these films, which is consistent with cinematic production of this time period. The way they use religious imagery reminds us that there is little possibility or hope for the most marginalized in their context of production.

CONCLUSION

Religion, particularly Catholicism, is an important part of many Mexican films from the Golden Age (1933–1964) to the present. Religious imagery and symbols, including representations of Catholic leaders, rituals, private expressions of devotion, and life in a religiously oriented community, allow these films to criticize their surrounding context. Part of this context includes the way the Mexican state has supported cultural programs, including the development of the Mexican film industry, and another part of this context is the changing influence of the Catholic Church in public life in the country.

The Mexican federal government has developed relationships with other powerful groups in the country and created new cultural programs in literature, art, and film. Indeed, since the Golden Age of Mexican film to the present, the Mexican government has bolstered the film industry: it has supported private film companies, developed its own cinematic ventures, and worked in collaboration with various other groups to train directors and produce and exhibit films.

In addition to seeking to influence the sphere of arts and culture, the state has also sought to control religion. Since the primary religion in Mexico is Catholicism, a good way for the Mexican government to expand power in the religious sphere is through a relationship with the Catholic Church. This relationship evolved from outright antagonism in the early part of the twentieth century, to allowing the Church to refashion itself as Mexico's moral compass in the 1950s, to recognizing a certain level of religious diversity and independence from state control in the early twenty-first century. The Catholic Church also experienced significant internal reforms in the 1960s and allowed for some left-leaning priests aligned with liberation theology to challenge its hierarchy. By the early twenty-first century, the religious panorama in Mexico had changed. The Catholic Church had an almost exclusive monopoly on religion in Mexico, but by the early twenty-first century, its power had somewhat lessened.

Over the course of these decades, then, the Catholic Church has been hugely influential, and its imagery and symbols would have been understandable for film audiences. Films, in turn, represent various aspects of Catholicism in its varied interpretations in Mexico. They do so to allude to the Church's changing relationship with the Mexican government, and over time, gradually include other Christian religious beliefs, as well as notable examples in which they represent Jewish communities in Mexico. These portrayals are an important way that films respond to their context.

The first chapter of this monograph examined three films. I proposed that allusions to Catholicism were one way that films engaged with the political and social changes in their context of production. A scene in *Río Escondido*, for instance, positions the protagonist Rosaura in a school building in such a way that her physical location, and the appearance of the inside of the school building, parallel that of a priest leading mass inside of a Catholic church. The film would have encouraged a sympathetic understanding of the revolutionary goal of free public education for all Mexican people by giving religious overtones to non-religious scenes that illustrated this goal.

Religious imagery was also part of the way that works from the Golden Age, and beyond, delineated acceptable behavior for male and female characters, and, by extension, for men and women in their context of production. It gave certain behaviors a stamp of approval and criticized others. For instance, the film *El seminarista* depicts benevolent patriarchs, and the strongmen who become them, in a positive way. The film approves of the protagonist, Miguel, as he does what he is told, first leaving seminary because he is ill, then teaching in a convent boarding school, where his students fall in love with him and where he does not take advantage of them. The film encapsulates these ideals in a scene where a student draws him with a halo, and presents Miguel living up to this angelic nature when he hears his uncle's deathbed confession. Miguel tells don Pancho that he is an honorable *charro*. My analysis of these scenes suggested that the film preferred Miguel's performance of benevolent patriarchy, even as it affirmed the rural strongman's ability to change. I also proposed that the religious imagery involved in the representation of these male characters reinforced how Miguel, don Pancho, and others embodied the then-prevailing idea that at home, men would be good fathers and husbands—if we understand "good" as imitating the president and revolutionary father. Women would follow their lead, and films typically presented them in ways that alluded to the archetypal interpretation of the virgin-whore dichotomy in Mexico, referencing the Virgin of Guadalupe or Malinche in some way. This chapter also demonstrated that the film *María Candelaria* strongly implies that its protagonist was pure and good because of her close relationship to the Virgin Mary, which the film illustrates with her traveling to a site of devotion to the Virgin in the early scenes of the film, and later on, after her fiancé is incarcerated, in scenes inside the local Catholic church where cinematic techniques almost make it seem as though a statue of the Virgin is crying with her. The film cements its understanding of María as good or pure, and her antagonist, an anonymous Indigenous woman, as bad, in scenes that depict María refusing to be painted nude and the anonymous character leading a mob that kills her.

In the second chapter of this book, many of the same tensions were present, in terms of the ideal roles for men and women in this historical context, as well as the fact that multiple films use religious imagery as a way to engage with their surroundings. That chapter examined films produced for popular audiences in the 1970s, as well as a film aimed at film festival audiences from the same time period. Two *ficheras*, *El oficio más antiguo del mundo* and *Las chicas malas del padre Méndez*, portrayed priests in brothels, and the latter was based on newspaper report of a priest who rescued sex workers. *El oficio más antiguo del mundo* upends the typical narrative as two sex workers rescue a priest, and the priest is so sympathetic that they confess their sins to him. This initially sympathetic and liberal priest turns out to be an imposter, which implies that liberal-seeming leaders in this context are also dishonest. Religious imagery in these films gave credence to a new iteration of the benevolent patriarch in *Las chicas malas del padre Méndez,* as he worked hard to supervise and control a group of nuns whose Social Work Institute tirelessly rescued sex workers. The much more well-known *Canoa: Memoria de un hecho vergonzoso* fictionalized a historical massacre in the town of San Miguel Canoa, instigated by its rabidly anti-communist local priest, Fr. Meza. This allegorical criticism of the Tlatelolco massacre, bolstered by the film's documentary style, criticizes the anti-communist leader in the film, as well as anti-communist presidents in the film's context.

Mexico experienced a new phase of economic insecurity under the guise of free trade, and a particular understanding of neoliberalism, in the 1990s and 2000s. In response to these international developments, the Mexican government changed its film laws, which meant that it closed its chain of movie theatres, deregulated ticket prices, and dramatically lowered the quotas for Mexican films that had to be shown on screens in Mexico. Films, and cinematic renderings of religious beliefs and practices, engaged with their context in new ways. In *Ángel de fuego*, the character Refugio's unique blend of Pentecostal (or charismatic) Christianity, Catholicism, and some of the director's own Jewish background enhances the film's disturbing portrayals of economically and socially marginalized groups in Mexico. When Schyfter's *Novia que te vea* brought Jewish communities to the screen, it was part of the growing presence of Judaism in Mexican film and literature. Indeed, more than the allusions to Jewish beliefs and practices as in Rotberg's work, *Novia que te vea* denoted a new stage of Mexican film development. It used a religious community that was much less familiar to its initial audiences, and discussed questions of identity and belonging in the film's storyline, using Indigenous characters and socialist ideas in ways that were relevant during the multiple historical periods in *Novia que te vea* as well as in the 1990s, the period in which the film was released. At the same time as directors Rotberg and Schyfter released these critically acclaimed works, director Carlos Carrera worked with others, such as screenwriter Vicente Leñero, to create one of the most controversial and highest grossing films in Mexican history: *El crimen del padre Amaro*. My analysis of that film focused on its representations of three priests and a female religious leader. The film likened the older priest Fr. Benito to the young and handsome Fr. Méndez, which I posited criticizes them both, and, by extension, both the old and new parties that controlled the country's federal government. T Dionisia's female-led religious practice proved that, within this film, there were no options for religion in Mexico that did not relate in some way to Catholicism, and that simply because there is a female leader, a religious group is not inherently good. This contrasts sharply with the character Fr. Natalio and the way that he lived out his beliefs with a group of peasants, likely demonstrating the screenwriter's support for the potential within certain understandings of Catholicism, as well as the potential of left-leaning leaders in the early twenty-first century.

Paying attention to religious allusions in each of these films, and in other films, reminds us that religion is a powerful tool. It can be used to subtly criticize some parts of a historical context, using imagery for a completely different goal than what might have been its original intention. It can be used to engage with the state when it might be hard to do so, if the state is supporting one's cinematic venture. As I draw this manuscript to a close in the fall of 2020, I am drawn to a line of a previous draft of my manuscript. There, I argued that the circus in Rotberg's *Ángel de fuego* refers to the neoliberal circus from hell of the 1990s, that film's context of production. Today, I add that its terrifying puppet show alludes to the political puppetry in that context, as well as in our own. I encourage us to continue to pay attention to films from our own context, and the ways that they employ religious imagery or symbols to incisively criticize events today.

NOTES

NOTES TO INTRODUCTION

1. The Virgin of Guadalupe appeared to Juan Diego in the same place where the Aztecs had worshipped the goddess Tonantzin. David Brading's *Mexican Phoenix: Our Lady of Guadalupe: Image and Tradition across Five Centuries* details the role of the Virgin of Guadalupe in Mexico.

2. Examples of orthodox Catholicism, approved by the hierarchy, include papal edicts, and specific versions or translations of the Bible and the missal, the book of services in a given year. Popular religious practice in Mexico usually relates to Catholic saints or significant apparitions of the Virgin Mary.

3. All translations are mine unless otherwise noted.

4. Other scholars of religion and film focus on how films may help audiences access the sacred or the transcendent, such as Paul Schrader's *Transcendental Style in Film: Ozu, Bresson, Dreyer* and Sheila J. Nayar's *The Sacred and the Cinema: Reconfiguring the "Genuinely" Religious Film.* The work of French Sulpician priest Amédée Ayfre (1922–1964) influences scholars of religion and film in Mexico, as his books were translated into Spanish; see, for example, *Conversion aux images? Les images de Dieu, les images et l'homme* (*Conversion by Image? Images of God, Images and Man*).

5. This play on words alludes to the Christian doctrine of the Trinity. According to the Catholic Catechism, the interpretation most relevant in the Mexican context, the Holy Trinity is the "central mystery of Christian faith and life . . . the source of all the other mysteries of faith, the light that enlightens them . . . the way and the means by which the one true God, Father, Son and Holy Spirit, reveals himself to men" ("Catechism").

6. Laura Isabel Serna's *Making Cinelandia: American Films and Mexican Film Culture Before the Golden Age* examines films from before this time period. Rielle Navitski's *Public Spectacles of Violence: Sensational Cinema and Journalism in Early Twentieth-Century Mexico and Brazil* also deals with this period as it analyzes silent cinema in both countries.

7. This title comes from Vicente Riva Palacio's novel *Monja y casada, virgen y mártir*, which was set during the Inquisition and published in 1903. Nuns, virgins, and married women are acceptable roles for Catholic women. Martyrs are also acceptable in the Catholic understanding and may call to mind women who died valiantly fighting for the Revolution.

8. Translations of Mexican film and cultural institutions in this paragraph and the two paragraphs that follow come from Misha MacLaird's *Aesthetics and Politics in the Mexican Film Industry.*

9. My study does not engage with films from the 1960s that were influenced by Latin American Nuevo Cine. According to critic Ana M. López, Nuevo Cine was influenced by movements such as "Third Cinema," "Imperfect Cinema," and "Cinema of Hunger" (311). López asserts that it was a "marginal, politicized, often clandestine cinematic practice" that tended to produce alternative types of films, although some films identified with this genre became commercial successes (309). Chapter 2 deals with the ways that the Mexican government and film industry appropriated this language for its own ends.

10. Gabriela Soto Laveaga's *Jungle Laboratories* elaborates on some of the ways that Echeverría tried to call Cárdenas's administration to mind.

11. Alma Adriana Aguilar Funes's "Cine y estado, dos aliados con fines constructivos" gives more information on film financing in the 1970s, pp. 67–100.

12. John R. May's 1998 edited collection, *La nueva imagen del cine religioso*, analyzes films from this perspective.

13. *Hojas de cine* is a collection of writing in periodicals that relates to the Nuevo cine latinoamericano movement. While it does not aim to address all Mexican film production, it is surprising that its second volume, which deals with Mexico, does not mention Catholicism in any meaningful way. Its third volume, about Central America the Caribbean, engages with popular religious expression, voodoo, and Catholicism in multiple cinemas (see for example Antonin).

NOTES TO CHAPTER 1

1. These films all star famous actors, and some of them participated in other films with religious overtones. For example, María Félix, the star of *Río Escondido*, also had a central role in a 1958 film with clear religious overtones, *Miércoles de ceniza* (*Ash Wednesday*). The film is based on a religious celebration and the film posters displayed the protagonist with an ashen cross on her forehead.

2. For more information about the PRI political party see Paul Gillingham and Benjamin T. Smith's edited collection, *Dictablanda.*

3. For more information see for example Miguel Alemán's *Discursos de Alemán.*

4. Vaccination campaigns in the historical context were rarely as peaceful. For more information about them, see Claudia Agostoni's "Control, Containment and Health Education in the Smallpox-Vaccination Campaigns in Mexico in the 1940s."

5. For more information see for example Janzen's *The National Body in Mexican Literature* (77).

6. Irma Cantú's "Malinche as Cinderellatl: Sweeping Female Agency in Search of a Global Readership" and Margo Glantz's edited collection *La Malinche, sus padres y sus hijos* both offer more nuanced interpretations of Malinche.

7. Mexican language plays with this concept of *chingar*, where women are *chingada* and the men are *chingón*. Critic Emily Hind explains the vocabulary of *chingar* and *chingada* for an English language audience (61). The verb *chingar* (to fuck), *el chingón* (the fucker), and *la chingada* (the fucked over, raped, or screwed) stem from this understanding of Malinche as *chingada* and Cortés as *chingón*.

8. It is often stated that the film won the Palme D'Or in Cannes in 1946; however, it simply received a diploma for participating in the contest (Ramón). *María Candelaria* sold well in Mexico, was exported to the US (Gaytán Fernández 26), and was popular in Spain. Some critics have wondered whether the plot was original or whether it adapted the plot of other works like *Janitzio*, but it remains a popular film (Vallejo 3; Taracena, "María Candelaria es un plagio"; Taracena, "María Candelaria o el don"; Laguna Sánchez).

9. Tierney explains that Fernández's work received significant funding from the SEP to develop educational materials. This financing was important to the release and circulation of his films (Tierney, *Emilio* 2–3).

10. According to a speech given by Delia Selene de Dios Vallejo in 2011, Diego Rivera was very critical of this film (3).

11. For more information about this particular incarnation of the child Jesus see, for example, Castro Sánchez's article "El niño de más de 450 años."

12. These are the Mexican film industry's equivalent to the Oscars

13. For more information on the Taller de Gráfica Popular see Ryan F. Long's chapter, "The People's Print Shop: Art, Politics, and the Taller de Gráfica Popular."

14. This opening scene is so important that it is copied in its entirety—by hand—in the 1983 summary of the film found in 2019 in the files on *Río Escondido* in the Centro de documentación archive at the Cineteca nacional (J. C. A. L.).

15. For more information about the rural education project, see for example Verónica Ruiz Lagier's article, "*El Maestro Rural* y la *Revista de Educación*. El sueño de transformar al país desde la editorial."

16. There were reportedly scenes that were too critical of the Catholic Church and, due to pressure from the Asociación Católica Mexicana, were suppressed ("Se suprimen").

17. For more information see Msgr. William P. Fray's article for lay Catholics, an explanation of theological concepts, like the role and function of the host in the Eucharist.

18. Olga Nájera-Ramírez's article, "Engendering Nationalism: Identity, Discourse, and the Mexican Charro," elaborates on the figure of the *charro*.

19. The actress, María Eugenia Llamas, played a similar role in other Golden Age films as well. For more information see *Hola!USA*'s article "Fallece María Eugenia Llamas, 'La Tucita,' a los 70 años de edad."

NOTES TO CHAPTER 2

1. There are multiple films in this decade that deal with the Catholic Church. Edgardo Reséndiz's "La iglesia y el cine mexicano" mentions several of them.

2. José María Fernández Unsáin's *La loca de los milagros* also alludes to religion. In this film, a wealthy woman experiencing ennui wants to create miracles via drugs for her friends.

3. For a comprehensive discussion of sex work, human trafficking, and consent, see Lorelei Lee's article "Cash/Consent: The War on Sex Work."

4. David Tombs's *Latin American Liberation Theology* provides a comprehensive introduction to this theology. The work of Enrique Dussel is also influential in this regard. He has published dozens of works since the 1970s, including *The Church in Latin America* (1992), an intervention that pertains directly to liberation theology.

5. David Agren's "In Mexico's Chiapas State, Bishop Ruiz Leaves Large Legacy" discusses Samuel Ruiz's life, and Tania Hernández Vicencio's "Sergio Méndez Arceo y su visión internacionalista" offers more information about Sergio Méndez Arceo.

6. Jaime M. Pensado and Enrique C. Ochoa's edited collection, *México Beyond 1968*, offers a comprehensive analysis of unrest in Mexico in this time period.

7. In Mexico, Indigenous is often synonymous with rural, even though not all Indigenous people are rural, and not all rural people are Indigenous. That is, rural people might be considered Indigenous by their urban counterparts, even if they do not practice a traditional culture or religion or worldview.

8. For more information about INI programs, and intellectual involvement in them, see for example Emily Hind (51–84).

9. An account of the experiences of this state violence can be found in María José Sagasti Lacalle, María Jiménez, Eufrosina Rodríguez, and Neil Harvey's *Las fuerzas de liberación nacional y los combates por la memoria, 1974–1977*.

10. The CCI (Central Campesina Independiente) was an organization for *campesinos* (peasants) upset with official unions for peasants and the *ejido* system and were one of the groups affiliated with the Party of the Poor. They ramped up their work under Echeverría's tenure, in part to show the false nature of his claims of working with peasants. According to Felipe Cazals, "The CCI attempted to find a path forward, but its efforts would later be betrayed by pervasive corruption. San Miguel Canoa is an example of this historic situation" (West 18). Martha L. Sepúlveda (16) and José de la Colina (13) reiterate that these men were from the CCI.

11. Tomás Pérez Turrent's *Luis Alcoriza* surveys the director and writer's life.

12. Prostitution is an important theme in Mexican history. For more information see for example Elisa Speckman Guerra and Fabiola Bailón Vásquez's edited collection, *Vicio, prostitución y delito*, and Adriana Sandoval's *De la literatura al cine: Versiones fílmicas de novelas mexicanas*. It has been an important topic in Mexican film since *Santa*.

13. Cosentino's article rightly refers to specific critics relevant to her topic there. The broader precedent undoubtedly includes the work of Dolores Tierney, whose monograph *Emilio Fernández: Pictures in the Margins* examines the work of this famous director, as well as the influence of a sociological approach to Mexican cultural studies in the work of critics such as Pedro Ángel Palou (*El fracaso del mestizo*) and Ignacio M. Sánchez Prado (*Screening Neoliberalism*).

14. This is from the screenplay; the words spoken in the film are the same. There are a number of clear parallels between the film and the screenplay, such as the use of subheadings. For this reason, I believe it appropriate to cite from the screenplay, even though there may be some differences between the two.

15. The director Fernández Unsáin and a colleague Armando Lemollé found a report on Fr. Méndez in the news and created this film based on real events in Uruapan, Michoacán ("Historias"; A. Serna 32).

16. Laura Turner's "Redheads: A Personal History" contextualizes misconceptions about red hair in the US and in the ideas of Catholic thinkers about biblical characters.

17. It was nominated for an Ariel for best picture and it won an Ariel for best screenplay. It also won a number of other national and international awards (Academia Mexicana).

18. Fr. Meza reportedly died under strange circumstances after he was "eventually removed from San Miguel Canoa by the Puebla curia and sent to another parish in the surrounding mountains. Rumor has it that shortly afterward he died of gunshot wounds received in a dust-up with some peasants" (West 16).

19. Transcription and translation are found in Leen's article.

NOTES TO CHAPTER 3

1. Political scientist Joy Langston's *Democratization and Authoritarian Party Survival: Mexico's PRI* explains this process.

2. Ignacio M. Sánchez Prado's "Mont Neoliberal Periodization: The Mexican 'Democratic Transition,' from Austrian Libertarianism to the 'War on Drugs'" analyzes this period and relates it to Mexican cultural production. Laura Podalsky's *The Politics of Affect and Emotion in Contemporary Latin American Cinema* engages with films from the 1990s and 2000s. Her work shows that Latin American films from this period also evoked different affective responses (7–8). These changes are not part of my analysis of Mexican cinema from this period, but considering audience responses remains important background to my work, particularly in light of the controversy generated by *El crimen del padre Amaro.*

3. Jorge I. Domínguez and Alejandro Poiré's edited collection, *Toward Mexico's Democratization: Parties, Campaigns, Elections, and Public Opinion* and Stephen Haber, Herbert Klein, Noel Maurer, and Kevin Middlebrook's *Mexico Since 1980* give more information about this time period.

4. For an account of the Zapatista uprising in Chiapas, see Andrés Oppenheimer's *México: En la frontera del caos.* This journalist goes into detail about the changes in Mexico after free trade, for good and for bad.

5. For an excellent summary of this debate regarding female directors and feminism see McClennen's article, "(De)Signing Women: Mexican Women Directors and Feminist Film."

6. For more information about children in film see, for example, Carolina Rocha and Georgia Seminet's edited collection *Representing History, Class, and Gender in Spain and Latin America: Children and Adolescents in Film.*

7. For further details on the *arrabal* genre see Carlos Monsiváis's essay, "Mythologies."

8. In the screenplay they reconcile at the end, but in the film they do not (Carro 8).

9. Incest in this film has very negative connotations. Nevertheless, it is a topic of debate among queer theorists. For a collection of debates around incest as an alternative or queer expression outside of patriarchal gender norms, see Elizabeth Barnes's edited collection *Incest and the Literary Imagination.*

10. In 2005, Gloria González-López's *Family Secrets* stated that there were no empirical studies of incest in Mexico. Her ethnographic work is based on the experiences of sixty women and sheds light on the fact that, in many cases of women who experience sexual violence, the perpetrator is a family member.

11. Rowan Renee is a photographer whose work reflects their experience of incest in twenty-first century United States. Their observations are relevant for this film and the Mexican context. In an interview with therapists, they

state: "The dysfunction in my family was so normalized it was difficult to recognize. As a child, you cannot see other possibilities so you don't know your experience is not normal" (Renee et al.).

12. Carolina Gabriela Vera Bérenger's 2006 thesis "Recuperación del documental audiovisual contemporáneo en la problemática social: Jóvenes, espiritualidad y religión" highlights that, since the 1990s, Mexico has experienced a transformation in terms of religion (81). She thus takes us into a more recent context and expands the scope and understanding of religion in Mexico.

13. The question of syncretism, that is, a religious inculturation of exchange between various forms of religious expression, is important in Latin America. In Mexico, it usually involves a combination of pre-conquest Indigenous traditions and Catholic practices. For more information about the definition of inculturation and why theologians prefer this term to syncretism, see Ramón Luzárraga's "Syncretism: Why Latin American and Caribbean Theologians Want to Replace a 'Fighting Word' in Theology." For information about the growth of non-Catholic religions in Latin America as they pertain to some feminine images of the divine, see for example Andrew Chestnut's chapter, "Conversion and the Products of Pneumacentric Religion in Latin America's Free Market of Faith."

14. Bernardo Barranco's *Las batallas del Estado laico: La reforma a la libertad religiosa* describes religious changes in this period in great detail.

15. Renée Sum Scott's chapter, "Rosa Nissán: Travesías por la memoria autobiográfica," Judith Morganroth Schneider's "Rosa Nissán's Reconstruction of Diasporic Consciousness: Reflections on Genealogy, Geography and Gender in *Las tierras prometidas*," and Manuel F. Medina's "The Female Stranger: Mexican and Jewish Gaze in Rosa Nissán's Imagined Spaces" give invaluable context for Rosa Nissán's work.

16. These remarks echo critic Guadalupe Cortina, who observes that "obras que cabe mencionar en cuanto a una representación tradicional y a veces negativa son *La hija del judío* de Justo Sierra (1908), *El libro rojo* de Vicente Riva Palacio (1905), *Malagato* de Josefina Estrada (1990) y *Morirás lejos* de José Emilio Pacheco (1967), por mencionar algunos" (works that are worth mentioning in terms of the traditional and sometimes negative representation are *The Daughter of The Jew* by Justo Sierra (1908), *The Red Book* de Vicente Riva Palacio (1905), *Malagato* by Josefina Estrada (1990) and *You Will Die in a Distant Land* by José Emilio Pacheco (1967)" (23).

17. This reception was not uniformly positive. Some critics like Jorge Ayala Blanco believed that the way the film portrayed women was especially at fault. For him, Jewish femininity of the 1990s, which he calls "la feminidad neo*kosher*[,] asegura la continuidad de la exclusión y de las perennes autoexclusiones, convencida de que éstas siguen siendo máximas soluciones" (neo*kosher* femininity[,] assures the continuity of exclusion and perennial self-exclusions, convinced that these are the best solutions) (n. p.).

18. The film *Novia que te vea* came into being after the writer Rosa Nissán participated in a workshop run by writer Elena Poniatowska. Poniatowska, an influential figure in the Mexican cultural sphere, recommended that Nissán develop what was then her novel-in-progress into a film (Rashkin 154).

19. In the film, Oshi identifies as part of the group of "turcos," as her maternal grandmother had emigrated from what is now Turkey and Persia (Halevi-Wise 272; Luna 120–21). She thus distinguishes herself from the Jewish community from Syria, the "árabes," who in English are often called Mizrahi. All her grandparents in the film speak the Ladino language, like other Jewish communities who have their roots in the expulsion from Spain in the fifteenth century. It is also called Judeo Spanish. For more information, see Tabea Alexa Linhard's "Ishica, ¿de quién sos tú?: Nostalgia for a Mother Tongue in Rosa Nissán's Novels," 458. Margalit Bejarano and Edna Aizenberg's edited collection, *Contemporary Sephardic Identity in the Americas: An Interdisciplinary Approach*, is a key text for understanding Sephardic Jewish identity and culture, as well as different interpretations of the term *Sephardic*, including the debate some scholars have over the boundaries between Sephardic and Mizrahi communities.

20. For a recent example of this attitude see Enrique Krauze's review of *Roma* in *The New York Times*, in which he states that the Indigenous women who accompany *criolla* families come from far away and long ago.

21. The actor Ernesto Laguardia, who portrays Saavedra, claims that Rifke integrates into the Mexican community when this character begins a sexual relationship with Saavedra. It represents "la integración de ella como judía a la comunidad mexicana, a las juventudes comunistas . . . ella se abre" (the integration of her as a Jewish person into the Mexican community and communist youth . . . she opens herself) (Arturo Pacheco).

22. Cristián H. Ricci's "Vigilar y castigar como modelo social" provides a historical and cultural context for the novel.

23. The novel was also controversial. According to Sergio González Rodríguez, "El Crimen del Padre Amaro fue durante mucho tiempo una lectura prohibida entre la sociedad católica en Portugal y en Brasil, y ahora el rebaño oscurantista quiere censurar la cinta mexicana basada en la novela" (*The Crime of Fr. Amaro* was for a long time a forbidden book in Brazilian and Portuguese Catholic society, and now the wave of regression would like to censure the Mexican film based on the novel) (6).

24. Producer Alfredo Ripstein asked Felipe Cazals and Vicente Leñero to work with him on this project. According to Leñero, the first attempt to film it did not work out. Alfredo Ripstein told him and Cazals that "como era judío, podía herir a los católicos con esta película. Entonces, Cazals lo mandó a la chingada" (since he was Jewish, he could damage Catholics with this film. And so, Cazals told him to go to hell) (Vértiz de la Fuente). Leñero goes on to explain that, three years later, he and Arturo Ripstein revisited the project with a new director, Carlos Carrera (Vértiz de la Fuente).

25. For more information about the controversy see newspaper articles such as "La organización de Católicos Unidos por México amenazan boicotear" and "Divide Amaro." Alfredo Joskowicz, the director of IMCINE, responded to the controversy in a statement, titled "Con relación a la película titulada 'El crimen del padre amaro.' "

26. On a related note, in 1999, Jorge Antonio Estrada Castellanos observed that, until recently, one had to confess if one watched a prohibited film (11). This practice may only have ended in more urban contexts and still been present when *El crimen* was released.

27. Other political parties in Mexico are thought to have conspired against the PRD in fraudulent elections, including the 1988 federal election when Cuauhtémoc Cárdenas, running for the presidency for the left-leaning Frente Democrático Nacional party, lost the election. Reding's article offers further explanation of these events.

28. Leñero was a prolific screenwriter. For a complete discussion of this aspect of his oeuvre, see Gustavo Ambrosio's "Vicente Leñero y su legado en el cine." Leñero's scripts and other parts of his work portray liberation theology in positive ways. See for example his novel, *El evangelio de Lucas Gavilán*, and its related theatrical work, *Jesucristo Gómez*. Leñero's discussion about Catholicism in an interview with Adela Salinas in 1997, "La opción por Jesucristo," sheds light on the author's religious views.

29. In this way, the film reminds scholars of Mexico in the twenty-first century that journalism is a very dangerous profession in that country. Numbers from the Committee to Protect Journalists suggest that three journalists were killed between 2000 and 2003, and that forty-five have been killed between 2000 and 2019 ("Mexico/Americas: Report").

30. Méndez Arceo was a powerful force for liberation theology in Mexico during the three decades he was a bishop. He was allowed to maintain his views, as long as he did so only within his diocese. For more information about him, see for example Robert Sean Mackin's "Becoming the Red Bishop of Cuernavaca."

31. Oswaldo Zavala's *Los cárteles no existen* provides more information about the relationship between the Mexican state and cartels, including questioning the idea that the boundary between them exists.

32. There is a long tradition of feminist engagement with the Catholic tradition; Elizabeth Schuessler Fiorenza is the most famous feminist theologian of the later part of the twentieth century. Her work, beginning with *In Memory of Her*, examines the role of women in biblical texts and in the Catholic Church. Sylvia Marcos's 2018 report, "Emerging Feminist Theologies," discusses the recent contributions of feminist theologians in Mexico.

WORKS CITED

Academia Mexicana de Artes y Ciencias Cinematográficas AC. "XVIII Entrega del Ariel (1976)." *Canoa* files collection, Centro de documentación collection, Cineteca Nacional, Mexico City, Mexico.

Agostoni, Claudia. "Control, Containment and Health Education in the Smallpox-Vaccination Campaigns in Mexico in the 1940s." *História, Ciências, Saúde—Manguinhos*, vol. 22, no. 2, 2015, pp. 1–15.

Agren, David. "In Mexico's Chiapas State, Bishop Ruiz Leaves Large Legacy." *National Catholic Reporter*, 28 Jan. 2016. https://www.ncronline.org/news/world/mexicos-chiapas-state-bishop-ruiz-leaves-large-legacy. Accessed 3 Oct. 2019.

Aguilar Funes, Alma Adriana. *Cine y estado, dos aliados con fines constructivos.* 2018. UNAM, Licenciatura thesis.

Agustín, José. *Tragicomedia mexicana 2: La vida en México de 1970 a 1982.* Planeta, 2007.

Alemán, Miguel. *Discursos de Alemán.* [Mexico, 1945].

Alfaro-Velcamp, Theresa. "'Reelizing' Arab and Jewish Ethnicity in Mexican Film." *The Americas*, vol. 63, no. 2, 2006, pp. 261–80.

Amador, María Luisa, and Jorge Ayala Blanco. *Cartelera cinematográfica: 1940–1949.* UNAM, CUEC, 1982.

Ambrosio, Gustavo. "Vicente Leñero y su legado en el cine." *Milenio*, 3 Dec. 2014. https://www.milenio.com/espectaculos/vicente-lenero-y-su-legado-en-el-cine. Accessed 28 Oct. 2019.

Amores perros. Directed by Alejandro González Iñárritu. Altavista Films, Zeta Film, 2001.

Ángel de fuego. Directed by Dana Rotberg. IMCINE, Producciones Metropolis, Una Productora Más, 1992.

Antebi, Susan. "A Rhetoric of Hygiene: Juan O'Gorman's Functionalism and the Futures of the Mexican Cityscape." *Journal of Latin American Cultural Studies*, vol. 21, no. 4, 2012, pp. 535–56.

Antonin, Arnold. "Haití: mito y razón." Leduc et al., vol. III, pp. 227–38.

Arredondo, Isabel. "Dana Rotberg." *Palabra de mujer: Historia oral de las directoras de cine mexicano (1988–1994)*, edited by Isabel Arredondo, Iberoamericana; Universidad Autónoma de Aguascalientes, 2001, pp. 167–70.

———. "Guita Schyfter." Arredondo, pp. 49–54.

Ashbrook, Tom. "Guillermo del Toro's Story." *On Point*, NPR, 23 Sep. 2010. https://www.wbur.org/onpoint/2010/09/23/guillermo-del-toro-film. Accessed 29 Nov. 2019.

Ayala Blanco, Jorge. "Schyfter y la feminidad neokosher." *El financiero*, 6 June 1994. *Novia que te vea* files, Centro de documentación collection, Cineteca Nacional, Mexico City, Mexico.

Ayfre, Amédée. *Conversion aux images? Les images et Dieu, les images et l'homme*. Éditions du Cerf, 1964.

Banco Nacional Cinematográfica, S. A. *Informe general sobre la actividad cinematográfica en el año 1976 relativo al Banco Nacional Cinematográfico, S. A. y a sus filiales*. El Banco, 1976.

Bancroft, Lundy. *Why Does He Do That?: Inside the Minds of Angry and Controlling Men*. Berkeley Publishing Group; Penguin, 2002.

Barnes, Elizabeth, editor. *Incest and the Literary Imagination*. UP of Florida, 2002.

Barranco, Bernardo. *Las batallas del Estado laico: La reforma a la libertad religiosa*. Grijalbo, 2016.

Bejarano, Margalit and Edna Aizenberg, editors. *Contemporary Sephardic Identity in the Americas: An Interdisciplinary Approach*. Syracuse UP, 2012.

Benjamin, Thomas. "A Time of Reconquest: History, the Maya Revival, and the Zapatista Rebellion in Chiapas." *The American Historical Review*, vol. 105, no. 2, 2000, pp. 417–50.

The Bible. The New Revised Standard Version, Thomas Nelson, 1989.

Blancarte, Roberto J. "La doctrina social del episcopado católico mexicano." *El pensamiento social de los católicos mexicanos*, edited by Roberto J. Blancarte, Fondo de Cultura Económica, 1996, pp. 19–38.

———. *Historia de la iglesia católica en México 1929–1982*. El Colegio Mexiquense; Fondo de Cultura Económica, 1992.

Bonfil, Carlos. "El crimen del padre Amaro." *La Jornada*, 18 Aug. 2002. https://www.jornada.com.mx/2002/08/18/03aa2cul.php?origen=opinion.html. Accessed 1 Aug. 2019.

———. "Las ciudades imaginarias del cine mexicano." *La jornada semanal*, 10 June 2001. https://www.jornada.com.mx/2001/06/10/sem-libros.htm. Accessed 4 Feb. 2019.

Boylan, Kristina A. "Gendering the Faith and Altering the Nation: Mexican Catholic Women's Activism, 1917–1940." *Sex in Revolution: Gender, Politics and Power in Modern Mexico*, edited by Jocelyn Olcott et al., Duke UP, 2006, pp. 199–222.

Brading, David. *Mexican Phoenix: Our Lady of Guadalupe: Image and Tradition Across Five Centuries*. Cambridge UP, 2001.

Brescia, Pablo. Rev. of *El crimen del padre Amaro* by Carlos Carrera. *Chasqui*, vol. 32, no. 2, 2003, pp. 184–86.

"Buñuel en México." 30 Oct. 2019–19 Apr. 2020, La Galería de la Cineteca Nacional, Mexico City, Mexico.

Cabrera, Daniela. "Gael Garcia Bernal is Heading to the Cannes Film Festival and Your Computer Screen." *Remezcla*, 1 May 2014. https://remezcla.com/film/gael-garcia-bernal-is-heading-to-the-cannes-film-festival-and-your-computer-screen. Accessed 19 Nov. 2019.

Cacho, Lydia. *Esclavas del poder: Un viaje al corazón de la trata sexual de mujeres y niñas en el mundo*. Grijalbo, 2010.

Canoa: Memoria de un hecho vergonzoso. Directed by Felipe Cazals, Sindicato de Trabajadores de la Producción Cinematográfica; CONACITE Uno, 1976.

Cantú, Irma. "Malinche as Cinderellatl: Sweeping Female Agency in Search of a Global Readership." *Colonial Itineraries of Contemporary Mexico: Literary and Cultural Inquiries*, edited by Oswaldo Estrada and Anna M. Nogar, U of Arizona P, 2014, pp. 147–71.

Cañada Martínez, Adriana. *La cotidianidad de la mujer rural en María Candelaria*. 2004. UNAM, Licenciatura thesis.

Carro, Nelson. "Introducción." *Ángel de fuego*, by Rotberg and Rodrigo, ediciones El Milagro, 1993, pp. 7–10.

Castro Ricalde, Maricruz. "Ciudadanos del margen: *Ángel de Fuego* de Diana Rotberg." *Nuestra América: Revista de Estudios sobre la Cultura Latinoamericana*, vol. 1, 2006, pp. 112–25.

"Catechism of the Catholic Church." The Vatican. http://www.vatican.va/archive/ccc_css/archive/catechism/p1s2c1p2.htm. Accessed 28 Nov. 2019.

Castro Sánchez, Aída. "El niño de más de 450 años." *El Universal*, 3 Feb. 2018. https://www.eluniversal.com.mx/colaboracion/mochilazo-en-el-tiempo/nacion/sociedad/el-nino-de-mas-de-450-anos. Accessed 1 Aug. 2019.

Chestnut, Andrew. "Conversion and the Products of Pneumacentric Religion in Latin America's Free Market of Faith." *Conversion of a Continent: Contemporary Religious Change in Latin America*, edited by Timothy J. Steigenga and Edward L. Clearly, Routledge, 2007, pp. 72–92.

Cima Films, S.A. *Las distintas etapas del amor.* México, 1968.

Colina, José de la. "La noche de las antorchas." *Tiempo de cine*, 14 Dec. 1975, p. 13.

Cortina, Guadalupe. *Invenciones multitudinarias: Escritoras judíomexicanas contemporáneas*. Juan de la Cuesta, 2000.

Cosentino, Olivia. "Re: Star studies." Received by Rebecca Janzen, 6 Nov. 2019.

———. "Starring Mexico: Female Stardom, Age and Mass Media Trajectories in the 20th Century." *The Routledge Companion to Gender, Sex and Latin*

American Culture, edited by Frederick Luis Aldama, Routledge, 2018, pp. 196–205.

Cunneen, Joseph. "Pain and Healing: Melodrama Stays on Surface; 'Ararat' Goes Deeper." *National Catholic Reporter,* 29 Nov. 2002, p. 16.

"Currículum Vitae. Guita Schyfter: Directora." Instituto Mexicano de Cinematografía. N.d. *Novia que te vea* files, Centro de documentación collection, Cineteca Nacional, Mexico City, Mexico.

Dalton, David S. *Mestizo Modernity: Race, Technology, and the Body in Postrevolutionary Mexico.* U of Florida P, 2018.

de la Mora, Sergio. " 'Tus pinches leyes yo me las paso por los huevos.' Isela Vega and Mexican Dirty Movies." Ruétalo and Tierney, pp. 245–57.

———. *Cinemachismo: Masculinities and Sexuality in Mexican Film.* U of Texas P, 2006.

de León, Concepción. "Alfonso Cuarón Keeps the Winning Streak Going for Mexican Directors." *The New York Times,* 28 Feb. 2019. https://www.nytimes.com/2019/02/28/style/oscars-roma-cuaron-mexican-directors.html. Accessed 8 Sept. 2020.

del Valle, Luis G. "Teología de la liberación en México." *El pensamiento social de los católicos mexicanos,* edited by Roberto J. Blancarte, Fondo de Cultura Económica, 1996, pp. 230–65.

Detweiler, Craig. "Christianity." Lyden, pp. 109–30.

Dever, Susan. *Celluloid Nationalism and Other Melodramas: From Post-Revolutionary Mexico to Fin de Siglo Mexamerica.* SUNY P, 2003.

"Divide Amaro." *El Universal,* 13 Aug. 2002. Secc. Espectáculos, *El crimen del padre Amaro* files, Centro de documentación collection, Cineteca Nacional, Mexico City, Mexico.

Domínguez, Jorge I., and Alejandro Poiré, editors. *Toward Mexico's Democratization: Parties, Campaigns, Elections, and Public Opinion.* Routledge, 1999.

Doremus, Anne. "Religion, the Church and Mexican Nationalism: The Films of Emilio Fernández." *Studies in Latin American Popular Culture,* vol. 22, 2003, pp. 149–63.

Dussel, Enrique. *The Church in Latin America.* Orbis, 1992.

Dyer, Richard. *Stars.* BFI Publishing, 1998.

Eça de Queirós, José María. *El crimen del padre Amaro* (*O Crime do padre Amaro*). Translated by Luz Monteagudo, Sirio and books4pocket, 2009.

El crimen del padre Amaro. Directed by Carlos Carrera, Alameda Films; Fondo para la Producción Cinematográfica de Calidad; Gobierno del Estado de Veracruz; IMCINE, 2002.

El derecho a la vida. Directed by Mauricio de la Serna, Cinematográfica Groves, 1959.

El grito. Directed by Leobardo López Arretche, Centro Universitario de Estudios Ceinmatográficos, 1968.

El oficio más antiguo del mundo. Advertising folder. Iconoteca collection. Cineteca Nacional. Mexico City, Mexico, 1970.

El oficio más antiguo del mundo. Directed by Luis Alcoriza, Cima Films, 1970. Re-released by Ardustry World Cinema, 2005.

El seminarista. Poster. Iconoteca collection. Cineteca Nacional. Mexico City, Mexico, 1949.

El seminarista. Directed by Roberto Rodríguez, Producciones Rodríguez Hermanos, 1949.

Estrada Castellanos, Jorge Antonio. *Imágenes de perversion: Cine y censura religiosa en Mexico*. 1999. Universidad Intercontinental, Licenciatura thesis.

Estrada Romero, Ana Luisa. *La trilogía de Cazals: Visión de una realidad cruel*. 1998. UNAM, Acatlán, Licenciatura thesis.

Feder, Elena. "Engendering the Nation, Nationalizing the Sacred: Guadalupanismo and the Cinematic (Re)Fromation of Mexican Consciousness." *National Identities and Sociopolitical Changes in Latin America*, edited by Mercedes F. Durán-Cogan and Antonio Gómez-Moriana, Routledge, 2001, pp. 229–68.

Fox, Claire F. "Pornography and 'the Popular' in Post-Revolutionary Mexico." *Visible Nations: Latin American Cinema and Video*, edited by Chon A. Noriega, U of Minnesota P, 2000, pp. 143–73.

Franco, Jean. *Plotting Women: Gender and Representation in Mexico*. Columbia UP, 1989.

Fray, Msgr. William P. "The Real Presence of Jesus Christ in the Sacrament of the Eucharist: Basic Questions and Answers." *United States Conference of Catholic Bishops*, 2001. http://www.usccb.org/prayer-and-worship/the-mass/order-of-mass/liturgy-of-the-eucharist/the-real-presence-of-jesus-christ-in-the-sacrament-of-the-eucharist-basic-questions-and-answers.cfm. Accessed 1 Nov., 2019.

García Orso, Luis. "*El crimen del padre Amaro*." *Xipe totek*, vol. 45, 2003, pp. 97–105.

———. *Imágenes del espíritu el en cine*. Obra nacional de la buena prensa, 2000.

García Riera, Emilio. *Breve historia del cine mexicano: Primer siglo 1897–1997*. Ediciones Mapa, 1998.

———. *Historia documental del cine mexicano*, vol. 1, 2nd ed., Universidad de Guadalajara, 1994.

———. *Historia documental del cine mexicano*, vol. 4, 2nd ed., Universidad de Guadalajara, 1994.

———. *Historia documental del cine mexicano*, vol. 14, 2nd ed., Universidad de Guadalajara, 1994.

———. *Historia documental del cine mexicano*, vol. 15, 2nd ed., Universidad de Guadalajara, 1994.

García Tsao, Leonardo. *Felipe Cazals habla de su cine*. Universidad de Guadalajara, 1994.

García, Gustavo. "El mito de la neutralidad." *El cine mexicano a través de la crítica*, edited by David R. Maciel, UNAM, 2001, pp. 292–94.

Gaytán Fernández, Francisco. "María Candelaria." *Journal of Film Preservation*, vol. 84, 2011, pp. 26–27.

Gillingham, Paul, and Benjamin T. Smith, editors. *Dictablanda: Politics, Work, and Culture in Mexico, 1938–1968*. Duke UP, 2014.

Glantz, Margo, coordinator. *La Malinche, sus padres y sus hijos*. Taurus, 2001.

González-López, Gloria. *Family Secrets. Stories of Incest and Sexual Violence in Mexico*. New York UP, 2015.

González Rodríguez, Sergio. "La vigencia del 'padre Amaro.' *Reforma*, 9 Aug. 2002, Secc. Gente, p. 6.

Haber, Stephen Herbert Klein, et al. *Mexico Since 1980*. Cambridge UP, 2009.

Haddu, Miriam. *Contemporary Mexican Cinema, 1989–1999: History, Space and Identity*. Edwin Mellen Press, 2007.

Halevi-Wise, Yael. "Puente entre naciones: idioma e identidad sefardí en *Novia que te vea* e *Hisho que te nazca* de Rosa Nissán." *Hispania*, vol. 81, no. 2, 1998, pp. 269–77.

Hatfield, Elia. "La trata de personas o la industria del sexo a través del cine mexicano." *Chasqui* vol. 47, issue 1, p. 144–59.

Hecho en México. Directed by Duncan Bridgeman, El Mall, Pantelion Fils, VideoCine, 2012.

Hernández Vicencio, Tania. "Sergio Méndez Arceo y su visión internacionalista." *Política y Cultura*, vol. 38, 2012, pp. 89–117.

Hershfield, Joanne. *Mexican Cinema/Mexican Woman, 1940–1950*. U of Arizona P, 1996.

Hind, Emily. *Femmenism and the Mexican Woman Intellectual from Sor Juana to Poniatowska: Boob Lit*. Palgrave Macmillan, 2010.

"Historias fílmicas: Las chicas malas del padre Méndez." N.d. *Las chicas malas del padre Méndez* files, Centro de documentación collection, Cineteca Nacional. Mexico City, Mexico.

Hola!USA. "Fallece María Eugenia Llamas, 'La Tucita,' a los 70 años de edad." 1 Sep. 2014. *Hola! USA*. https://us.hola.com/cine/201409017942/maria-eugenia-llamas-fallecimiento. Accessed 1 Aug. 2019.

Huerta Ortiz, César. "A 50 años de Canoa: una pistola, un cura y amenazas de muerte." *Reforma*, 14 Sept. 2018. *Canoa* files, Centro de documentación collection, Cineteca Nacional, Mexico City, Mexico.

Hughes, Jennifer Scheper. *Biography of a Mexican Crucifix: Lived Religion and Local Faith from the Conquest to the Present*. Oxford UP, 2010.

Instituto Nacional de Estadística, Geografía e Informática. *La diversidad religiosa en México*. Instituto Nacional de Estadística, Geografía e Informática (INEGI), 2005.

Instituto Nacional de Estadística y Geografía (México). *Panorama de las religiones en México 2010*. Instituto Nacional de Estadística y Geografía, Secretaría de Gobernación (INEGI), 2011.

Irwin, Robert McKee. *Mexican Masculinities*. U of Minnesota P, 2003.

J. C. A. L. "Río Escondido." 18 Nov. 1983. *Río Escondido* files, Centro de documentación collection. Cineteca Nacional. Mexico City, Mexico.

Jablonska Zaborowska, Aleksandra. "El campo simbólico-religioso en el cine mexicano actual." *Boletín Americanista*, vol. LXV.2, no.71, 2015, pp. 117–30.

Janzen, Rebecca. *The National Body in Mexican Literature: Collective Challenges to Biopolitical Control*. Palgrave-Macmillan, 2015.

Jesús el niño Dios. Directed by Miguel Zacarías, Panorama Films, 1969.

Jesús nuestro Señor. Directed by Miguel Zacarías, Panorama Films, Producciones Zacarías S. A., 1970.

Jesús, María y José. Directed by Miguel Zacarías, Panorama Films, Producciones Zacarías S. A., 1970.

Jolly, Jennifer. *Creating Pátzcuaro, Creating Mexico: Art, Tourism, and Nation Building under Lázaro Cárdenas*. U of Texas P, 2018.

José María Fernández Unsaín. Memoria del cine mexicano. Directed by César Roel, IMCINE; CONACULTA, 1993.

Joskowicz, Alfredo. "Con relación a la película titulada 'El crimen del padre Amaro,' El Instituto Mexicano de Cinematografía (IMCINE) Informa lo siguiente." *Reforma*, 7 Aug. 2002, Secc. Cultura, p. 4.

Keating, Shannon. "Let's Talk About that Confessional Scene in 'Fleabag.'" *Buzzfeed*, 20 May 2019. http://www.buzzfeednews.com/article/shannon keating/fleabag-season-2-phoebe-waller-bridge-hot-priest. Accessed 27 Nov. 2019.

King, John. *Magical Reels: A History of Cinema in Latin America*. Verso, 2000.

Kloppe-Santamaría, Gema. "Lynching and the Politics of State Formation in Post-Revolutionary Puebla (1930s–50s)." *Journal of Latin American Studies*, vol. 51, no. 3, 2019, pp. 499–521. https://doi.org/10.1017/S002 2216X18001104.

Krauze, Enrique. "'Roma': Una historia de amor y servidumbre." *The New York Times*, 14 Dec. 2018. https://www.nytimes.com/es/2018/12/14/opinion-roma-cuaron-krauze. Accessed 28 Oct. 2019.

La guerra de las monjas. Flyer. 1970. Centro de documentación collection, Cineteca Nacional, Mexico City, Mexico.

La loca de los milagros. Directed by José María Fernández Unsáin, Cima Films, Estudios América, 1975.

La virgen de Guadalupe. Directed by Alfredo Salazar, Cinematográfica Calderón, 1976.

"La organización de Católicos Unidos por México amenazan boicotear la cinta." *Esto*, 9 Aug. 2002, p. B8.

Laguna Sánchez, José. "El plagio posible del filme 'María Candelaria': Las coincidencias con 'Janitizio'" *El Universal*, 25 Oct. 1986. Secc. Cultura, *María Candelaria* files, Centro de documentación collection, Cineteca Nacional, Mexico City, Mexico.

Lahr-Vivaz, Elena. *Mexican Melodrama: Film and Nation from the Golden Age to the New Wave*. U of Arizona P, 2016.

Langston, Joy. *Democratization and Authoritarian Party Survival: Mexico's PRI*. Oxford UP, 2017.

Las chicas malas del padre Méndez. Directed by José María Fernández Unsáin, Artistas Mexicanos Asociados; Películas Rodríguez, 1970.

Lay Arellano, Israel Tonatiuh. *Análisis del proceso de la iniciativa de la Ley de la Industria Cinematográfica de 1998*. 2005. Universidad de Guadalajara, Master's thesis.

Leduc, Paul et al., coordinators. *Hojas de cine: Testimonios y documentos del nuevo cine latinoamericano*, vol. III. Centroamérica y el Caribe. Fundación mexicana de cineastas; Universidad Autónoma Metropolitana; Secretaría de educación pública, 1988.

Lee, Lorelei. "Cash/Consent: The War on Sex Work." *n + 1*, no. 35, 2019. https://nplusonemag.com/issue-35/essays/cashconsent. Accessed 4 Nov. 2019.

Leen, Catherine. "The Sound of Silence: The *corrido* as Counterculture in Felipe Cazals' *Canoa*." *Modern Languages Open*, Dec. 2016, pp. 1–16.

Leñero, Vicente. "La opción de Jesucristo." Interview with Adela Salinas. *Dios y los escritores mexicanos*, edited by Adela Salinas, Nueva Imagen, 1997, pp. 75–81.

———. "Unión adúltera con el poder." *Proceso*, 18 Aug. 2002. https://www.proceso.com.mx/188055/union-adultera-con-el-poder. Accessed 1 Aug. 2019.

———. *El evangelio de Lucas Gavilán*. First published 1979. Joaquín Mortiz, 2007.

———. *Jesucristo Gómez*. Océano, 1983.

"Letanías lauretanas." *Devocionario católico*. 2000. https://www.devocionario.com/maria/lauretanas_1.html. Accessed 23 Oct. 2019.

Linhard, Tabea Alexa. "Ishica, ¿de quién sos tú?: Nostalgia for a Mother Tongue in Rosa Nissán's Novels." *Hispania*, vol. 92, no. 3, 2009, pp. 456–64.

Lockhart, Darrell B, editor. *Critical Approaches to Jewish-Mexican Literature* (Aproximaciones críticas a la literature judeomexicana.) Chasqui, 2013.

Long, Ryan F. "The People's Print Shop: Art, Politics, and the Taller de Gráfica Popular." *Modern Mexican Culture: Critical Foundations*, edited by Stuart A. Day. U of Arizona P, 2017, pp. 84–106.

———. *Fictions of Totality: The Mexican Novel, 1968, and the National-Popular State*. Purdue UP, 2008.

López Aranda, Susana. "Dana Rotberg: Entre la realidad y la imaginación," *Dicine*, vol. 46, 1992, pp. 8–9.

López Ramírez, Mario. "El crimen del padre Amaro." Ficha de filme nacional. 2013. *El crimen del padre Amaro* files, Centro de documentación collection, Cineteca Nacional, Mexico City, Mexico.

López-Vallejo y García, Ma. Luisa. *La religión en el cine mexico (ensayo)*. 1978. UNAM, Licenciatura thesis.

López, Ana M. "Tears and Desire: Women and Melodrama in the 'Old' Mexican Cinema." *Mediating Two Worlds: Cinematic Encounters in the Americas*, edited by John King et al., BFI, 1993, pp. 147–64.

Los caifanes. Directed by Juan Ibáñez, Estudios América; Cinematográfica Marte, 1967.

Los que hicieron nuestro cine: Luis Alcoriza. Directed by Alejandro Pelayo Rangel, Producción de Unidad de Televisión Educativa y Cultural de la SEP, 1983.

Losada, Matt. Rev. of *Canoa. A Shameful Memory. Cineaste* Summer 2007, pp. 63–64.

Luna, Ilana Dann. *Adapting Gender: Mexican Feminisms from Literature to Film*. SUNY P, 2018.

Luna Elizarrarás, Sara Minerva. *Corrupción, legitimidad y género en el México del 'Milagro': Discursos públicos en torno a la figura del Presidente Adolfo Ruiz Cortines*. 2012. UNAM, MA thesis.

Luzárraga, Ramón. "Syncretism: Why Latin American and Caribbean Theologians Want to Replace a 'Fighting Word' in Theology." *Journal of Moral Theology*, vol. 2, no. 2, 2013, pp. 89–108.

Lyden, John, editor. *Routledge Companion to Religion and Film*. Routledge, 2009.

Lyden, John. "Introduction." Lyden, pp. 1–10.

Mackin, Robert Sean. "Becoming the Red Bishop of Cuernavaca: Rethinking Gill's Religious Competition Model." *Sociology of Religion*, vol. 64, no. 4, 2003, pp. 499–514.

MacLaird, Misha. *Aesthetics and Politics in the Mexican Film Industry*. Palgrave-Macmillan, 2013.

Marcos, Sylvia. "Emerging Feminist Theologies: Overview of the *JFSR* Live Roundtable in Cuernavaca, Mexico." *Journal of Feminist Studies in Religion*, vol. 34, no. 2, 2018, pp. 89–92. doi: 10.2979/jfemistudreli.34.2.08.

María Candelaria (*Xochimilco*). Directed by Emilio Fernández, Films Mundiales, 1944.

Marshall, April D. "Naming Clues to the Layers of Transgression in *El crimen del padre Amaro*." *Names: A Journal of Onomastics*, vol. 62, no. 2, pp. 100–6. https://doi.org/10.1179/0027773814Z.00000000078.

May, John R., editor. *La nueva imagen del cine religioso*. Universidad Pontifica de Salamanca, 1998.

McClennen, Sophia. "(De)Signing Women: Mexican Women Directors and Feminist Film." *Revista de Estudios Hispánicos*, vol. 36, 2002, pp. 69–96.

Medina Torres, Beatriz. *Una perspectiva ideológica del cine echeverrista caso de estudio: producción cinematográfica de 1975 y 1976 (Canoa, Longitud de Guerra y Cascabel)*. 1993. UNAM, Acatlán, Licenciatura thesis.

Medina, Manuel F. "The Female Stranger: Mexican and Jewish Gaze in Rosa Nissán's Imagined Spaces." Lockhart, pp. 143–54.

Mennell, D. Jan. "Memoria, *midrash* y metamorfósis en *Novia Que Te Vea* de Guita Schyfter: un diálogo textual-visual." *Chasqui*, vol. 29, no. 1, 2000, pp. 50–63.

Merino, Orlando, and Jaime García Estrada. *Alfredo Joskowicz: Una vida para el cine*. UNAM; CONACULTA, 2012.

"Mexico/Americas: Report." *Committee to Protect Journalists*. 8 Oct. 2019. https://cpj.org/americas/mexico. Accessed 23 Oct. 2019.

Miércoles de ceniza. Directed by Roberto Gavaldón, Cinematográfica Filmex; Azteca Films, 1958.

Mis padres se divorcian. Directed by Julián Soler, Cinematográfica Filmex, 1959.

Monja, casada, virgen y mártir. Directed by Juan Bustillo Oro, Industrial Cinematográfica, 1935.

Monsiváis, Carlos. "Mythologies." In *Mexican Cinema*, edited by Paulo Antonio Paranaguá, BFI-IMCINE, 1995, pp. 124–25.

———. "Sociedad y cultura." *Entre la guerra y la estabilidad política: el México de los '40*, edited by Rafael Loyola, Grijalbo, 1990, pp. 259–80.

———. *El Estado laico y sus malquerientes*. UNAM, 2008.

Mora, Carl J. *Mexican Cinema: Reflections of a Society, 1896–2004*. 3rd ed., U of California P, 2005.

Mora Lomelí, Raúl H. *Dios en el cine*. Instituto Tecnológico y de Estudios Superiores de Occidente; U Iberoamericana, León, 2005.

Morán, Alicia Adriana. *La crítica de un irreverente: el catolicismo en diez obras mexicanas de Luis Buñuel (1950–2006)*. 2007. UNAM, Licenciatura thesis.

Morganroth Schneider, Judith. "Rosa Nissán's Reconstruction of Diasporic Consciousness: Reflections on Genealogy, Geography and Gender in *Las tierras prometidas*." Lockhart, pp. 132–42.

Muñoz, María L. O. "Populism, Indigenismo and Indigenous Mobilization in Echeverría's Mexico." *Populism in 20th Century Mexico: The Presidencies of Lázaro Cárdenas and Luis Echeverría*, edited by Amelia M. Kiddle and María L. O. Muñoz, U of Arizona P, 2010, pp. 122–34.

Muro González, Víctor Gabriel. "Iglesia y movimientos sociales en México: 1972–1987." *Estudios Sociológicos*, vol. 9, no. 27, 1991, pp. 541–57.

Nájera-Ramírez, Olga. "Engendering Nationalism: Identity, Discourse, and the Mexican Charro," *Anthropological Quarterly*, vol. 67, no. 1, 1994, pp. 1–14.

Naveja, Juan María. "Estado-Iglesia: conflicto en puerta por una película." *Milenio*, 28 July 2002, Secc. Cultura, pp. 35–36.

Navitski, Rielle. *Public Spectacles of Violence: Sensational Cinema and Journalism in Early Twentieth-Century Mexico and Brazil*. Duke UP, 2017.

Nayar, Sheila J. *The Sacred and the Cinema: Reconfiguring the "Genuinely" Religious Film*. Continuum, 2012.

Noble, Andrea. *Mexican National Cinema*. Routledge, 2005.

Novia que te vea. Directed by Guita Schyfter, Fondo de Fomento a la Calidad Cinematográfica; Instituto Mexicano de Cinematografía; Producciones Arte Nuevo, 1994.

Oppenheimer, Andrés. *México: En la frontera del caos*. Javier Vergara Editor, 1996.

Ortega Mendoza, Jesús. "Para ver cine: Ángel de fuego." *El Universal*, 24 Feb. 1993, secc. Universo joven, p. 3.

Ortigão, Ramalho. "Literatura de observación: *El crimen del padre Amaro*." Translated by Javier Coca Senade and Raquel R. Aguilera. *Revista de occidente*, vol. 264, 2003, pp. 118–34.

Pacheco, Adriana. "El salón de baile en la Época de Oro del cine mexicano: espacio de conflicto entre el estado laico y la sociedad católica." *Chasqui*, vol. 42, no. 2, 2013, pp. 31–46.

Pacheco, Arturo. "Ernesto Laguardia protagonizará escenas eróticas con Maya Mishalska en cine." *El heraldo*, 16 June 1992. *Novia que te vea* files, Centro de documentación collection, Cineteca Nacional, Mexico City, Mexico.

Pacific Rim. Directed by Guillermo del Toro, Warner Bros., Legendary Entertainment, Double Dare You, 2013.

Palou, Pedro Ángel. *El fracaso del mestizo*. Ariel, 2014.

Paz, Octavio. *El laberinto de la soledad. Postdata. Vuelta a "El laberinto de la soledad*." First published 1981. Fondo de Cultura Económica, 2012.

———. *The Labyrinth of Solitude, the Other Mexico, and Other Essays*. Translated by Lysander Kemp, Grove Press, 1985.

Pensado, Jaime M., and Enrique C. Ochoa, editors. *México Beyond 1968: Revolutionaries, Radicals, and Repression During the Global Sixties and Subversive Seventies*. U of Arizona P, 2018.

Peredo Castro, Francisco. "Catholicism and Mexican Cinema: A Secular State, a Deeply Conservative Society and a Powerful Catholic Hierarchy." *Moralizing Cinema: Film, Catholicism, and Power*, edited by Daniel Biltereyst and Daniela Treveri Gennari, Routledge, 2015, pp. 66–81.

Pérez, Jorge. *Confessional Cinema: Religion, Film, and Modernity in Spain's Development Years, 1960–1975*. U of Toronto P, 2017.

Pérez-Anzaldo, Guadalupe. *Memorias pluridimensionales en la narrativa mexicana: Las mujeres judeomexicanas cuentan sus historias*. Ediciones Eón, 2009.

Pérez Turrent, Tomás. "Crises and Renovations (1965–1991)." *Mexican Cinema*, edited by Paulo Antonio Paranaguá, translated by Ana M. López, IMCINE; British Film Institute; CONACULTA, 1995, pp. 94–115.

———. *Luis Alcoriza*. Cine Iberoamericano de Huelva, 1997.

Pilcher, Jeffrey M. "The Gay Caballero: Machismo, Homosexuality, and the Nation in Golden Age Film." *Masculinity and Sexuality in Modern Mexico*, edited by Víctor M. González, and Anne Rubenstein, U of New Mexico P, 2012, pp. 161–75.

Plate, S. Brent. "Religion and World Cinema." *Continuum Companion to Religion and Film*, edited by William L. Blizek, Continuum, 2009, pp. 89–100.

Podalsky, Laura. *The Politics of Affect and Emotion in Contemporary Latin American Cinema: Argentina: Brazil, Cuba, and Mexico.* Palgrave, 2010.

Pope Pius XI. "Vigilanti Cura." *Mundo cinematográfico*, 29 June 1936, pp. 7–18.

Pope Pius XII. "Discurso al mundo cinematográfico." *Mundo cinematográfico*, 28 Oct. 1955, pp. 33–47.

Pridgeon, Stephanie. *Revolutionary Visions: Jewish Life and Politics in Latin American Film*. U of Toronto P, 2021.

Ramírez Berg, Charles. *Cinema of Solitude: A Critical Solitude of Mexican Film, 1967–1983.* U of Texas P, 1992.

Ramón, David. "*María Candelaria*: Una película mítica." *Historias Recuperadas: María Candelaria, Emilio Fernández*. Difusión Cultural UNAM, 2004, n.p.

Rashkin, Elissa. *Women Filmmakers in Mexico: The Country of Which We Dream.* U of Texas P, 2001.

Reding, Andrew. "Mexico at a Crossroads: The 1988 Election and Beyond." *World Policy Journal*, vol. 5, no. 4, 1988, pp. 615–49.

The Reliable Source. "The Telenovela Life of Mexico's New President." *The Washington Post*, 3 July 2012. https://www.washingtonpost.com/blogs/reliable-source/post/the-telenovela-life-of-mexicos-new-president/2012/07/03/gJQA1TATLW_blog.html. Accessed 16 Oct. 2019.

Renee, Rowan, et al. "Interrogating the Limits of Trauma Language: A Conversation on Sexual Abuse Narratives in Art Marking and Storytelling." *Guernica*, vol. 1, July 2017. http://www.guernicamag.com/interrogating-the-limits-of-trauma-language. Accessed 4 Nov. 2019.

Reséndiz, Edgardo. "La iglesia y el cine mexicano." *Reforma*, 9 Aug 2002, section Gente, p. 1.

Ricci, Cristián H. "Vigilar y castigar como modelo social en *El crimen del padre Amaro* de Eça de Queirós." *Espéculo: Revista de estudios literarios*, vol. 22, 2002. https://webs.ucm.es/info/especulo/numero22/p_amaro.html. Accessed 1 Feb. 2019.

Río Escondido. Directed by Emilio Fernández, Producciones Raúl de Anda, 1948.

Ríos Alfaro, Lorena. "La idea de *Novia que te vea* la tenía clara desde 85, no la extraje del libro de Rosa Nissan." *Uno más uno*, 8 Jul. 1994. *Novia que te vea* files, Centro de documentación collection, Cineteca Nacional, Mexico City, Mexico.

Riva Palacio, Vicente. *Monja y casada, virgen y mártir.* J. Ballescá, 1903.

Roberts-Camps, Traci. "The Female Body as Spectacle: *Ángel de fuego* and *La mujer del pueblo*: Otilia Rauda by Dana Rotberg." *Transmodernity*, vol. 2, no. 2, 2013, pp. 1–19.

Rocha, Carolina, and Georgia Seminet, editors. *Representing History, Class, and Gender in Spain and Latin America: Children and Adolescents in Film.* Palgrave-Macmillan, 2012.

Román, Ernesto. "Río escondido." *Miradas al acervo*, edited by Roberto Ortiz Escobar, CONACULTA; Cineteca Nacional, 2003, pp. 58–61.

Rotberg, Diana, and Omar A. Rodrigo. *Ángel de fuego.* Ediciones El Milagro, 1993.

Rotberg, Diana. "A Malena, yo no la juzgo." Interview with Isabel Arredondo. *Palabra de mujer: historia oral de las directoras de cine mexicano (1988–1994)*, edited by Isabel Arredondo, Iberoamericana; Universidad Autónoma de Aguascalientes, 2001, pp. 170–89.

Ruétalo, Victoria, and Dolores Tierney, editors. *Latsploitation, Exploitation Cinemas, and Latin America.* Routledge, 2009.

Ruiz Lagier, Verónica. "*El Maestro Rural* y la *Revista de Educación*. El sueño de transformar al país desde la editorial." *Signos históricos*, vol. 29, 2013, pp. 36–63.

Sagasti Lacalle, María José, et al. *Las fuerzas de liberación nacional y los combates por la memoria, 1974–1977: Cuadernos de trabajo Dignificar la Historia II.* Grupo Editorial de La Casa de Todas y Todos, 2016.

Saldaña Serrano, Javier. "Innecesarias y restrictivas las modificaciones constitucionales en materia de libertad religiosa en México (artículos 24 y 40)." *Revista Mexicana de Derecho Constitucional*, no. 29, 2013, pp. 285–311.

Saldarriaga, Patricia. "The Imagery of Jerusalem in the Colonial City." *The Transatlantic Hispanic Baroque: Complex Identities in the Atlantic World*, edited by Harald E. Braun and Jesús Pérez-Magallón, Ashgage, 2014, pp. 237–51.

Sánchez Prado, Ignacio M. "Alegorías sin pueblo: el cine echeverrista y la crisis del contrato social de la cultura mexicana." *Chasqui*, vol. 44, no. 2, 2015, pp. 50–67.

———. "El mestizaje en el corazón de la utopía: La raza cósmica entre Aztlán y América Latina." *Revista Canadiense de Estudios Hispánicos*, vol. 33, no. 2, 2009, pp. 381–404.

———. "Mont Neoliberal Periodization: The Mexican 'Democratic Transition,' from Austrian Libertarianism to the 'War on Drugs.'" *World Literature, Neoliberalism, and the Culture of Discontent*, edited by Sharae Deckard and Stephen Shapiro, Palgrave-Macmillan, 2019, pp. 93–110.

———. *Screening Neoliberalism: Mexican Cinema 1988–2012.* Vanderbilt UP, 2014.

Sánchez, Francisco. "El oficio más antiguo del mundo." *Revista mexicana de cultura*, p. 7. Hemeroteca digital, UNAM, Mexico City.

Sandoval, Adriana. *De la literatura al cine: Versiones fílmicas de novelas mexicanas.* UNAM, 2005.

Scarlett, Elizabeth. *Religion and Spanish Film: Luis Buñuel, the Franco Era, and Contemporary Directors.* U of Michigan P, 2015.

Schaefer, Claudia. *Bored to Distraction: Cinema and Excess in End-of-the-Century Mexico and Spain.* SUNY P, 2003.

Schuessler Fiorenza, Elizabeth. *In Memory of Her: A Feminist Theological Reconstruction of Christian Origins.* Crossroad, 1983.

"Se suprimen escenas a 'Río escondido.'" *Cinéma Reporter*, 29 Nov. 1947. *Río Escondido* files, Centro de documentación collection, Cineteca Nacional, Mexico City, Mexico.

Sepúlveda, Martha L. "Sobre Canoa." *Revista otro cine*, no. 4, Oct.–Dec. 1975, pp. 16–18.

Serna, Armando. "Las chicas malas del padre Méndez." N.d., pp. 32–35. *Las chicas malas del padre Méndez* files, Centro de documentación collection, Mexico City, Mexico.

Serna, Laura Isabel. *Making Cinelandia: American Films and Mexican Film Culture Before the Golden Age.* Duke UP, 2014.

Schrader, Paul. *Transcendental Style in Film: Ozu, Bresson, Dreyer.* Da Capo Press, 1976.

Silva Martínez, Marco A. "Rosa Nissán: ¡Novia que te filmen!" *El Nacional*, 4 Jul. 1993. *Novia que te vea* files, Centro de documentación collection, Cineteca Nacional, Mexico City, Mexico.

Sison, Antonio D. "Postcolonial Religious Syncretism: Focus on the Philippines, Peru, and Mexico." Lyden, pp. 178–93.

Solórzano, Fernanda. "*Canoa*, introducción al horror." *Letras Libres*, 14 Apr. 2016. https://www.letraslibres.com/mexico/cinetv/canoa-introduccion-al-horror. Accessed 14 Jan. 2019.

Soto Laveaga, Gabriela. *Jungle Laboratories: Mexican Peasants, National Projects, and the Making of the Pill.* Duke UP, 2009.

Soutar, Jethro. *Gael García Bernal and the Latin American New Wave.* Portico, 2008.

Speckman Guerra, Elisa, and Fabiola Bailón Vásquez, editors. *Vicio, prostitución y delito: mujeres transgresoras en los siglos XIX y XX.* UNAM, 2016.

Steinberg, Samuel. *Photopoetics at Tlatelolco: Afterimages of Mexico, 1968.* U of Texas P, 2016.

Sum Scott, Renée. "Rosa Nissán: travesías por la memoria autobiográfica." Lockhart, pp. 122–31.

Taracena, Alfonso. "'María Candelaria' o el don de la originalidad." *El universal*, 31 Oct. 1986. Secc. Cultura, *María Candelaria* files, Centro de documentación collection, Cineteca Nacional, Mexico City, Mexico.

Taracena, Alfonso. "María Candelaria es un plagio." *El universal*, 23 Oct. 1986. Secc. Cultura, *María Candelaria* files, Centro de documentación collection, Cineteca Nacional, Mexico City, Mexico.

Thornton, Niamh. *Revolution and Rebellion in Mexican Film.* Bloomsbury, 2013.

Tierney, Dolores, et al. "New Latin American Stardom." D'Lugo et al., pp. 164–79.

Tierney, Dolores. *Emilio Fernández: Pictures in the Margins.* Manchester UP, 2007.

Tombs, David. *Latin American Liberation Theology.* Brill, 2002.

Tuñón, Julia. "Femininity, *Indigenismo*, and Nation: Film Representation by Emilio 'El Indio' Fernández." *Sex in Revolution. Render, Politics, and Power in Modern Mexico*, edited by Jocelyn Olcott et al., Duke UP, 2006, pp. 81–96.

———. "María Candelaria: Emilio Fernández, Mexico, 1943." *The Cinema of Latin America*, edited by Alberto Elena and Marina Díaz López, Wallflower, 2003, pp. 45–52.

———. *Mujeres de Luz y Sombra en el cine mexicano: La construcción de una imagen (1939–1952).* El Colegio de México, 1998.

Turner, Laura. "Redheads: A Personal History." *The Toast*, 28 June 2016. https://the-toast.net/2016/06/28/redheads-a-personal-history. Accessed 4 Dec. 2019.

Vallejo, Delia Selene de Dios. "María Candelaria." Transcript of Talk for the Cine, Club de género of the Federación Internacional de Mujeres Universitarias, Federación mexicana de universitarias, UNAM, Museo de la Mujer, 31 May 2011. *María Candelaria* collection, Centro de documentación collection, Cineteca Nacional, Mexico City, Mexico.

Venkatesh, Vinodh. *New Maricón Cinema: Outing Latin American Film.* U of Texas P, 2016.

Vera Bérenger, Carolina Gabriela. *Recuperación del documental audiovisual contemporáneo en la problemática social: jóvenes, espiritualidad y religión.* 2006. UNAM, Licenciatura thesis.

Verástique, Bernardino. *Michoacán and Eden: Vasco de Quiroga and the Evangelization of Western Mexico.* U of Texas P, 2000.

Vértiz de la Fuente, Claudia. "Leñero y Carrera, un diálogo sobre 'El crimen del padre Amaro.'" *Proceso*, 26 June 2013. https://www.proceso.com.mx/345997/lenero-y-carrera-un-dialogo-sobre-el-crimen-del-padre-amaro. Accessed 21 Feb. 2019.

Viñas, Moisés. "Las adaptaciones mexicanas de Eca de Queiroz." *Ovaciones*, 26 Aug. 2002, Secc. Espectáculos, pp. 6–7.

West, Dennis. "Revisiting the Scene of the Crime: An Interview with Felipe Cazals." Translated by Dennis West and Joan M. West. *Cineaste*, summer 2015, pp. 15–19.

Williams, Gareth. *The Mexican Exception: Sovereignty, Police and Democracy.* Palgrave Macmillan, 2011.

Yarri, Donna. Rev. of *The Crime of Father Amaro* (*El crimen del padre Amaro*). *Journal of Religion & Film*, vol. 8, no. 2. https://digitalcommons.unomaha.edu/jrf/vol8/iss2/20. Accessed 1 Feb. 2019.

Zavala, Oswaldo. *Los cárteles no existen: narcotráfico y cultura en México.* Malpaso, 2018.

INDEX

www.ingramcontent.com/pod-product-compliance
Lightning Source LLC
LaVergne TN
LVHW040758070826
844660LV00025B/1190

* 9 7 8 1 4 3 8 4 8 5 3 0 0 *